What Is Religion?

AN INTRODUCTION

John F. Haught

Paulist Press
New York and New Jersey

Interior art and cover design by John Davis Gummere.

Library of Congress Cataloging-in-Publication Data

Haught, John F.
    What is religion? : an introduction / by John F. Haught.
      p.   cm.
    Includes bibliographical references.
    ISBN 0-8091-3117-X
    1. Religion. I. Title.
  BL48.H365   1989
  200—dc20   89-39734
                                            CIP

Published by Paulist Press
997 Macarthur Boulevard
Mahwah, New Jersey 07430

Printed and bound in the
United States of America

Contents

Preface

This book is an introduction to religion intended especially for college students, but also for other interested readers. It offers an appreciative and critical understanding of one of the most important dimensions of human life. It is not an exhaustive survey of world religions, nor does it follow the format of those textbooks that seek to cover as many religions as possible. Instead it isolates and reflects upon what informed students of the subject take to be the essential features of religious existence. I have provided sketches of the main traditions (in Part I), but I do so in order to make room (in Parts II, III, and IV) for a theoretical and evaluative examination of the central aspects of religion.

I would like to express my gratitude to Chester Gillis for reading the manuscript and to my wife Evelyn for her many helpful corrections. Special thanks also to Donald Brophy of Paulist Press for his kind encouragement and wise editorial advice.

I should alert readers to several stylistic and structural features in the text. First, for the sake of simplicity I have not used diacritical marks in transliterating terms employed by the Asian religions. Second, I use the ecumenical designation "B.C.E." (Before the Common Era) instead of the more traditional "B.C." (Before Christ). Third, biblical citations, unless otherwise indicated, are from the *Revised Standard Version*. And finally, from the very start I interpret religion in terms of the idea of "mystery." If this notion seems too enigmatic to some readers they may wish, before proceeding too far into the text, to scan Chapter 10 where I describe at length what I mean by it.

TO THE MEMORY OF MY FATHER

Introduction

Picture the following scenes. Cave dwellers in Western Europe 35,000 years ago are burying one of the children of their tribe, taking pains to arrange the body in a deliberate pattern, and adorning it with special ornaments and pigmentation. An aged ascetic in India sits quietly in contemplation at the edge of a forest. A Buddhist monk in Sri Lanka walks effortlessly along a pebbled pathway meditating in a monastery garden. A prophet in ancient Israel announces the coming of the "Day of the Lord."

Such gestures usually go by the name "religion." And the purpose of this book is to make some sense of this amazingly diverse and persistent phenomenon. Activities like those just mentioned have been going on for thousands of years, and in spite of the modern suspicion of religion they are likely to continue for a lot longer. For years, too, scholars have been trying to understand religion, but they are still at a loss to say exactly what it is. Nonetheless, they keep trying, and the present book continues the effort to understand what is perhaps the most distinctively human of all our habits.

Why do people engage in religious activity? What do they hope to accomplish by such exceptional modes of consciousness and conduct? What good does religion do? Is it any longer an essential aspect of human existence, even granted that it has certainly been prevalent throughout human history? Is it an honest approach to life, or is it perhaps an escapist business that we can easily dispense with today? What connection does it have to morality, to the way we decide what is good or bad, to the way we behave? Are its many ideas about "another dimension" or an "ultimate reality" truthful or illusory? Is it compatible with reason and science? Does religion make us any happier than we would otherwise be? How does it link up with the rest of life? These are some of the questions we shall address in this text.

1

The Distinctiveness of Religion

I doubt that I would be using the term "religion," or that the reader would have any idea of what I am talking about, unless we had already tacitly agreed that there is indeed something distinct about the phenomena to which the word "religion" seems to be pointing. But it is not easy to put a finger on exactly what this is. Literally thousands of scholars have attempted to define religion, always with less than satisfying results. No matter how carefully they "define" religion, other experts will eagerly indicate what the definition has left out.

Nevertheless, our detaching a certain type of activity from the totality of human life and labelling it "religion" is given considerable assistance by the fact that such gestures as those four listed at the beginning are already clearly different from "ordinary" ways of behaving. They stand out on their own, at least as far as our modern way of looking at things is concerned. It is difficult to avoid noticing their quality of being "set apart." Religious activity often takes place in what seems to be artificially contrived time, space or modes of consciousness. Sacred places, liturgical calendars, meditative moods, extraordinary fastings, self-denials, exceptional private or communal actions, praying, sacrificing, meditating, prophesying—all of these give the impression of being stylized deviations from normality. They have a quality of caricature, of play-acting and sometimes unnaturalness to them. They stand out so obviously from the everyday that it is difficult to avoid giving such commotion a special name. In our time this name is "religion."

Actually "religion" is a relatively modern concept. The ancient world had no word for what we are calling religion, partly because religion blended so intimately with the rest of life and did not contrast sharply with profane or ordinary life the way it does today. It was not as noticeable, perhaps because it was so pervasive. It is our modern sense of a mundane or secular sphere that makes religious activity stand forth more obtrusively to us. We want to define and understand religion more carefully than religious people of the past would have been interested in doing.

In order to arrive at any instructive interpretation of religion we need first to look at a range of "data" from which we can draw such insight. Obviously we cannot explore many of the manifestations of religion in this text. We have to be quite selective. But in order to gain some breadth, in Part I we shall look at four radically distinct groupings of religious experience as the basis for our investigations. In Part II we shall abstract four distinct "ways" of being religious from the brief descriptions presented in Part I. Then in Part III we shall begin to ask "why" people have turned to religion. There we shall see how religion fits into and grows out of other, more "natural," aspects of human life and awareness. And finally, in Part IV we shall ask some critical questions about religion, in particular whether its reference to an "ultimate" reality or an "ultimate" kind of fulfillment is a plausible interpretation of reality and human existence. In order to sharpen these critical questions we shall bring religion into conversation with modern skepticism.

Dialogue with Skepticism

We cannot discuss religion seriously today without being aware of the suspicion in which it is held by much modern thought. And so I shall situate my discussion of religion in the context of a "conversation" with modern secularism and skepticism. Such an approach is more fruitful than one that ignores the fact that for many people today "religion" has completely lost its meaning and appeal. Taking seriously the arguments of skeptics and critics of religion may actually lead us to a deeper appreciation of religion. This will help us in our efforts to extract what is essential to it and allow us better to discriminate the wholesome from the unwholesome aspects of it.

It is no secret that secularism now threatens religion in many parts of the world. Modern science, the Renaissance and the Enlightenment have together produced a new preoccupation with our "immediate environment," or with what some religious people might call "this world." As a result of modern infatuation with the exclusively "secular" realm, the province of "mystery" upon which religions have been nurtured seems to have diminished or disappeared altogether, and the world of immediacy, the one available to us in ordinary experience and scientific inquiry, has been enshrined as the only real one. The religious outlook seems to have

I Expressions of Religion	II Ways of Religion	III Aims of Religion	IV Critiques of Religion
Early Religion	Sacramentalism	Reassurance	Secularism
Hinduism	Mysticism	Mystery	Skepticism
Buddhism	Silence	Adventure	Nihilism
Prophetic Religion	Action	Morality	Humanism

lost its luster for many sincere people today, especially in the academic world. Thus we cannot understand religion in a satisfactory way, even in an introductory work such as this one, without taking a look also at the modern distaste for or indifference to religion.

With modern skepticism we must face the fact that the story of religion has not been a uniformly edifying one. After all, religion is something done by human beings, all of whom are inclined at times to narrow-mindedness and evil. That their religious life and ideas often display tendencies toward childishness, resentment, escapism, ethnocentrism, sexism, elitism, absolutism and various forms of oppression or exclusivism should not completely surprise us. So we need not close our eyes, as we often do, to the dark side of religion. Alfred North Whitehead is correct when he says that religion ". . . has emerged into human experience mixed with the crudest fancies of barbaric imagination." But he may also be correct in observing that the religious vision is "our one ground for optimism," and that "apart from it, human life is a flash of occasional enjoyments lighting up a mass of pain and misery, a bagatelle of transient experience." (Whitehead, 1967 a, p. 192) In other words, we may seek the wholesome, enlivening core of religion and distinguish this from its shadier side. Indeed that is exactly what authentic religious life is all about: a search for the essence, kernel, substance or depth of any religious tradition into which we may have been born or with which we may have become associated. Genuine religiousness requires a constant search for the essence of religion. And some acquaintance with modern skepticism is today an important aspect of this search.

Religion as Route-finding

One of the most accessible ways to understand religion in an introductory way is offered by the British scholar John Bowker. He sees religion as a "route-finding" through the severest barriers interfering with the continuity of human life. Religions formulate "ways" to move us past the most frustrating "compounds of limitations" that we have to deal with as we make our way through life. Obstacles or limits to the continuity of human life arise in extraordinarily frustrating ways at times, and religion is a response to the most unbending of the limitations that interfere with human life-ways. Many limits, of course, can eventually be hurdled or pushed back by non-religious techniques. But then the focus of religion will shift toward the *most stubborn obstacles* to the continuity of life, the obvious ones being suffering and death, the unrepeatable nature of the past, the capriciousness of fate, the feelings of powerlessness, guilt and meaninglessness. And it is especially in connection with these apparently intransigent roadblocks that the kind of route-finding we call religion begins to take distinct form. (Bowker, 1973) Eventually religion discerns a realm of what we shall call "mystery" looming up beyond life's limits. And in various ways it seeks to connect us to this mystery in which alone fulfillment is deemed possible.

It is quite easy to recognize "religions." Their symbols, rites and teachings, though connected with the rest of life, tend to cluster in higher density around what are identified as the *ultimate* limits to our quest for perfection. The function of religions is to fortify our trust that there is some "way through" the barriers that block the road toward ultimate fulfillment. And the plausibility of religions, as Bowker points out, depends upon the effectiveness of the paths they make through the most difficult obstacles. This interpretation of religion as a kind of route-finding, even though it does not take into account every aspect of religion, cuts right to the heart of our subject. And thinking of religion in terms of the "limits" of our experience will also help us to locate it more precisely in terms of the other aspects of our lives.

Why Study Religion?

If you have read this morning's paper, or followed the course of world events recently, you may have noticed how often the conflicts that dominate the news result directly from the high degree of importance people attribute to their own beliefs and traditions. It is obvious, but it is also worth repeating often, that people take their beliefs, ideologies and especially their religions very seriously. The conflicts between Iran and Iraq, Israel and the PLO, Catholics and Protestants in Northern Ireland, Christians and Marxists in various parts of the world, Sikhs and Hindus in India, fundamentalists and liberals, creationists and evolutionists, and countless other such battles—these would not occur unless people put great stake in preserving a way of thinking, a tradition, a set of meanings that provides the basis for their way of life. More often than not there is a strongly religious dimension at the heart of international, social and political conflicts.

If we fail to understand the religious convictions that give purpose to the lives of others and ourselves, there can be little hope for resolving many of the disputes that now endanger human life on earth. Some scholars have even gone so far as to propose that the major source of world strife is our failure to understand the religions and ideologies of others. Bowker, for example, notices that religions, like nations, are typically "systems" possessing distinct boundaries. These boundaries, clearly defined by traditions, scriptures and doctrines, are considered essential in order to give a definiteness and stability to the religious system and to keep it from being diluted into a vagueness that would fail to motivate its adherents. Most religions have deemed it necessary therefore to defend and fortify their doctrinal boundaries. They must do so in order to ensure the transmission of their highly valued information about ultimate issues on to the next generation.

Hence religions have by and large been rather conservative bodies. They have placed enormous significance on preserving for posterity the specific sense of route-finding that they have found successful in combating the threat of disorder. For example, official teachers in the Roman Catholic Church seek to exclude certain theologians who propose disturbing new interpretations of traditional teachings. Or Islamic revolutionaries chastise religious thinkers who want to accommodate Islam to the modern world. Such reactions illustrate religion's sensitivity to the invasion of any alternative visions that appear to challenge the "successful" approach of a specific tradition. It is not surprising then that "border incidents" would arise when one view of the most important side of life brushes up against an alternative religious or secular vision. Conflicts occur largely because people take their religions so seriously. Their religions are *important* to them, and maybe we have not yet fully understood why this is so. The search for such understanding is one very good reason to study religion. (Bowker, 1988)

We have failed to appreciate the importance of religion to Muslim terrorists, Sikh militants or Buddhist pacifists, often fancying that only our own approaches can be truly successful in negotiating the limits placed on human experience. It may not even occur to us that others have defined or identified the "compound of limitations" and the most significant questions that give rise to their religious systems in a way that differs considerably from our own. And so we fail to grasp the most important dimension of their lives. For this reason alone the study of religion is perhaps one of the most important components of any serious educational process.

But there are also other reasons for studying religion. One of the most important is simply that of wanting to know how far our environment extends. What are the full dimensions of our surroundings? Religions have almost universally made at least some kind of reference to "another dimension," one that we shall refer to as "mystery." They have been dissatisfied with any suggestion that the immediate environment, or the superficial world of appearances, is the sum total of reality. In one way or another they have pushed beyond whatever "seems" to be the case or whatever "seems" to limit our lives. For the most part they have not advocated a flight out of life and into the "beyond." In fact, contrary to what many modern caricatures of religion have maintained, religions generally attempt to reconcile people to the facts of their existence here and now. But more often than not they provide this contextualization by speaking of a realm of beyondness, of mystery, of "transcendence" (from the Latin, *transcendo*, "to pass beyond") or of ultimate perfection. This transcendent realm or experience is not always a special or clearly defined "place." Nor is it always considered a scene of survival after death. At least originally most of the major religions were not terribly obsessed with personal immortality. But the great religious teachers do share a premonition that what we ordinarily perceive to be the limits to reality can "somehow" be gotten beyond. And they think it essential for our happiness or "enjoyment" *here and now* that we acquire the awareness of an ultimate environment, or perhaps an extraordinary "enlightenment," that lies "beyond" our immediate experience. As we shall see, this impression of some type of "beyond" began to dawn very early in the history of religion. And it reached its most intense pitch in the centuries immediately preceding the Common Era (somewhere around 600 B.C.E.). What are we to make today of this quest for a realm of mystery or perfection situated beyond the immediacy of the here and now?

Other reasons for studying religion may be more personal, and each individual will approach the subject matter of this book with different questions and expectations. One of the most obvious has to do with our own search for identity and meaning. Most readers probably already have some connection with one religious tradition or another, although I am not going to presume that this is true of all. And our traditions (even if they are purely

APPROXIMATE RELIGIOUS AFFILIATION WORLDWIDE
(BY PERCENTAGE)

Christians	24 %
Muslims	14 %
Hindus	12.6%
Buddhists	6.3%
Jews	.4%
Others: religious and non-religious	42.7%

secular ones) have given us some sense of who we are and what our goals in life may be. But these aims are always in flux and never fully defined. The feeling of being "unfinished" is universal, and it may lead at times toward a wider vision of ourselves in relation to the rest of the world. There may be no better way of seeking such expansiveness than by a sympathetic "passing over" into the religious world of others. (Dunne, 1972) We may have to make our way through the firm boundaries of our own religious system at times in order to get a perspective both on it and on the others that make up our complex world. Learning to appreciate what others have identified as the basic limits on life can help us in our own efforts toward self-definition. Traveling with them as they seek religiously to transcend life's limits can be a deeply rewarding personal journey.

Finally, the serious study of religions, our own along with those of others, may itself be one of the most important ways in which the ageless religious quest wends its way forward in our own time. In fact, contemporary interest in "comparative religions" or "world religions" or the "history of religions" is itself a fundamentally religious concern and not mere curiosity. For it has been aroused by a new awareness of limitations, as have all creative religious developments in the past. In this case it is a recognition of the *limitations of our own traditions,* a new awareness that our own religious systems with their firm boundaries may in some way be confining and restraining us even while providing a needed impression of order, security, and point of departure.

Religion as a Response to Suffering

Religions seek to provide pathways through the "limits" that interfere with the human longing for ultimate fulfillment. We can understand what is distinctive about the various religious teachings if we single out a universally troublesome obstacle, and observe how it is surmounted by the particular kind of route-finding characteristic of each tradition. And since in one way or another the problem of suffering is the concern of all religion, we shall be especially interested in how it is addressed in each case. Since each of us knows at least something about suffering, and has sought some way through it, such a focus will serve to draw us also into the circles of meaning sketched by religions as a response to the problem of pain.

The fact of death is the extreme instance of human suffering. And the entire story of religion, in one way or another, responds to this most definitive of limits. More than any other limit, our own sense of having-to-die draws us into conversation with all the religious traditions. Approaching our subject in terms of the problem of suffering and death cannot communicate all the relevant features of a religion, but it may get us initially involved with it.

Religion and Theology

Religion is not exactly the same thing as theology. Theology is reflection on religion, usually undertaken by those already committed to a religious system. Theology seeks to understand a religion in terms that will communicate its teachings to a specific audience. Depending on what that audience is, theology will take on different shapes at different times.

Religion first comes to expression in the "naive" form of symbols, myths and rituals. But because the symbolic language of religion is never completely clear, it invites constant interpretation. It is the function of theology to provide this interpretation. Symbols beg to be interpreted, and so religion inevitably gives rise to theology. Sometimes it is difficult to say where religion leaves off and theology begins, since they are so closely related. But a good sign of theological work is the "codification" of a religious system into a formalized set of teachings. These teachings are usually called *dogma*. The various "creeds" of religions are results of theological reflection. For example, the Nicene Creed recited by Christians ("I believe in God, the Father Almighty . . .," "I believe in Jesus Christ, His only Son, our Lord," etc.) is the end product of enormous and painful theological discussion about the meaning of the basic religious symbols of Christian faith. The "Five Pillars" of Islam and the "Four Noble Truths of Buddhism" are also the result of the codification process undertaken by theological reflection.

But theology is not only concerned with producing formulas and dogmas. It is also at times *critical* reflection on the meaning of religious symbolism and teaching. Theology is the work of religious people who like the rest of us have inquiring and critical minds and who apply their reason to the understanding of religion. Sometimes theology leads to the refinement of symbols and sometimes it leads to further confusion. But it cannot be avoided by religions. Religions demand continuing reflection and criticism, partly because of their extravagant claims, and partly because they tend at times to close themselves off from alternative perspectives.

What we are calling religion in this book includes both the primordial symbolic representations of a sense of "mystery" as well as theological reflections on and codifications of the symbols.

CHRONOLOGY

125,000–30,000 **BCE**	Neanderthals
33,000–8,000	Cro-Magnons
2000–1750	Period of biblical patriarchs
1750–1200	Aryans invade India; beginnings of Vedic religion
1250	Israel's Exodus from Egypt
1000	Zoroaster
800–400	The "Axial" Age
	The Upanishads
700's	The classical biblical prophets Amos, Hosea, Isaiah, Micah
500's	Mahavira (origins of Jainism)
	Gautama, the Buddha
	Lao-tzu (Tao Te Ching)
	Confucius
165	Maccabean revolt in Israel
6–26 **CE**	Jesus of Nazareth
	The Conversion of Paul
60–125	The Writing of the gospels
354–430	St. Augustine
570–632	Muhammad
788–838	Shankara
750–1258	Abbasid Caliphate
1095–1291	The Crusades
1225–1274	Thomas Aquinas
1483–1546	Martin Luther
1491–1556	Ignatius Loyola
1509–1564	John Calvin
1500–1700	Mogul Empire
1600's	Origins of modern science
1859	Darwin's *Origin of Species*
1817–1892	Bahaullah (founder of Ba'hai)
1962–65	Second Vatican Council

A Personal Note

Recent studies of textbooks used in colleges and high schools have concluded that students usually find them intolerably dull. The main reason for this is that textbooks often simply list facts without providing any scheme for interpreting the data or without hazarding any value judgments that might pull the students into a lively conversation with the subject matter. I have found the same to be true of many introductory surveys of religion. Having used some of these in my own classes, I have often wished that in addition to presenting the important data about religion, the authors would risk some theoretical interpretation of it. I shall try to avoid here the pallid neutrality of the typical introductory text. This book will not only set forth a scheme for making sense of religion, but it will also seek criteria for determining what is and what is not authentically religious.

That I do find something "authentic" in religion will become clear as we go along. But will this favorable disposition toward religion on my part exclude the possibility of objectivity? Would not a more neutral approach, by someone perhaps indifferent to religion and personally unmoved by it, be more trustworthy? And would not a more dispassionate approach allow the data to emerge without being skewed by an a priori favorable assessment? I have to admit that a lot can be learned about religion employing such a detached method. And this text will utilize the results of scientifically disinterested studies of religion. But, important as such external accounts might be, I think that religion can be discussed more "objectively" by someone who is personally excited by it as well as willing to learn from those who are outsiders to it. I trust that students of music would not want to be instructed by a teacher who was tone deaf. People who cannot resonate with a melody, or who remain unmoved by it, might be able to tell you much about music theory or the physics of harmony. But they could not lead you very far inside the rich world of music.

Likewise those who are interested in religion only from the point of view of psychology, history, anthropology or sociology and other "scientific" approaches may not have the last word about it. Perhaps they should not have the first word either. For that reason I have gambled that students and other readers of this book, including those who will disagree with my interpretations and conclusions, will not be put off by the fact that I am generally stirred by the substance of human religious expression. In certain areas of knowledge such personal involvement is not an obstacle to, but a condition of, objectivity. Religion, I think, is one of them.

PART I

Expressions of Religion

Early Religion

Religion has never completely outgrown its origins. Just as adolescents and adults remain in some way continuous with their own infancy and childhood, religion today is still connected to the very earliest rituals, symbols and inklings of mystery that occurred thousands of years ago at the dawn of religious experience among our remotest ancestors. We would do well, difficult though it may be, to get some feeling for the beginnings of the religious story. For "primitive" religion still survives at a deep level even in contemporary spiritual endeavor. And if we were to lose touch with it, or pretend that it is no longer smoldering beneath the accumulations of later religious developments, it would be like forgetting our own childhood.

It would not be wise for us to repress the religious longings of our race's infancy. Modern psychology takes it as axiomatic that we must stay in touch with our earliest psychic experiences, simply for the sake of wholeness and sanity. The same may be said of our collective recollection of religious origins. Retrieving the earliest religious premonitions of mystery would be not only intellectually satisfying, but also spiritually healing.

How Do We Learn about Early Religion?

The primary way of gaining access to an understanding of the religion of early hunting and gathering societies, though it is not without its own difficulties, is to study the parallels that still exist in isolated preliterate tribal groupings (such as in Africa, Australia, South America and New Guinea). Though these have inevitably undergone some mutation as a result of modern developments in agriculture, travel and communication, they are probably similar in many ways to the earliest forms of tribal existence. Such societies have practices and ideas that may go back thousands of years, and it is even possible that they have remained relatively untouched by global history. There is, in any case, a staying power in religion that exists precisely in order to conquer time and to preserve a people's "life-ways." And so in many cases we may presume the comparative antiquity of religious myths and rituals.

It is difficult to determine just how long ago religious activity began. Did the prehominids such as *Australopithecus* of four million years ago have anything like a religious life? Or did *homo habilis* of two million years ago, from whom we have evidence of tool-making, of life in common, but not of formalized ritual? We simply do not know. The first clear evidence of anything like religious activity can be found in archeological remains from the Old Stone Age. Remnants indicating ritualistic activity have turned up especially at sites ranging from Western Europe to the Ural Mountains, almost always in caves inhabited during the period from 50,000 to 10,000 B.C.E. The evidence is often quite meager, and so we have to be somewhat imaginative in our reconstruction of any religious activity that occurred during this period. But many scholars conclude that ritual and a symbolic or mythic understanding of the world was already present in the lives of the hunters and gatherers during the Paleolithic period.

Artifacts and paintings left by Neanderthals and Cro-Magnons indicate the early sparks of what would later flame out into the great religions of the world. Understandably these fragile vestiges of early religion have as their constant theme the close dependency of humans on nature, and especially the animals. For example, the most famous of all the cave paintings, "The Dancing Sorcerer," found at Ariège, France, seems to depict a shaman or sorcerer, the most important religious personality during the

Prehistoric cave painting, called "The Dancing Sorcerer," discovered in Ariège, France.

pre-agricultural period, clad in a costume composed of mixed animal features. The painting may be an expression of the close kinship hunting societies felt with the beasts upon whose existence they depended for food and clothing.

Such felt kinship with nature was a major facet of what, for lack of a more suitable term, has traditionally been called "primitive" religion. (By the term "primitive" we in no way imply inferiority, but simply chronological primacy.) Since hunting was a most important aspect of early human life, it is not surprising that it would be overlaid with enormous religious significance. Religion has often been expressed in terms of what makes the difference between life and death, survival and extinction, of what may be called a people's "ultimate concern." This is an expression used by theologian Paul Tillich to characterize religion's tendency to find something of utmost importance, that is, something that has an "ultimate" significance for people. And for early humans the success of the hunt was certainly a matter of ultimate concern.

Hence prayers and rites in preparation for the chase, appeasement of the spirits of slain animals, and eventually sacrifices to the spirits controlling nature, must have characterized the earliest forms of religion. Later, when agriculture began to emerge in the Neolithic period, starting about ten thousand years ago, the religious focus would begin to shift toward the earth and its fertility as the primary concern. But from the Paleolithic period to the end of the last Ice Age religion centered mostly around the close dependency of humans on the kingdom of the animals.

Totemism

Hunting and gathering societies often have a special relation with a particular animal, such as a bear, a wolf or a snake. Such an animal is called a *totem* (a term used by North American Indians). The totem is treated with a special reverence that seems to bear some of the marks of religion. Relation to the totem serves to bind a people to its ancestors, as well as to a common set of meanings and life-styles. Often the violations of customs associated with the totem are considered forbidden or *taboo*. Thus totemism is a social phenomenon, but it has religious overtones as well. Identification with the totem is a way of merging with sacred reality.

This close relationship with animal life has never been completely lost. It is evident in the few hunting and gathering societies that still exist, perhaps not significantly changed since prehistoric times. And remnants of the early sense of kinship with the animals still lie buried beneath later levels of religious consciousness that developed during the agricultural period and beyond. To a large extent the religion of hunters and gatherers is a thing of the long forgotten past, but among many environmentally sensitive people today there is a strong appreciation of our need to recapture the primal feeling of connectedness and interdependency with the animal kingdom. One of the vital lessons we can learn from the earliest forms of religion is the bonding we have with the rest of life.

Panvitalism

Early religion is also characterized by "panvitalism," the perception that all things are alive. The world of most preliterate peoples is experienced almost as a womb-like medium of vitality in which nature, animals and humans all abide. Living things and persons borrow the energy to live from this environing life-force. They emerge mysteriously from the life-environment, and when they die, they somehow blend into it again. Death seems unreal. If everything is alive, how can any animal or person really be dead? This quandary may have led very early to the conviction of some vague sort of survival beyond death. (Jonas, 7–26)

How different this panvitalistic world is from ours! The universe of modern science is pervasively dead material stuff, with only a thin veneer of life precariously clinging to our planet. Death is the rule for our scientific consciousness, and life the exception. But in the "primitive" view life seemed present everywhere. The encompassing cycle of the seasons, the growth of vegetation, the wealth of animal life, the amazing fertility of humans—all of these impressed our ancestors with the utter aliveness of the universe. (Jonas, 9–10)

Preoccupation with Death

It is no wonder, then, that death could not easily be accepted as just another fact of nature. And there is archeological evidence that religious interpretations of death began to occur as early as the Old Stone Age. In caves of Western Europe dating from this time there are clear signs of a kind of ritual associated with burial. The arrangement of ornaments, bracelets, tools and weapons around the corpse, and the red ochre pigmentation (perhaps a symbol of blood and new life) poured over the bones of the dead, indicate a special crisis felt in the death of one's fellows. The traumatic sense of absence experienced in the departure of a member of the social unit summoned forth touching attempts to find a path through this most extreme of all human frustrations.

There may even have been a primal intuition that something of the person survives death, that there is perhaps an animating principle or "soul" that lives on after the person has died. Students of religion speculate that ancient burial patterns, such as the arrangement of bodies in the fetal position, or in the posture of sleep, provide hints of belief in rebirth after death. At least it is clear that death was a most impressive and mysterious experience and that the earliest expressions of religion had a lot to do with coming to grips with death. Death has always remained one of the "muses" of religion, and religion would probably not be of much interest to people unless it helped them in some way to cope with their mortality. This basic occasion for religious conjecture, namely our having-to-die, has not changed in importance over the last hundred thousand years. "The prospect of death wonderfully concentrates the mind." So said Samuel Johnson, and the history of religion seems to back him up.

Animism

The most obvious way in which "primitive" religion deals with death is through *animism* (from the Latin *anima*, soul, life, spirit). Animism is the belief that a spiritual dimension exists along with the bodies of animals and humans. Often a single human or animal possesses several souls or spirits. Animism, vestiges of which survive in all the major religions of the world today, goes hand in hand with panvitalism. And it may well have arisen in early crises over the apparent finality of death, as a way of salvaging the primeval world-view of panvitalism. For if, as panvitalism insists, everything is alive, then it is difficult to accept the thought that anything can be dead. Death must be an illusion if everything is alive. (Jonas, 9–10) And so the life-principle of the dead, the *anima*, must still be a presence to be reckoned with, even though the person or animal is empirically lifeless. In animism the person or animal still lives on as a spiritual presence or as several souls. And these souls continue to inhabit and haunt the world of the living. Sometimes they are consoling presences, but at other times they can return in order to torment or punish. The animist world is filled with fear as well as fascination.

The Sense of the Sacred

Still, we must be careful not to conclude that religion originated simply out of a need to accommodate death. Such an interpretation will not adequately account for religion as far as the religious person is concerned. For it seems to the religious person that religion originates in the encounter with an objective dimension of "mystery" or with what has been called "the sacred" or "the holy." If we asked our paleolithic or neolithic ancestors why they practiced religious rituals in connection with hunting, death and fertility, they would hardly be inclined to answer in terms of our modern social sciences. They would not tell us they were acting religiously for the purpose of survival or simply in order to confront the overwhelming threat of death. Nor would they be content with a purely Darwinian explanation of religion as an adaptive device allowing natural selection to preserve our species. Instead they would insist that they were responding to a "presence." Their religion, they would stipulate, is a *communion* with holy or sacred powers. Can we completely ignore their own testimony, as modern scientific studies of religion have usually done, in our attempt to understand their religion?

Other Characteristics of Early Religion

Early religion also gave rise to certain kinds of acts and expressions that have remained, in some form or another, part of religion up to the present. These are symbol, myth, ritual, magic, prayer, sacrifice and shamanism.

Symbol. Ever since its paleolithic beginnings religion has been inseparable from what we may call *symbolic consciousness*. Indeed its unique kind of symbolism is what makes it possible for us to recognize religion at any time or place, and to distinguish it from other aspects of human life and consciousness.

Generally speaking, a symbol is any object, aspect of nature, event, person or expression which by pointing to one thing directly points to something else indirectly. What the symbol refers to is "beyond" the immediately or literally given object employed as the symbol. At the same time, however, the symbolized reality is also "inside" the symbol. And the symbolized reality can be grasped only by way of the symbol. This is because the symbol *participates* in the reality to which it points. (Tillich, 1957, 41ff.; Ricoeur, 1974, 12–13)

Symbols should be distinguished from signs. Signs have an arbitrariness not present in symbols. For instance, a red traffic light standing for "stop" has no intrinsic connection with the act of putting on the brakes. There is no inherent reason why the color green could not have served just as well to signal the need to halt at an intersection. It is just that convention, human agreement, has decided that red will have this meaning.

A symbol, on the other hand, is naturally, and not just conventionally, connected with what it stands for. The totem, for example, is a symbol and not a mere sign. It is not just an indiscriminate indicator, but an actual embodiment of the sacral character of reality. In a later religious development the person of Jesus of Nazareth becomes the central religious "symbol" for Christians. Christians perceive this man not just as an arbitrary pointer to God, but as an indispensable participatory embodiment (incarnation) of the ultimate mystery that his person symbolizes.

And symbols also point *beyond* themselves. Religious symbols in particular attempt to transport us beyond the immediate environment. They open up to our consciousness an "ultimate environment" quite other than the ordinary. The sense of "beyondness," and the sharp religious differentiation of the immediate world from the "transcendent" realm, is not yet highly developed in early religion. But even here the beginnings at least of a sense of transcendence or "beyondness" seem to be present.

Symbols are the primary language of religion. They point out a way through the most imposing limitations, such as suffering, the hostility of others, the indifference of nature and finally death itself. By their very nature symbols pull us away from any complete immersion in immediacy. Because they naturally aim "beyond" themselves they are understandably the central mode of expression in religion. They are the primary access human consciousness has to "mystery."

Myth. When symbols are unfolded in the form of a story we have *myth* (from the Greek, *mythos,* story). A myth is simply a symbolic narrative, usually referring to events that took place in some realm beyond the immediate one, and thereby giving people an awareness of their deepest origins, a wider vision of reality, and a sure knowledge of their specific identity. A myth does this by telling the story of how things came to be. It narrates, for example, the heroic deeds and foundational events in the lives of ancestors of the social unit. Or by telling of how suffering and evil appeared, a myth may point a way out of the straits people find to be the most frustrating. It is especially in myths that the central ideas of religion have always been embodied, and it is in religious myths that the possibilities of finding a way through the limitations on life are most vividly presented.

Most "theology" is simply reflection on the "myths" which embody the substance of religious views of the world. Theology takes these myths seriously, if not always literally. For theology, myth does not mean fiction or illusion. Rather, myth is an irreplaceable way of expressing the essence of mystery. The role of theology is not to remove or replace but to interpret the myths by which religion attempts to depict the character of ultimate reality.

We have no records of the earliest myths of preliterate societies, but we can safely presume that people have been telling such stories ever since they began to mark time. And we may also suppose that the most important stories had to do with how things came to be the way they are, that is, with "origins." Religion has been inseparable from the quest for origins and stories about the beginnings.

Ritual. Ritual is the communal *acting out* of the symbolic and mythic sense of having found a path through the most severe limitations on human existence. It is not sufficient for us humans merely to *think* our way through the restrictions that life and death impose upon us. We are bodily beings, feeling beings, acting beings, and not simply thinking ones. Rational arguments alone have never been able to cut a path through the limits on life. Merely thinking our way through difficulties seldom works. And so a ritualistic drama or acting out of a sense of "breaking through" is an intrinsic part of most religion, from the Stone Age up to the present. Moreover, even where a sense of the sacred is no longer prominent, as in secularized societies, the ritualistic impulse is still present. Some kind of ritualistic activity is essential to human social existence. Rituals are ways in which people communally celebrate the meanings that give them their identities. And in this way rituals function to provide social solidarity.

The most important rituals are called *rites of passage*, and they have to do with transitions from one stage of life to another. By participating in such rites one's identity undergoes an adventurous transformation, usually involving a widening and deepening of relationship to the community or to nature.

Take, for example, the rite of initiation. At a certain time in the life of a young member of a preliterate society, often during early adolescence, it is time to break away from childhood and enter decisively into the adult world or into full membership in the life of the society. In order to dramatize this moment of transition a formalized "rite of passage" is usually prescribed. This initiation rite often involves undergoing a kind of "death," such as being sent out into the desert alone, or being inserted into a hollow place (such as a grave, log, tent or cave) symbolizing burial. At the end of the rite, which may last many days in some cases, and often involves severe pain and discomfort, the initiate is "reborn" into a new life and a new identity.

The survival of initiation rites into our own day indicates their enormous psychological and spiritual importance for our species. But in general they do not have the same significance for us today that they had in the past, perhaps much to our detriment. The Christian sacraments of baptism and confirmation are referred to as "rites of initiation." And the Jewish practice of bar mitzvah is another vestige of the ancient ritual of passage. But how often do these lead one dramatically into a whole new life? Depth psychologists have sometimes lamented the absence of powerful rites of passage in the lives of people today, for they recognize the power such rites have traditionally had in bringing about a sense of purpose and commitment that people need in order to live full and happy lives.

Magic. It is striking to notice the physical location of many of the primitive paintings and drawings that survive from the Paleolithic period. They are often situated in places where no one could see them without making an exceptional effort. Etched in nooks and crannies on remote and nearly inaccessible cave walls and ceilings, or on rock projections far off the beaten path, it is highly unlikely that this art was intended purely to capture the attention of passers-by. What then was its objective? Quite possibly it was magic. (Maringer, 1960, 108) Paintings of animals pierced with arrows and spears abound. These paintings suggest a strong desire to influence the hunt by way of a kind of sympathetic "picture magic." Before setting out for the hunt one would assure success in advance by drawing a vivid picture of the coveted beast and garnishing it with a projectile. Early art has suggestions of such magic, but along with magic there may also be a simple desire to express the native human longing for beauty which has played a vital role in the unfolding of religious consciousness in general.

The tendency toward magical manipulation of events is not confined to early religion. For even in most later religious developments elements of magic survive. Sir James G. Frazer, in his famous book, *The Golden Bough*, theorized that religion developed later than magic, after preliterate people began to notice that magical techniques do not always work. Today scholars do not accept his theory that religion developed out of magic, but they are nonetheless alert to the prominent role magic has played and continues to play in the story of religion.

In the light of later religious developments it would seem that magic has little to do with religion. For magic is a manipulative attempt to control the powers of nature. It is an attitude or practice quite at variance with the posture of trust, surrender and gratitude that belong to so much of religion. Magic is what people resort to when religious trust fails. It is more likely a precursor of science than of religion, for both science and magic have in common the search for causal laws by which to predict and control the future course of events. Religion, on the other hand, generally renounces such control. Nevertheless, in the actual unfolding of the religious story a temptation to magic has been a constant one, and much religion, as practiced, is mixed up with magic.

Prayer and Sacrifice. We can safely assume that prayer and sacrifice were also vital components of early religion. Prayer is both petition and expression of gratitude to the sacred power or powers that are believed to govern nature and human life. Sacrifice, a word derived from the Latin "to make holy," is also at heart both petitionary and thankful. In sacrificial offerings of fruit or animals, and even of humans, the objective is not merely to appease spirits in order to ensure continuing benefits. Sacrifice is also a gesture indicating a people's grateful envisagement of the gifts of food and life as belonging to a wider world than just that of self-interest. By sacrificing significant items in their lives people situate their world within a divine framework. They offer sacrifice not simply in order to manipulate fate, but so that their offerings might continually be seen as part of a deeper and more meaningful order. Thus sacrificial rites are another way in which religious people break out of the circle of the purely human or purely natural. Elements of this sacrificial impulse survive to this day in the Christian "sacrifice" of the Mass.

If we were to look with the interests of a social scientist at the evolution of mammalian life on our planet, and then if we tried to point to an activity that clearly distinguishes humans from other mammals, we might be tempted to say that it is the human propensity to offer prayer and sacrifice. Most of our human characteristics have close parallels in the behavioral patterns of other species, but there is nothing in the latter that comes close to praying and sacrificing. Animals have mates, raise families, hunt and gather, communicate with one another, have a certain degree of sensitivity and ability to adapt to the world in creative ways. They even have "rituals," like the dancing of bees and the courting of birds. But only humans, as far as we know, pray and offer sacrifice. And since prayer and sacrifice are so much a part of religion, it could be argued that religiousness is our most distinctively human characteristic.

Shamanism. One of the most compelling phenomena observable in preliterate religion, and especially of the pre-agricultural period, is *shamanism*. The name "shaman" is Siberian in origin, designating one who seems to have a special capacity for "ecstasy," for going beyond the bounds of ordinary life and entering into a realm apart. Variations on "shamanism" are found in many primal religions, for example, the "medicine man" of native Americans or the "witch doctor" of some African tribes.

And in a derivative sense shamanism still lives on in the major religions. (Eliade, 1972; Carmody, 1985)

A shaman is a special type of route-finder, a kind of "scout" of the other world. He (or at times "she") is often portrayed as journeying to the "underworld" or the heavens, or sometimes as simply being a medium through which strange powers make their way into a people's life. It would seem that the shaman is invested with so much significance because of the people's need to find a way through their sense of limitations. The shaman provides this way.

The personality of the shaman is psychologically a disturbing one. The initial stages of becoming a shaman often involve a period of insanity or sociopathic behavior. This is a torturous episode in the shaman's life, since he runs the risk of losing his bearings altogether. If things go right, however, he finds a spiritual helper, either another shaman or some mythic being of his dreams, who has already undertaken the perilous journey into the spiritual world and who can accompany him as he explores and masters the perilous geography of the mysterious realms.

Initially shamanistic activity strikes us as bizarre, but it is not difficult to understand why the shaman is so important. His frenetic actions, séances and trances, precisely because they appear "mad" to other people, break down the boundaries of the everyday world and open up a refreshing (and frightening) realm of new possibilities beyond. The shaman's importance may lie less in what he experiences personally than in his functioning as a hint to the social group that there is indeed a way to break through the limitations on life. Even if occasionally he seems to get lost, he is nonetheless widening the wall that threatens to enclose a people's life. Apparently the human spirit has never been able to suffer indefinitely the suffocation of fixed boundaries. And so the need for a touch of madness to break down the barriers of normality that confine it is almost inevitable. The shaman is needed in order to provide new breathing space, to signal a salvation beyond the monotony of everyday life. This may account for the prestige often bestowed upon the shaman. It also explains how the shaman may be admired and respected even if his wild activity is purely theatrical and deceptive, as it occasionally is.

Do we have any remnants of shamanism today outside of extant hunting and gathering societies, or with the exception of a few exotic cults scattered here and there? There are vestigially shamanistic elements present in the great traditions, but the role of the shaman has largely given way to that played by prophets, priests and priestesses, or other religious officials who began to appear with the rise of agriculture. Still, even in our so-called secular culture there are some interesting parallels to shamanism. It has been suggested, for example, that psychiatrists or depth psychologists provide a similar function for at least some people today. These modern medicine men and women are often invested with supernormal powers by their patients, and they are expected to bring a sort of salvation by widening our psychic horizons. Aware of the limits to the continuity of life, people have always longed for access to a realm of wholeness beyond the brokenness or banality of normal experience, and it has been a long habit of ours to turn special individuals into conveyors of liberation. Thus when priests, sorcerers and prophets no longer have socially prominent roles, and are not invoked to carry on the tradition of shamanism, less sacral personages such as psychiatrists, mental health experts and other gurus of human potential are called upon to fulfill the role of the shaman.

Agriculture and the Religious Significance of Fertility

Around 8000 B.C.E., when the glaciers of the late Ice Age began to recede, the economy of people, first in the Near East and later in Europe and elsewhere, began to shift toward the cultivation of crops and domestication of animals. As this "economic" revolution occurred, a dramatic change took place in the story of early religion. During this period the earth and its fertility became the primary issues of religious concern. The fecundity of nature and its cycles of birth, death and rebirth began to shape the religious imagination in a new way. And the images that were born in the religious awareness of the agricultural revolution have provided the central metaphors and myths of the world's religions ever since. Think, for example, of the savior figure undergoing death and resurrection in Christianity or in Egyptian religion. Both Christ and Osiris die, descend into the depths, and then come to life again. The imaginative basis of these journeys lies in the agricultural experience of grains of wheat, or other seeds, perishing in order to produce new life. The religions of the world owe a supreme debt to the agricultural revolution and the new images of route-finding it called forth.

Agricultural religions are fascinated by the presumably miraculous energy behind the cycles of growth, fertility and rebirth in plants, animals and humans. This energy seems to come ultimately from the earth. Because the earth's fertility is so much like that of a woman's, scholars are now noticing more than they did in the past just how prominently the figure of the mother-goddess emerges in the Neolithic period. Such an esteemed position, according to many scholars, may not always have been accorded to women in the hunting period, since it was probably the men who went looking for means of survival and held the positions of honor, while women dealt with more domestic chores. Nor have women been dominant in most later religious developments, even though it is especially women who have kept religion alive and insured its transmission to their children. But the figure of the woman, and the mother in particular, was especially important in some societies of the early agricultural period, and possibly even before.

The Perennial Issues in Religion

Reflection stimulated by the shocking realities of fertility and death holds a pre-eminent place in the early phases of religion. This fact alone can serve to bring us near to prehistoric religion in spirit, since sex and death are still as much on our minds as on those of our religious forbears. The difference may be that they often coped better than we. Their ritualistic activity arose as part of an effort to deal with the overwhelming power behind the energies of sex, the miracle of life and the capriciousness of death. When we no longer have such rituals to organize the uncontrollable aspects of our experience, we may be less able than many of our ancestors to adapt to them or integrate them into our lives. One very good reason for our studying religion today, even if we are "non-religious" ourselves, is to see how it has helped most people of the past to cope with the twin mysteries of sex and death.

Premonitions of God?

Is there an anticipation of anything like the idea of God present in early religious awareness? Interestingly, preliterate religion, at least in cases that we can easily observe today, does at times make reference to a more or less remote spiritual being. This deity is seen as the creator of the world, giver of the moral law, or pictured as supreme over the other figures in primal mythology. At times people pray to this divinity, but more often than not they ignore it in everyday life, and instead they give their attention to more immediate and personal gods, goddesses and spirits. Scholars of "primitive" religion refer to the remote deity as the "high god," since it is often pictured as inhabiting the sky. This remote being is sometimes called a *deus otiosus,* an idle god serving no useful purpose. (Eliade, 1958, 38–123)

But is this notion of a high god a predecessor of monotheism? Does it prefigure belief in one god such as we find in Judaism, Christianity and Islam? Earlier in this century Wilhelm Schmidt put forth the intriguing theory that monotheism was the earliest form of religion, and belief in the high god a diluted and pale remnant of pristine monotheism. Accordingly, he saw polytheism (belief in many gods) as an even further deviation from the purity of a primordial monotheistic revelation. Such a view is not accepted by most scholars today, since there seems to be little evidence to support it. Most contemporary ideas on the origin of religion are now influenced by the evolutionary thinking that began to appear at the end of the last century. In this evolutionary scheme the idea of God appears relatively late in the story of religion. This approach would discourage us from looking for evidence of monotheism in early religion. What we can see at least dimly, though, is a primal sense of what we shall call "mystery." And it is especially this sense of mystery that links later religions with early ones.

In more recent times many peoples have made a sharp distinction between realities that are "sacred" and deserve our religious reverence, and things that are everyday or matter-of-fact and therefore taken for granted. Because of our modern understanding of religion we may be inclined to place a sharp division between the sacred and the secular. But in primitive tribal existence everyday life and religion form an indivisible unity. And so we do not find there any strongly developed sense of the supernatural. There is an awareness of the "unknown," of the sacred and unmanageable energy in all things, but no crisp notion of a *distinct* realm of transcendence set apart. Such a religious distinction comes later, and it will help us to delineate early religion from most of the so-called "major" religious traditions.

Even so, the primal expressions of religion leave us with the strong impression of at least a partial break from the immediacy of the given world. In animism, for example, there are the first stages of a piercing

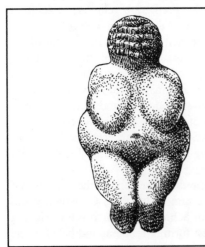

A neolithic "Venus," found in Willendorf, Austria.
An obvious fertility figure.

through to another dimension, even though the latter is quite vague and not yet peopled with deities like those we observe in the Greek pantheon or in Roman, Egyptian and Sumerian religions. In that remote sense it is tempting to say that there is a vague "premonition of God," but it would not be wise to impose "theistic" features on early religion.

Conclusion

It is impossible to summarize clearly and adequately the way primitive religion confronts the problem of suffering. All of the aspects of religion mentioned above are part of this enterprise. However, a special place must be given to what we have called animism. The primal intuition that there is more to humans (and even animals and plants) than meets the empirical eye still survives in some form in most religions today as part of their own paths. Belief in a dimension of existence more subtle and durable than mortal bodiliness has provided millions with the suspicion that there is a wider world encompassing our immediate one. And this belief makes living in this one tolerable and meaningful. It provides a way out, beyond the anguish of suffering, fate and death.

Thus, even in the earliest phases of human existence there seems to have dawned the sense of a realm of "mystery" which will remain a constant aspect of religion. Later we shall have to clarify more carefully what we mean by "mystery." But we may discern at least the beginnings of the "mystic" sense in the animism, sacrifices, rituals, shamanism and myths of early religion.

2.

Hinduism

By the middle of the first millennium B.C.E. a monumental new development had occurred in the story of religion. In Asia as well as the Near East the primal intuition of mystery had undergone a dramatic transformation. While elements of "primitive" religion and myth still lived on (and continue to survive at a certain level in popular religion to this day), theological reflection on religion had moved closer to an explicit awareness of the transcendence and oneness of an "ultimate reality."

The earliest phases of religion do not appear to have had a clear impression of the unity and transcendence of the divine. And even though later developments in religion had multiplied gods and goddesses, and had proliferated into countless complex rituals and cults, a sharp sense of the divine as a radically transcendent unity did not arise until the middle centuries of the first thousand years B.C.E. At this time a new theological sensitivity began to consolidate the religious experience of the sacred into an absolute oneness beyond all individual objects of experience, and even beyond the gods themselves.

This innovative theological development had grown up out of disillusionment with the often magical and crude features of much popular religious practice. It was motivated by the desire to place religious life on a more substantial foundation. In the case of Buddhism, which appeared during this same period, disgust with the superficial state of religion in India was so unsparing that the Buddha and his disciples questioned seriously the value of any talk about ultimate reality at all. But in other parts of the religious world, instead of being abandoned, the idea of an ultimate divine reality received an attention and devotion that has remained perhaps the single most significant feature of religion up until modern times. This new sense of "the divine" did not mean exactly the same thing in

India as in the West, but it shares with Judaism, Christianity and Islam the connotation of an ultimate mystery of sacral *oneness* beyond the world of ordinary experience.

The "monotheistic" movement in religion was not always popular. The prophets of Israel, some of whom were contemporary with this epochal religious trend, encountered stiff resistance to their reformist ideas that Yahweh is the *one* trustworthy God. In India, China, Persia and the Hellenistic world similar intuitions of a single transcendent mystery came up against the polytheism (belief in many gods and goddesses) of the religious masses. And in Hinduism we meet one of the most striking examples of the timeless struggle between "God and the gods."

Central Teachings of Hinduism

One of the most direct ways of gaining acquaintance with a religious tradition is to examine how it helps its devotees come to grips with the universal fact of human suffering. We can "get inside" of a religion, in some small degree at least, if we learn how it responds to pain and to the fact of death. This is especially true of our attempts to appreciate the religions of India. These religious traditions initially seem exotic and even forbidding. But if we remember that they are venerable attempts to break through the limitations that have frustrated *all* of us, we may then become part of their own circle of meaning. And although their symbols and doctrines initially seem culturally alien to us, there is a universal element in them that speaks to us as well.

In central Asia for a period of more than thirty-five hundred years a family of religions known collectively as "Hinduism" has flourished. The term "Hinduism" is derived from the name of the Indus river in India. It is commonly used to designate a complex group of religious attitudes, practices and ideas ranging from extremely "primitive" sacrificial cults to some of the most "sophisticated" metaphysical thinking the world has yet seen. It is impossible to find a common set of meanings that ties this rich body of religious traditions tightly together into a consistent whole. Its elements are so diverse that they defy easy systematization. So in order to gain an initial understanding of Hinduism we must look for general tendencies that we can abstract from the morass of religious phenomena that gives it some vague sort of identity. One way of doing this is to focus on several ways in which Hindu religious notions have dealt with the problem of suffering.

Central Hindu teachings tell us that our ordinary life is caught up in an endless procession of events known (in the Sanskrit language) as *samsara*. *Samsara* binds us to the transient and imperfect world which is the abode of suffering. It prevents us from reaching the liberation, or *moksha*, that we long for. *Samsara* is the condition of being caught up in time and perishability, of being vulnerable to weakness, ignorance, pain or unhappiness in general. But it is, above all, the condition of being tied to the cycle of rebirth.

For people in and around the world of India the imperfection of life, the sense of its inadequacies and lack of fulfillment, is usually symbolized by the likelihood of rebirth. Most of us have an intuition that the present life we are living is not completely satisfactory. Either through our own fault or because of injustice and fate, the threads of our lives never seem to be tied up in a perfectly neat way. We remain unfinished, never completely rounded off. In the East this feeling of not being fulfilled is given expression in the doctrine of "reincarnation". This is the belief that after we die in our typically incomplete condition we may be reborn into lower or higher forms of being. We might come back as a worm, fish or other animal, as a king or even a god or goddess, depending on our conduct in this and previous lives. And this cycle may be repeated millions of times.

The notion of reincarnation may seem strange to non-Asians, although recently it has begun to gain more appeal among some Westerners. But in India and many other places in the East the sense of not yet having attained one's true destiny is epitomized in the uncomfortable prospect of undergoing a series of births and rebirths from which there is no easy escape. The "unsatisfactoriness" of ordinary, unliberated life is vividly captured in this ancient image of the cycle of rebirths that stands in the way of *moksha*, of ultimate freedom.

To be faced with a long succession of deaths and rebirths, of being again and again "reincarnated" in a variety of lesser or higher beings, vividly captures for the Eastern mind what it means to be separated from one's essential being. At the same time, however, the concept of rebirth also makes allowance at least for an *eventual* liberation from the frustrating world of *samsara*. One is not destined to remain forever bound to the cycle of rebirth. There are pathways through which one can come to ultimate deliverance, sometimes by one's own efforts, at other times by the sheer grace of God. And this promise of final deliverance makes the notion of rebirth less severe than the idea of eternal punishment in hell.

The woes of entanglement in *samsara* are in turn the working out of a more fundamental metaphysical principle, the law of *karma*. *Karma* is the inflexible principle that gives consistency and predictability to the universe. Like our laws of physics it is relentless and immutable. All things must follow its rigorous demands. In a sense *karma* is something for which we may be grateful since it prevents any whimsical deviations from the routines that make all levels of the universe function. But its workings also consign us to a fatalistic cycle of rebirths if our actions and lives are not in accordance with the demands of duty (*dharma*). Just as the laws of physics state that for every action there is a corresponding reaction, the law of *karma* holds that we must reap exactly what we sow. The "law" of *karma* keeps us locked into the world of *samsara* and rebirth as long as we have not found the appropriate way to liberation. Being consigned to the world of suffering in *samsara* is simply the application to our own existence of the remorseless *karma* that rules the world.

Ignorance and Salvation

As long as we remain enmeshed in *samsara* we are in a state of ignorance, or *avidya* (literally "unknowing") about our true situation, and this ignorance is the proximate cause of our suffering. *Avidya* means that we as individuals *do not know who we really are*. We are ordinarily oblivious to our real identity. Immersed as we are in the normal routines of life and labor, we remain out of touch with our inner being. Our ignorance turns reality into a mere veil (*maya*) that covers up the truth about the world and ourselves. What we *take* to be real is usually in fact *maya*, illusion, and not reality at all. As in the case of other great religions, Hinduism is alert to the ways in which we allow ourselves to be deceived. The notions of *avidya* and *maya* point to this common state of deception.

But just what is the true inner state of our being, the core identity that eludes our grasp and remains covered up by our ignorance? Important teachings of Hinduism give a breathtaking answer to this question: in our deepest selves *we are essentially at one with God* (or *Brahman*). And salvation means to realize this unity. For some Hindu teachers the unity is an actual identity with *Brahman* (ultimate reality); for others it is not a literal identity of the self and God, but rather a difference-in-unity. In whatever way we understand it, though, Hindus generally hold that we are for the most part unaware of this unity with *Brahman*, thus rendering our lives unsatisfactory. The experience of *moksha* would then consist of the blissful awareness that our existence is not separate and isolated, but one with ultimate reality.

Hindu religion, to reiterate, locates the roots of suffering in our ignorance of this unity. Ignorance is the result not simply of intellectual dullness but of a way of living that strays off the course of genuine devotion to duty or *dharma*. *Avidya* implies missing the whole point of life because of an attachment to things that are unworthy of us and too small for us. At the center of our being we are identical with, or at least intimately related to, the

Godhead, and so attachment to finite things leaves us deeply distracted and dissatisfied. We superficially shape our sense of selfhood by our relations with mere objects, or our place in society, or our careers, even though our true identity is that of being in union with the divine. The process of salvation then would consist of finding the pathway out of this ignorance. Various types of *yoga*, meditation, devotion to a special deity, and the performance of good works, provide the pathways to liberation.

Hindus express their belief in the identity of the Self with God in a couple of famous short doctrinal formulas: *"Atman Brahman,"* which means that the Self is one with God; and *"tat tvam asi"* ("that art thou") implying "you are one with ultimate reality." What these expressions mean is too rich to say in a few words, and only actual experience, not mere reading about them, can lead one to an understanding of them. But, according to the ninth century Hindu philosopher Shankara, both items point to the belief that all things and persons are at the root of their being in complete unity with God. There is no separate identity or ego. The ego's impression of a distinct identity is an illusion. In the world of *maya* and *samsara* things and selves merely *appear* to be distinct, diverse and real. But actually *Brahman* alone is real. If we could fully understand this, according to Shankara and many other Hindus, we would perceive that our suffering has no independent reality either. The purpose of life is to experience the ultimate unity of all things, and in this experience suffering dissolves into joy.

Hindu Scriptures

The religious history encompassed by the name "Hinduism" can be divided roughly into three periods, the first running from about 1500 to 600 B.C.E., the second occurring in the years surrounding the sixth century B.C.E., and the third consisting of the complex development of Hindu devotional life from the sixth century up to the present. Major themes of the first period's religious life are represented in a body of sacred writings known as the *Vedas,* and those of the second period in the *Upanishads,* meditations later attached to the *Vedas.* The religious life of the first phase, the Vedic period, is dominated by sacrifices and ritually-oriented practice, together with a growing emphasis on the priestly class. However, the time of the *Upanishads,* beginning not long before the sixth century B.C.E., expresses misgivings about the cumbersome features of a religious life reduced to rituals and sacrifices. In the *Upanishads* we observe a turn away from the polytheism and ritual complexity that clings to ceremonial cults. There is a gradual conversion to a more explicit belief in the transcendence and unity of the divine, that is, of *Brahman*. The *Upanishads* do not abandon the vivid myths of the Vedas, and they strive to remain in touch with the rich Vedic sacrificial tradition. But at the same time they interpret the stories in the *Vedas* as pointing to an ultimate oneness beyond the plurality of the gods. They refer to this ultimate reality as *Brahman*, and they teach us that coming to consciousness of our union with *Brahman* is the final purpose of our existence, as well as the solution to our suffering and mortality.

During the same general time period in which Upanishadic religion emerged (around the sixth century B.C.E.) both Buddhism and Jainism appeared in India, and they too represent a distaste for the multiplication of gods and many burdensome religious practices. In fact, this period is a pivotal time in the story of religion the world over. In China, Europe and the Near East, as well as in India, there occurred almost simultaneous unifying and simplifying developments in religious speculation. In the movement known as Taoism in China, in the emerging metaphysics of the pre-Socratic philosophers in the West, in the Zoroastrian religion in Persia, in the belief in one God concerned with justice in the religion of Israel, and in the Brahmanism of the *Upanishads,* there occurred a major planetary shift of religious consciousness. Theological reflection began to move religion away from exclusive preoccupation with a multiplicity of deities and devils, and toward the transcendent "oneness" perceived beneath, beyond or within the world.

Philosopher Karl Jaspers was so impressed with the widespread perception of an ultimate transcendent unity and the corresponding critique of polytheism during this period that he called it the *axial age*. The centuries surrounding 600 B.C.E. may be the most crucial in the historical unfolding of religion on the earth. It will be useful for us to refer often to this "axial age" as we move further in our inquiry into religion.

Within the Hindu tradition it is especially the *Upanishads* that express the axial emergence of a sense of ultimate "oneness" underlying all appearances. And this impression of a divine unity is a powerful response to the problem of sorrow, suffering and death. Here is a sample of Upanishadic teaching:

> The universe is a tree eternally existing, its root aloft, its branches spread below. The pure root of the tree is Brahman, the immortal, in whom the three worlds have their being, whom none can transcend, who is verily Self.
> The whole universe came forth from Brahman and moves in

Brahman. Mighty and awful is he, like to a thunderbolt crashing loud through the heavens. For those who attain him death has no terror.

In fear of him fire burns, the sun shines, the rains fall, the winds blow, and death kills.

If a man fails to attain Brahman before he casts off his body, he must again put on a body in the world of created things.

In one's own soul Brahman is realized clearly, as if seen in a mirror. . . .

When all the senses are stilled, when the mind is at rest, when the intellect wavers not—then, say the wise, is reached the highest state.

This calm of the senses and the mind has been defined as yoga. He who attains it is freed from delusion.

In one not freed from delusion this calm is uncertain, unreal: it comes and goes. Brahman words cannot reveal, mind cannot reach, eyes cannot see. How then, save through those who know him, can he be known?

There are two selves, the apparent self and the real Self. Of these it is the real Self, and he alone, who must be felt as truly existing. To the man who has felt him as truly existing he reveals his inmost nature. (*Katha Upanishad*, in Prabhavananda and Manchester, 1957, 23f.)

The theological revolutions that occurred during the axial age deflated the importance of sacrifices and rituals that dominated the Vedic period. Such religious practices can go only so far in helping us deal with suffering and death. Belief in many personal gods may give a familiar face to the often harsh and impersonal universe, and they can thereby make it more habitable. Attachment to specific deities, praying and sacrificing to them, is one way of seeking liberation from suffering, and for many peoples of the world it is enough. However, the *Upanishads* are not satisfied with the ages-old sacrificial cults and the proliferation of prayers and practices focusing on a pantheon of lesser deities. They encourage us to ground our religious lives in a more permanent Being beyond the transient symbolic representations found in all types of popular religion. They by no means discard popular piety with its rich narratives and symbolic patterns of thought. But they survey the ancient stories in search of a more fundamental reality, deeper and more lasting than all the gods and goddesses of which they tell. The Sanskrit term *Brahman* is used by Hindus to name the ultimate unity that gives all things their being, and that manifests itself in each apparently separate and unique existence.

SUBTLE ESSENCE OF ALL THINGS

When Svetaketu was twelve years old, his father Uddalaka said to him, "Svetaketu, you must now go to school and study. None of our family, my child, is ignorant of Brahman."

Thereupon Svetaketu went to a teacher and studied for twelve years. After committing to memory all the Vedas, he returned home full of pride in his learning.

His father, noticing the young man's conceit, said to him: "Svetaketu, have you asked for that knowledge by which we hear the unhearable, by which we perceive the unperceivable, by which we know the unknowable?"

"What is that knowledge, sir?" asked Svetaketu.

"My child, as by knowing one lump of clay, all things made of clay are known, the difference being only in name and arising from speech, and the truth being that all are clay; as by knowing a nugget of gold, all things made of gold are known, the difference being only in name and arising from speech, and the truth being that all are gold—exactly so is that knowledge, knowing which we know all."

"But surely those venerable teachers of mine are ignorant of this knowledge; for if they had possessed it, they would have taught it to me. Do you therefore, sir, give me that knowledge."

"Be it so," said Uddalaka, and continued thus:

"In the beginning there was Existence, One only, without a second. Some say that in the beginning there was non-existence only, and that out of that the universe was born. But how could such a thing be? How could existence be born of non-existence? No, my son, in the beginning there was Existence alone—One only, without a second. He, the One, thought to himself: Let me be many, let me grow forth. Thus out of himself he projected the universe; and having projected out of himself the universe, he entered into every being. All that is has its self in him alone. Of all things he is the subtle essence. He is the truth. He is the Self, And that, Svetaketu, THAT ART THOU."

From Max Müller, ed. *The Sacred Books of the East*. Oxford: Clarendon Press, 1897.

Suffering as the Illusion of Separation

If it can be demonstrated that the realm in which sorrow makes its abode is not really real, if it can be shown that it is only a scheme of appearances and no more than that, then suffering can be placed in an entirely new perspective. It need no longer be taken so seriously, for in fact it has no genuine existence. It is only painful as long as we think (in our typical state of ignorance) that this world of suffering is the real world, and that our apparent self is our real Self. The *Upanishads* teach us that the world of diversity and suffering is not the real world and that our apparent, suffering self is not real either. This unrealistic impression of things gives rise to the world of *maya*, a word usually translated as "illusion" but signifying much more than a wrong impression. *Maya* is the illusory world in which diversity, differentiation and separate selfhood seem to be real in themselves rather than manifestations of an underlying oneness. Suffering is an aspect of the unreal world of *maya*. Thus if we could arrive at the point of acknowledging the illusory nature of *maya*, then suffering could be vanquished.

According to the *Upanishads* the universe is originally an undifferentiated unity. *Brahman*, or what might be called "Being," is itself undivided, non-dual. But because of the narrowness of our human vision we ordinarily experience being in its plurality and diversity without sensing the unity underlying the diversity. And our abiding in the condition of *maya*, in which we are unaware of the unity of all things, is the cause of suffering.

If the individual person actually experiences (and not merely "thinks" of) his or her suffering as inseparable from the ultimate unity of things, it then no longer qualifies as unconquerable suffering. For what causes the agony of suffering is the isolation that comes with it, our conviction that it is disconnected from the rest of things. Pain loses its sting if it can be linked to a larger unity in which its seeming independence is dissolved. In the midst of suffering we often feel extremely alone, and this privacy compounds the anguish. But if our suffering is situated in the larger perspective of an ultimate unity and meaning, the edge is taken off of it. The *Upanishads* and the many later Hindu teachings based on them respond to the problem of suffering by convincing sufferers that they belong to a permanent unity of being. The concrete experience of belonging to this unity is itself salvific. In theistic religions of the West also salvation is sometimes called "atonement" (at-*one*-ment). Bringing about a sense of oneness, of deep belonging, is in some way or another the method of all religious salvation from suffering.

How often we are able actually to experience our suffering in terms of a wider and deeper unity is another question, of course. But the *Upa-*

nishads point to the intriguing possibility of our overcoming suffering if we could just see things the right way. *Seeing* things rightly is the main pathway through the limitations on life. Genuine liberation, *moksha*, is possible if things and selves are illuminated properly. But this means defeating the illusion of separateness and diversity. It means above all overcoming the impression that our inmost self, *Atman*, is different from *Brahman*. To see ourselves and our apparent suffering as *Brahman* is the solution to the problem of sorrow, pain and anxiety. This does not mean that we cease to feel suffering or pain. But

> . . .[t]he individual who has an adequate grasp of *Brahman* will find that suffering falls away in significance. Since everything that happens is a manifestation of *Brahman*, it follows that true understanding only arises when the accidents of time and space are penetrated and are seen to reveal *Brahman*. *Brahman* pervades all things without being exhausted in any one of them; which means that suffering or sorrow cannot be the final truth about existence. (Bowker, 1970, 227)

But how does such perception of the ultimate unity of things actually become possible for us? Certainly not by reading a book or taking a class in religion. One may find release from suffering and the cycle of rebirths only by concrete participation in the special meditative practices, devotional life or pursuit of duty and discipleship prescribed by various aspects of Hindu teaching. And in the development of Hinduism, continuing up to our own day, we find an extremely rich variety of such ways to liberation. Some of these are described in the most famous of all Hindu texts, the *Bhagavadgita*.

The *Bhagavadgita*

We are more than just rational or feeling beings who can simply think, wish or feel our suffering away. We are also acting beings, and Hinduism is aware of this fact. One must act appropriately, following the demands of duty, in order to find release from the cycle of rebirths. And appropriate acting means working not for the sake of the rewards or fruit of one's efforts, but simply for the sake of duty itself. One must learn to be detached from the many things that absorb our attention and distract us from discovery of the *Atman*, the Ultimate Self beneath the ego. And detachment from concern for the fruits of our labor is one way to reach this goal.

The theme of devotion to duty without being obsessed with the fruits of action, that is without focusing on the possible outcomes of one's efforts, is one of the most impressive contributions of Hinduism to the world of religion. And this ideal is nowhere more beautifully presented than in the most famous of all Hindu writings, the *Bhagavadgita*. The *Gita* is not a part of the *Vedas* or the *Upanishads*, but it is the most widely read Hindu religious document. Its value lies partly in the fact that it sets forth clearly the main ways of release from *samsara*. Reading this accessible work is one of the best ways to become familiar with Hindu religious ideas and practices.

The *Gita* is part of a larger narrative concerned with an ancient feud between two clans descended from the same ancestor. At a decisive moment in the epic the hero of one of the clans, a warrior named Arjuna, realizes just prior to battle that he is about to slay members of his own blood line. Understandably he is anxious about entering into the fray. Turning to his charioteer, Krishna, who is the famous Hindu deity, *Vishnu*, incarnate as a man, Arjuna expresses his reservations about fighting his own kin. It would be a shirking of his duty were he not to fight, but it would violate the sacred obligation to care for his family if he participated in their slaughter. Arjuna fears that he will inevitably violate the sacred *dharma*, the right order of things, no matter what decision he makes. And so he agonizes over his impossible situation, seeking help from Krishna:

> When I see my own people arrayed and eager for fight, O Krishna, my limbs quail, my mouth goes dry, my body shakes and my hair stands on end. . . . I do not long for victory, O Krishna, nor do I foresee any good by slaying my own people in the fight. . . . So it is not right that we slay our kinsmen. . . . Indeed how can we be happy, O Madhava (Krishna), if we kill our own people? . . . In the ruin of a family its ancient laws are destroyed: and when the laws perish, the whole family yields to lawlessness. . . . Having spoken thus on the field of battle, Arjuna sank down on the seat of his chariot, casting away his bow and arrow, his spirit overwhelmed by sorrow. (1, 28–47)

All of us face difficult situations and moral dilemmas at times, perhaps not so severe as Arjuna's, but nevertheless, just as impossible. And we wonder how we should act, or where we might gain the courage to act appropriately. The answer Krishna gives to Arjuna's crisis is that of the *Upanishads*. It is a distinctively religious response, lifting the whole conversation above the plain of ethical conflict and placing it in a wider perspective. And within this wider framework the ethical conflict is relativized in importance. It is a good example of how religion "works" by introducing a wide, mystery-filled perspective beyond ethical or everyday worries.

In the first place, Krishna responds, death is not a threat to the self since the self is inseparable from the eternal *Brahman*. Krishna tells Arjuna:

> "Wise men do not grieve for the dead or for the living. Never was there a time when I was not, nor thou, nor these lords of men, nor will there ever be a time hereafter when we shall cease to be. . . . Know thou that that by which all this is pervaded is indestructible. Of this immutable being, no one can bring about the destruction." (2, 11–12)

Thus it is knowledge of our unity with *the indestructible nature of ultimate reality* that can give us courage in the face of the apparent transience of life. The truly real abides forever. And so, feeling our inherent connection with it, we may plunge into life without fear that our actions will inflict irreparable damage. The eternal and unitary nature of ultimate reality make it foolish for us to take ourselves, or any particular thing or person with ultimate seriousness. Even ethical dilemmas are not of final importance. Only *Brahman* is ultimate. All else is relative, and knowledge of the eternal ground of all things can eliminate our anxiety. Krishna's words to Arjuna echo the *Upanishad's* groping for a transcendent unity that eternally rescues the world and ourselves from the apparent condition of separateness and perishability.

This is one side of Krishna's response to Arjuna's suffering, but there is another as well: Krishna tells Arjuna to act without concern for the results of his efforts. This advice initially sounds peculiar to our pragmatic, goal-oriented way of approaching ordinary life. We usually organize our activity in order to attain certain ends or rewards for our labor. To act without attending to the consequences of one's action sounds like an impossible and even foolish command. And yet Krishna's advice epitomizes Hindu religious wisdom by setting forth a path to freedom that carries us beyond the requirements of a purely pragmatic existence. If we could undertake our work without worrying excessively about whether it leads to the goals we prefer, we might experience the beginnings of liberation. Krishna's advice is not entirely different from what biblical religion refers to as following the "will of God." For Jews, Muslims and Christians this imperative also initially seems burdensome, but the religiously wise testify to its ultimately liberating consequences. Religions often tell of the need to be ready to detach ourselves from what we, in our separate identities and limited perspectives, would like to happen. And they all exhort us to surrender ourselves and our efforts to a wider, transcendent scheme, the ends of which are not within our view. We are asked by the great teachings simply to trust that *in the final analysis,* and in a way that we are not able to see at the present moment, things will work out for the best.

Such, for instance, seems to be the instruction of the *Gita.* "To action alone hast thou a right and never at all to its fruit; let not the fruits of action be thy motive; neither let there be in thee any attachment to inaction." This theme of "detachment" is a major facet of all the great religious teachings. And though it may initially seem severe, its final intention is that of liberation into a wider world of mystery.

The Stages of Life

Hinduism also sets forth a series of life stages that will ideally lead to liberation. These are not open to all because restraints of caste and gender disallow participation by outcastes and women. But for males there are three life stages, those of student, householder and retiree. And in some cases there is a fourth possibility, though not strictly speaking a stage, that of the *sannyasin,* one who altogether renounces the world by taking up the life of an *ascetic.*

The first stage, that of the student, is of different durations for boys of different castes. Its purpose, however, is to instill in youth a sense of their tradition, of duty and identity at a time before they become too preoccupied with the encumbrances of being a householder. The second stage, that of householder, is the time for entering into the affairs of society, raising a family, seeking success in business or other professions, leaving one's mark on the world. Hinduism looks kindly on, and even enthusiastically promotes, worldly ambition and the pleasures that accompany a successful life. It can do so because it knows that there is a time for everything, and that the day will come when one has had enough of the pursuit of riches and secular achievements.

The middle years of life are the time for full engagement with the world. But the energies of such a life eventually ebb, and so the Hindu organization of life leads naturally to a third stage, that of retirement. Traditionally this stage is a time for contemplation. Removed from the obligations of family life and labor, a retiree could depart to the forest or some other remote place. There he could begin to practice more intensely the devotional life prescribed by the *Upanishads.* In short, one could come closer to the Self and the mystery of *Brahman.*

Finally, a fourth possibility is open even beyond that of retirement. Actually one may slip into this "stage" at any point in life, and so it does not presuppose successful negotiation of the other three stages. It is that of the *sannyasin*. Partly influenced by the emergence of Jainism and Buddhism, the *sannyasi* is one who takes up the ascetic life, that is, a life of renouncing all the pleasures of the world and all social status and identity in order to devote himself fully and without distraction to the goal of union with God.

The Caste System

Indian society is hierarchically ordered into several levels or castes. At the highest echelon are the priests or Brahmins. Right beneath them are the Kshatriyas, made up of warriors and nobles. Then at the next lower rung of the social ladder are the Vaishyas who consist of farmers and those engaged in commerce. Beneath them are the Shudras, the servant class. Finally, lowest of all, are the outcastes or the untouchables. These are considered "filthy" and so are given the most degrading kinds of employment. They are said to deserve their lot because of misdeeds in some previous life.

Our reaction to this system is understandably one of shock at the injustice it seems to perpetrate. But we must recognize that the caste system goes hand in hand with the doctrines of *karma* and reincarnation. Religiously speaking, it does not seem to many Hindus to be unjust. People end up in a particular class because their deeds have deserved it. After all, they might also have been reincarnated as vermin or rodents. The caste system is an expression of a cosmic system of retribution that transcends any particular person's life. Without the stratification into social levels such as the caste system provides there would be little visible evidence that one can get closer to the point of breaking out of the cycle of rebirth. Members of a lower class will therefore usually accept the interpretation that their lowly situation is the result of bad *karma*. And the existence of more privileged classes into which they might eventually be reborn is a visible reminder of possibilities of salvation that they might not be aware of if society were purely homogeneous.

Modern skeptics and those more at home with the prophetic religions of the West cannot help asking, though, whether this caste system is perhaps a classic case of "religious legitimation." (See Chapter 11) Is the religious teaching about *karma* and reincarnation an ingenious ideology designed only for the purpose of preserving the social status quo, keeping people content with their unjust social lot? Or is it an indispensable symbolic way of teaching the timeless doctrines of *karma* and reincarnation?

Bhakti

In spite of the *Upanishads'* lofty ideals of devotion to the transcendent
One, popular religious piety needs more diversity and color. The rather
impersonal notion of *Brahman* may seem somewhat austere and abstract to
the average devotee. Psychologically speaking religious individuals in all
the traditions need to see a personal face on the ultimate mystery. Even the
great theologians at times have their own favorite deities that link them to
the one ultimate reality of theological reflection. People ordinarily require
some vivid representation of the godhead. Religions in the concrete seem
to revolve around images, places of worship, charismatic leaders and teachers, sacred writings, elaborate rituals, processions, celebrations, doctrines
and codes of conduct. At times religious people seem to get lost in the
colorful multiplicity of objects of worship and convoluted practices. Religions have very specific, anthropomorphic (human-like) and sometimes
therio-morphic (animal-like) representations of the sacred. What are we to
make of this tendency of religions to relate to very specific gods, goddesses
and images of God?

The great religious reformers since the first millennium B.C.E. are
often wary of a possible temptation to "idolatry" (= worship of images or
idols). Whenever we take this or that representation of deity too seriously
we are likely to miss the deeper reality it represents. Religious reformers
often fear that we are thereby substituting an image for what is in reality
imageless. We are confusing something finite with an infinite mystery
incapable of representation. But popular religion keeps turning up with
diverse devotional practices and many colorful images of God. This is
especially true of Hinduism, but to a considerable degree of all the other
religious traditions as well.

In Hindu piety there is a need to relate to ultimate reality by way of
intermediary deities. Two of the most popular are *Vishnu* and *Shiva.* These
and thousands of other deities continue to nourish the religious lives of
devout Hindus. Today the majority of Indians are devotees of either *Vishnu*
(the renewer of worlds) or of *Shiva* (the destroyer of worlds). The respec-
tive sects devoted to them are known as Vaishnavism and Shaivism.

In subcultures of India it is normal also to find a small statue of one of
the other innumerable gods in the average household. Elaborate ceremonies centering on these figures are undertaken daily by Hindu families,
and the result is the feeling of "personally" relating to God by way of such
intermediary images. Although a Muslim, Christian or Jew might suspect
idolatry in these rituals, Hindu religious teachers give a more lenient
interpretation. The images do not compete with *Brahman.* Rather they
point to or "symbolize" the divine in a very lively and wholesome way.

There are millions of gods, but still only one God. This God needs a face, and popular religion is only too eager to provide as many as are required.

Devotion to the gods is called *bhakti*. In *bhakti* one chooses a god or goddess such as *Vishnu, Shiva, Kali* or *Krishna* in order to establish an interpersonal relationship with the Godhead. In an analogous way Christians relate to God by way of prayerful devotion to the figure of Christ or one or more of the saints. Most religious people seem to need something like *bhakti*, devotion to a particular deity, as their way toward union with the Absolute. Very few are able to relate to God without the help of vivid images that arouse feelings of love, gratitude and piety. And so the colorful personal deities of folk religion are venerated not just by the uneducated, but to some degree also by mystics and philosophers. A feeling of the warmth of dialogue with God is of importance for most religious people, including scholars and mystics. And in India innumerable gods of hearth, home and village saturate the religious life of seers as well as the masses.

This devotional, and seemingly polytheistic, style of religious life might seem to be in conflict with the *Upanishads'* emphasis on the need for relation with the one mystery of *Brahman*. But, at least for most Hindu theologians, there need be no contradiction. In fact the oscillating back and forth between the poles of unity and diversity ensures the liveliness of the religious tradition as a whole.

Conclusion

The earliest phases of the Hindu tradition are similar to those we associated with "primitive" religion. But during the axial period a question was raised about whether the gods and goddesses of popular piety any longer had religious significance, and if so, how should they be situated with reference to the one ultimate reality. In surveying the variety of responses Hindus give to this question we take note of one of the major issues that still enchants all religious inquirers: is ultimate reality impersonal, or is God somehow personal? On the one hand, if God is a person, does that not make Him or Her too small, encapsulating the infinite in the finite clothing of gender, moods and actions that are proper to weak mortals? But if God is impersonal, how could human persons ever establish any meaningful relationship with the divine? Hindu theological reflection continues to wrestle with these questions.

3

Buddhism

Sometime during the sixth century before the Common Era a man named Siddhartha, who was later to be called the Buddha, was born into the wealthy clan of Gautama near Benares in India. He spent his early years in the security and affluence of a prince. Groomed by his father to live out his days in the royal style, he was educated, married, had a son and did what was expected of one who would someday become king. However, around the age of thirty he suddenly became aware of the "unsatisfactoriness" of life. Until this time his father had protected him from the uglier realities of the world. But one day, during a brief excursion from the palace, Gautama (as he was also called) observed three striking instances of human misery. First he came upon a man ravaged by the wrinkles and sufferings of old age; then he saw someone beset with disease; and finally he witnessed the body of a dead person. His charioteer explained to him that these are examples of the pervasive reality of human misery. On the same occasion Gautama also noticed a monk who had renounced the world and taken up a life of strict asceticism, and he marvelled at the state of peace the ascetic seemed to have achieved in the face of all the suffering around him.

Deeply disturbed by the specter of human suffering, Gautama began to rethink his life. How, he pondered, could anyone be happy, given the threats of suffering, old age and death? Not by any means a new question, since it is universal, it pressed upon him in a way that he could not ignore. And he abruptly came to the conclusion that he could no longer persist in the luxurious style that had buffered him from the harsh facts of life.

According to legend, on the very night of his encounter with the miseries of life Gautama began his spiritual pilgrimage. He took a drastic step that might strike many of us as curious, but in the story it symbolizes his special need to remove himself completely and dramatically from his former way of living. He went to his wife's bedroom, bade farewell to her and his infant son, and rode off into the dark. He had made an irrevocable commitment to find an answer to the questions aroused by his experience of the negativities of life, and a complete turnaround seemed the only way to begin.

Thus he broke utterly with his past, forsaking his former life in what Buddhists have called "the Great Going Out" or "the Great Renunciation." Buddhist teachings hold that in some way or other, not necessarily in so dramatic a way perhaps, each of us as well can find peace only after we have broken from a life of clinging to ourselves, ambitions, things and other persons as though they were permanent. And in Gautama's renunciation of an illusory, shallow and unsatisfying existence, his followers are given an abiding model that might motivate them also to undertake a similar renunciation within the special context of their own lives.

But where would Gautama look for an answer to the riddle of human suffering? At first he tried what many a sensitive soul at that time would have done. He sought out a guru or teacher who would fill him with knowledge and wisdom. But this tactic proved fruitless. As Gautama was to learn, mere discipleship alone would not bring salvation, for one has to experience life on one's own. Simply following doctrines imposed by another fails to touch you at the core of your being and consciousness.

Taking another approach then Gautama experimented with a severe spiritual discipline of the senses. He joined a small band of monks, and for six years he followed the regime of the ascetics who fasted and wandered aimlessly about trying to purify their souls completely of bodily and sensual inclinations. Legend has it that Gautama outfasted all the other monks in quest of lasting release from sorrow. But again, this self-punishing discipline failed to bring happiness. Gautama remained deeply dissatisfied, still attached to the wheel of rebirths. He must have said to himself: "What more can one do than I have done in order to find peace. I have tried everything, and nothing seems to bring me any closer to my goal. Is there no answer to the problem of suffering? Are there any other paths available?"

In spite of temptations to despair Gautama refused to abandon his quest, and this grittiness has endeared him to his followers for two and a half thousand years. The elaborate descriptions of his perseverance provide for Buddhists of all types the basis for trust in the meaning of their own lives as a search for final freedom. For those who have not yet found peace amidst their struggles the story of Gautama's endurance remains a bulwark of enormous strength. His followers' drawing upon the Buddha's personal courage is not entirely unlike the Christian's receiving strength to face the trials of life by identifying with the sufferings of Christ, or the

Stoic's gaining strength from the tale of Socrates' intrepid stance in the face of execution. In all such cases the knowledge that liberation was eventually attained by the master provides incentive for the disciples to go forward in spite of frustration.

One day, having reached a point of near starvation from fasting, and realizing that the punishment of his senses had brought him no closer to his goal, Gautama went to a tavern and ate a normal meal. The ascetic's life had failed to bring him release, and the act of eating signalled a new turn in his quest. This act shocked his former monastic associates, and so they abandoned him. But Gautama, in his utter aloneness, journeyed to the banks of a river and sat down under a fig tree, or what has come to be called the *bodhi* tree. Vowing not to arise until he had found the answer to his tormenting questions, he fell into a deep meditative trance. After a long period of time (one that has been highly exaggerated in the legendary accounts), and after overcoming nearly irresistible temptations to veer from his objective, "enlightenment" came. In a moment of sudden illumination Gautama "saw the light" and found the solution to the problem of pain. Henceforth he was the Buddha, the Enlightened One. No longer tied to the oppressive cycle of rebirths, he had entered into the bliss of *nirvana*.

We do not know exactly what the Buddha's experience of enlightenment was like. In Buddhist teachings, each person must experience it himself or herself in order to understand it. Silence is the most appropriate response to the experience. Enlightenment cannot be put into words that would adequately communicate its content. But Buddhist tradition has handed down at least some of the substance of Gautama's illumination in the formulations known as the Four Noble Truths and the Eightfold Path. In the midst of his enlightenment it occurred to Gautama that suffering ceases and happiness begins only in the moment that one stops "clinging" to things and even to life itself. Renunciation of clinging (*tanha*) is the "way" to salvation. And under the *bodhi* tree (the tree of enlightenment) this sincere searcher experienced the blissful results of his "way of renunciation." Henceforth he has rightly earned the name of Siddhartha, that is, "one who has reached the goal." And the Buddha's having reached this goal has given hope and happiness to millions of others.

The Central Teachings of the Buddha

It is easy to see why so many people in all parts of the world can readily become entranced by the story of the Buddha. It is also easy to understand why the path he taught, now known as "Buddhism," eventually became a "world religion," speaking to people of all ethnic and cultural backgrounds even where other religions like Christianity have failed. For Buddhism's message is simple and uncomplicated. And it addresses directly a central preoccupation that each one of us has: how can I find release from suffering, sorrow and disappointment? It cuts right through all speculative theological questions about whether God does or does not exist, what the next life might be like, or whether the world has a creator or not, and goes directly to the problem of suffering. Putting theology aside it gives us its Four Noble Truths:

1. All life is suffering.
2. The cause of suffering is "desire" (or our instinct for clinging).
3. To find release from suffering we must let go of our desires.
4. And the way to accomplish this is by following an appropriate path of thinking, acting and meditating.

1. The First Noble Truth: Life is suffering (*dukkha*). If you have ever had the feeling that you did not quite fit into a situation, whether it be school, family, country, church, or even the universe, you are already in a position to understand one of the fundamental concepts of Buddhism, namely, *dukkha*. This term originally described the sensation of a bone being out of joint. It is usually translated as "suffering," but keep in mind the original meaning. For when the teachings of the Buddha begin with the simple pronouncement that all life is *dukkha,* this means not only physical suffering, but the frustration of never quite being able to get our lives together. It points to the universal experience of humans that there is always something unsatisfactory or "out of joint" in their lives.

Suffering is universal. "All life is suffering," according to Buddhism. But, Buddhist wisdom observes, there is something in us that refuses to face this fact. Mechanisms of denial cause us to see reality through rose-colored glasses. Our propensity for wishful thinking leads us to spin illusions about ourselves and our own situation in the world. And so, convinced that the pervasive unsatisfactoriness of existence will just disappear someday, we deny that life is *dukkha*. But this "ignorance" simply compounds the disappointment that inevitably occurs when our wishes remain unfulfilled.

The First Noble Truth invites us to give up our illusions. It asks us to look squarely at the unsatisfactory complexion of life. And once we face this harsh fact head on, something remarkable happens: we begin to behold the possibility of release from the misery of suffering. But until we acknowledge that life is unsatisfactory we remain caught up in the cycle of rebirths.

2. The Second Noble Truth: The cause of suffering is desire or clinging (*tanha*). What makes suffering so much a part of life is the sheer transience of things. The fact that nothing lasts and that all things perish may be the hardest truth of all for us to accept. And Buddhism associates suffering so closely with impermanence that we cannot accept the First Noble Truth without admitting the pervasive perishability of all things and life itself. In order to conquer the transience in life we follow our spontaneous tendency to cling to something solid and secure. The Pali word Buddhists use to name this clinging instinct is *tanha*.

Literally *tanha* means "thirst," but it designates much more. It is our inclination for turning the impermanent aspects of our lives and experience into the illusion that they are permanent. Simple reflection on our immediate experience tells us that nothing lasts. Everything is subject to perishing, whether the moments of our experience, the things we worship, our possessions, the persons we love, our careers, and our very life. There is nothing that endures. And yet we attach ourselves tightly to things and persons, to the impermanent moments of our lives and the achievements of our past. We want to hold onto them so dearly that we endow them with a fictitious substantiality. They take on the semblance of enduring realities that give our lives a false sense of permanence and security as long as we are attached to them. In our proclivity for dropping anchor in some sort of fixed and final reality we even give to ourselves an immortal "soul" (*Atman*), and to reality an ultimate unity immune to all perishing (*Brahman*). But both of these ideas are without foundation in immediate experience, at least according to Buddhism. Belief in the soul and devotion to an unchanging deity are ways of evading reality. They are products of *tanha*, of our persistent temptation to vanquish the transience (or "emptiness") of our experience and of the entire world.

In contrast, Hinduism and Western theism deal with the fact of perishability by positing the reality of the imperishable God in whose being and providential care all things are rescued from their impermanence. This intuition of permanence is the way in which many of the religions make our lives of suffering and impermanence bearable. But Buddhism proposes another "solution" to suffering and loss. It confronts our terror at the prospect of perishing by fully embracing impermanence and refusing to absorb it into any fixed scheme of transcendence and ultimate unity. Instead of taking flight from perishing, it confronts perishing head on. Instead of taking refuge in a haven of divine permanence beyond or above the flux of things, Buddhism exhorts us to accept the fleetingness of life and all that accompanies it. In this way salvation may be attained.

Like Hinduism, Buddhism accepts the doctrines of *karma, samsara* and rebirth. But the Second Noble Truth emphasizes that what keeps us locked into the cycle of rebirth is desire. All forms of *tanha* leave us caught up in the unsatisfactory world of *samsara*. And so any "way" that could decisively release us from the wheel of rebirths would surely catch our attention. Buddhism shows its followers this way with a clarity and simplicity seldom found elsewhere among the religions.

3. The Third Noble Truth: Suffering can be surmounted by abandoning the inclination to cling (*tanha*). The way to transcend sorrow is to extinguish the possessiveness of *tanha*, to renounce our thirst for permanence and substantiality. This "extinguishing" is quite literally what is meant by *nirvana*. The attainment of *nirvana* entails the bliss of enlightenment which is the "goal" of life. *Nirvana*, salvation from suffering, can be accomplished without the help of God or the gods, at least according to some of the central Buddhist teachings. Hence, each one of us must work out our own salvation. And Buddhism, like other religions, provides a discipline, a set of directives, a path, whereby we might find deliverance. This discipline is embodied in the Fourth Noble Truth.

4. The Fourth Noble Truth: *Nirvana* can be attained by following the appropriate way of wisdom, morality and meditation. This way is set forth in the *Eightfold Path* which consists of the attitudes, ethical actions and spiritual exercises that will lead one to the extinguishing of desire. Specifically, this Eightfold Path includes: right views, right intentions, right speech, right action, right livelihood, right effort, right mindfulness, and right concentration.

Buddhist ethical teachings are relatively straightforward. They challenge us without being impossible to follow. In fact, the Buddha's prescriptions are referred to as a "middle way." They seek to avoid the strict fastings and self-punishment of the ascetics on the one hand and an unchallenging leniency on the other. A famous Buddhist text sets forth this "middle path" together with the Four Noble Truths:

> And what, monks, is the Middle Path, of which the Tathagata
> [the Buddha] has gained enlightenment, which produces insight
> and knowledge, and tends to calm, to higher knowledge, enlight-
> enment, Nirvana? This is the Eightfold Way, namely right view,
> right intention, right speech, right action, right livelihood, right
> effort, right mindfulness, right concentration. This, monks, is the

Middle Path, of which Tathagata has gained enlightenment,
which produces insight and knowledge, and tends to calm, to
higher knowledge, enlightenment, Nirvana.

Now this, monks, is the noble truth of pain: birth is painful,
old age is painful, death is painful, sorrow, lamentation, dejec-
tion, and despair are painful. Contact with unpleasant things is
painful, not getting what one wishes is painful. In short the five
groups of grasping are painful.

Now this, monks, is the noble truth of the cause of pain: the
craving which tends to rebirth, combined with pleasure and lust,
finding pleasure here and there, namely the craving for passion,
the craving for existence, the craving for nonexistence.

Now this, monks, is the noble truth of the cessation of pain:
the cessation without a remainder of craving, the abandonment,
forsaking, release, non-attachment.

Now this, monks, is the noble truth of the way that leads to
the cessation of pain: this is the noble Eightfold Way, namely,
right views, right intention, right speech, right action, right livelihood, right effort, right mindfulness, right concentration. (*Pali
Sermons, Samyatta*, V, Thomas, trans., 29–33)

This method is easily listed, but not necessarily that simple to put into
practice. Salvation, release from suffering, does not come cheaply. We
have to pay a price. Like all the great traditions, Buddhism offers no
shortcuts to salvation. This sobriety is what distinguishes the main religious traditions from the "cheap grace" of more convenient ways. Calm
comes only after the storm, victory only after combat. Enormous risk and
struggle are required if the goal of life is to have any depth of significance
to it. To find liberation from the cycle of rebirth a discipline is essential,
such as is laid out in the Eightfold Path.

But Buddhism does not make the path to fulfillment impossible. In
general it steers a "middle road" between severity and licentiousness in
life. It does not require an excessively arduous asceticism, such as fasting
to the point of starvation, or other forms of self-punishment that we find in
other religions at times (although there are some exceptions in sub-systems
of Buddhism as well). Nor does it allow the luxury of "quietism" according
to which we have to do nothing at all in order to find salvation. It sets forth
the moderate "via media," between the extremes, as the path to *nirvana*.
This is the function of the Eightfold Path.

Because of the vagueness of its precepts, however, there is much
latitude for interpretation of exactly how to live our lives, and, as a result,
differing traditions have arisen within Buddhism. Some of these are quite

strict, requiring monasticism and celibacy as the condition for living the ethical life. Others are less severe and try to reach the average person involved in family life and worldly affairs. As a general rule, though, Buddhism lays down the following minimal ethical "commandments": do not kill, do not steal, avoid excessive sexual indulgence, do not lie, do not take alcohol or drugs.

Compassion

Over and above these prescriptions Buddhism admonishes its adherents to cultivate the right interior dispositions that might guide them toward peace and fruitful relations with others, and eventually to *nirvana*. Above all, compassion should govern our actions, and this will produce "good karma," while greediness, envy and lust will produce the unhappiness of "bad karma." And like the other great traditions, Buddhism provides its devotees with an exemplar of the compassionate ethical life, namely, the Buddha himself.

Though enlightenment begins with renunciation, it bears fruit in compassion. Having had the great experience of enlightenment, the Buddha may have been tempted to enjoy his attainment alone, and Buddhist writings provide colorful accounts of this temptation. He might have remained completely silent. But in the end Gautama could not resist the deeper urge to share his experience of salvation with others. Even though his enlightenment could not be put into words, he could at least provide others with some of the clues to its attainment.

After tasting of *nirvana* a great compassion for suffering humanity came over him, and he immediately travelled to the nearby city of Benares to spread the good news that release from suffering is indeed possible for all. There in the deer park he delivered his first sermon and gathered his earliest band of followers, perhaps including the monks who had earlier forsaken him. Here were the beginnings of a new "world religion." Before he died in old age of food poisoning, Gautama shared with numerous others the serenity and peace he had found at the end of his spiritual journey.

In demonstrating compassion for others the Buddha became the model for one of the most intriguing ideals of religious existence we will ever encounter, namely the *bodhisattva*. The *bodhisattva* (which means "one who is to become a Buddha") is a model of unselfish love for others. Originating in the Buddha's own love of humanity, this exemplar of religious authenticity developed in a branch of Buddhism called Mahayana (which is to be distinguished from the other main Buddhist tradition, usually known as the Hinayana). Mahayana (meaning the "large vessel"), unlike Hinayana ("small vessel") Buddhism, teaches that we may not necessarily find salvation on our own and without assistance. We need to feel the compassion of those who, like the Buddha himself, have experienced or come close to *nirvana* and can therefore guide us to this goal. The guide who may show us this path is called the *bodhisattva*.

The *bodhisattva*, in the teachings of Mahayana Buddhism, is one who is already far along the path toward enlightenment and *nirvana*. (Everyone, incidentally, is a potential *bodhisattva*.) But just at the moment when *nirvana* has occurred, or is about to occur, the *bodhisattva* pauses and decides that it is not yet the right time to enter fully into the blissful state of fulfillment. Why not? Because the mass of living beings still remains stuck in the cycle of rebirths, sorrow and suffering. Too many fellow living beings have not yet attained the bliss of *nirvana*. It would not be appropriate to enter into the rapture of final liberation as long as even one of them remains suffering outside. Thus the *bodhisattva*, filled with compassion and fellow-feeling, renounces even *nirvana*. In a memorable Mahayana text the *bodhisattva* is pictured as uttering such sentiments as these:

> All creatures are in pain. All suffer from bad and hindering karma. All that mass of pain and evil I take in my own body. Assuredly I must bear the burden of all beings for I have resolved to save them all. I must set them all free, I must save the whole world from the forest of birth, old age, disease, and rebirth . . . For all beings are caught in the net of craving, encompassed by ignorance, held by the desire for existence; they are doomed to destruction, shut in a cage of pain.
>
> It is better that I alone suffer than that all beings sink to the world of misfortune. There I shall give myself into bondage, to redeem all the world from the forest of purgatory, from rebirth as beasts, from the realm of death. I shall bear all grief and pain in my own body for the good of all things living. I must so bring to fruition the root of goodness that all beings find the utmost joy, unheard of joy, the joy of omniscience. (*Siksasamuccaya*, adapted from de Bary, 84–85)

The Buddhist "Religion"

We saw in Hinduism a clear example of the religious search for unity beyond the diversity of experience. But this mystical longing for "the One" beyond the many can be found in other great religious and philosophical traditions as well. Generally speaking, the "axial" religions arrived at a more vivid impression than ever before that there is a single divine mystery beyond all particular things. The sense of this unifying transcendent reality challenged religious people to look for the meaning and goal of their lives beyond the immediacy, plurality and diversity of everyday experience. At times it invited them to seek perfection beyond "this world" altogether, in an eternal domain surpassing all mundane understanding.

Nevertheless, people cannot avoid being aware of the plurality and diversity of things and persons, and they are constantly beset by an impression of the impermanence of the world and all things in it. How do we know that there is a unity and permanence beyond this plurality and impermanence that we experience? Might it not be the case that the conviction of ultimate Unity is simply a coating that we ourselves devise and superimpose upon the flux and multiplicity of experience? Are we obliged in all honesty to gather up the moments of our experience, as the *Upanishads* or the Hebrew prophets urge us to do, into an encompassing unity that we might call "God"? What if reality consisted for us solely of a plurality of transient, impermanent moments, and the impression of one God abiding eternally and permanently beyond the world's multiplicity were not part of our experience? And what if even the idea that we are each a substantial self with an enduring personality were also a fiction? If we saw things this way we might be close to some of the teachings of Buddhism.

Such ideas, however, would make us immediately question whether Buddhism can legitimately be called a "religion." In our search for an answer to the question "what is religion?" we are usually prone to focus on the idea of the sacred or the supernatural. But Buddhism does not seem to have much to do with God, at least explicitly. We are tempted to define religion as belief in "transcendent reality," or as devotion to a "totally other" dimension of reality. Religion commonly means belief in and worship of an "ultimate reality" beyond our immediate world. But preoccupation with the supernatural is not characteristic of Buddhism. Even though Buddhists accept the reality of "gods," these deities are themselves subject to rebirth and are part of the natural, rather than any supernatural, world. If by religion we mean the quest for transcendent reality, or the sense of God, or the sacred, or even the "One" of Hinduism, then Buddhism does not look much like a religion, at least initially.

However, Buddhism may still be called a religion for two reasons. In the first place it is intensely concerned with the "route-finding" we have associated with every phase of the religious story. Like other religions, it holds out a way to *ultimate* salvation, to a final liberation or fulfillment. It is not a secularistic type of atheism. It is a radical response to the situation of human suffering, and it seeks to move us beyond the limits on life in a decisive way. If we view religions as clear-cut ways of "breaking through" limitations, then Buddhism is a religion, even if it differs from others in its understanding of the nature of reality. In fact few religions have made ultimate salvation from suffering more central to their concern than has Buddhism.

In the second place, Buddhism belongs to the story of religion because in its own unique way it opens us up to a dimension of "mystery." It may not speak explicitly of God or the sacred. But in its very advocacy of "silence" about ultimate reality it nonetheless promotes in its participants a movement of self-transcendence. Like all religions, it urges us to distrust the superficiality of appearances and sense-experience. It seeks to expand our sense of reality far beyond that of the modern secularist view, according to which reality is no more than what is given in science and ordinary experience. Like all religions Buddhism seeks to deepen and widen our awareness, to move us beyond the surface of the ordinary and the illusory, to awaken us to the unknown. In order to experience this awakening we must learn to be silent, even to the point of not speaking or thinking about ultimate reality at all. As we shall note later, this exhortation to silence about God is not peculiar to Buddhism, but is found in other traditions as well.

The religion known as *Jainism* is one such example. Jainism originated almost simultaneously with Buddhism in the sixth century B.C.E. Its founder was a man named Mahavira. It has few followers today, most of them in the Bombay region of India. In Jainism as well as Buddhism, the primary focus is not on the reality of the divine but on how to find release from the limits of our ordinary existence. In both cases the Upanishadic convictions about the ultimate unity of all things in *Brahman* are ignored, and the attention of their devotees is shifted toward the working out of salvation on our own, without the help of God or the gods. Since neither of these religions originally required divine reality for reaching salvation, they have been called "atheistic" at times. However, the term "atheism" can be quite misleading if we think of it in terms of what passes as unbelief today. For both Jainism and Buddhism were born within an environment in which a "sense of mystery" was taken for granted, something usually ignored by Western secularistic atheism. Although they do not speak of an ultimate reality in the sense of God or *Brahman*, nevertheless an aura of mystery hovers over these religions. They are both expressions of the perennial religious tendency to transcend the limits of our worldly experience, even if at times they discourage any attempts to portray pictorially what lies beyond the limits of life as we ordinarily experience it. They are both to be included within the world of religion precisely because they are concerned with providing extraordinary, non-secular ways of forging a path through the compound of limitations that frustrates the life journey of human beings.

Buddhist Developments

Immediately after the Buddha's Deer Park Sermon, a community of those devoted to the new "way" was formed. This *sangha*, as it was called, became the prototype of Buddhism's ongoing social orientation. While the Buddhist religion is very much about the individual's salvation, it recognizes the need for some type of communal existence as the context for the individual's quest. Thus the Buddha's followers of later times deem it important to express their devotion not only to the Buddha and his teaching, but also to the *sangha*, the community that conveys the tradition. Gautama's followers have expressed a three-fold piety in the "Three Jewels" of Buddhism: "I put my trust in the Buddha; I put my trust in the *dharma* (the Buddha's teachings); I put my trust in the *sangha*."

But it was not always perfectly clear exactly who the Buddha was, what his teachings were, and what the structure of the *sangha* was supposed to be. As a result, different Buddhist factions, sects and traditions have splintered forth in the Asian world. Some of these give the monastic life priority, and they even make it a condition of salvation. Theravada Buddhism is the best known representative of this type. It emphasizes that each person must work out his or her own salvation, and that the life of a monk or nun is the most appropriate way to eventual release from the cycle of rebirth. Other Buddhist traditions, especially those associated with Mahayana, give more emphasis to the laity. Mahayana Buddhism began to resemble other kinds of religion in more specific detail. At times it turned the Buddha himself into something like a deity. And it promoted worship of various incarnations of the "buddha-nature" in other figures, especially those who embodied the role of the *bodhisattva*. Mahayana even cultivated a notion of "ultimate reality" around the concept of "emptiness," and it tended at times to emphasize the role of "divine grace" in the journey to salvation.

In some forms of Buddhism there is a religiousness that differs little from the kind of *bhakti*, or devotion to special deities, that we observed in Hinduism. And several popular expressions of Buddhism even indulge the practices of shamanism and sacrifice, as well as magic. Many Buddhists have their own versions of "gods" around which their devotional life centers. Though the Buddha was silent on the God-question, many of his followers have exhibited the ageless longing for vivid representations of ultimate reality. As a result, deities, rituals, prayers, festivals and other forms of worship have added religious diversity to Buddhism.

Therefore, it can be quite misleading to call Buddhism an "atheistic" religion. Even its founder never dogmatically denied the existence of God. It was just that questions about the existence of God, immortality of the soul and the creation of the world were simply not his concern. Rather, like a doctor caught up immediately in the suffering of a patient, Gautama was more preoccupied with delivering his fellow humans from suffering as soon as possible than he was with giving them the answers to metaphysical questions. Such answers might satisfy our theological curiosity, but would they significantly lessen our suffering? The Buddha in his compassion was interested only in showing us the way out of our suffering. If you had been shot with an arrow, would you not rather have someone immediately remove it and heal your wound than waste time discussing where the arrow came from, who shot you, whether the tip was stone or steel, etc.? If life is suffering, as the First Noble Truth states, then now is no time to get involved in philosophical disputes that have little bearing on actual deliverance from suffering.

The historical development of all religious traditions time and again leads away from the apparent "purity" of their foundational moments. And this is as true of Buddhism as of Judaism, Christianity and Islam. The religion of the masses of people generally takes on a colorful symbolic and "sacramental" character that may be interpreted by "purists" as a perversion of the pristine insights of the religion's founders. For example, some popular religious practices of Roman Catholicism have often evoked a sense of disgust in Christian reformers who want to adhere more strictly to what they consider to be the basic truths of prophetic faith. In Buddhism, as well, a number of controversial historical developments (which we cannot detail here) culminated in popular forms of piety that synthesized religious aspects of whatever culture it happened to penetrate. Strict Buddhists may look upon such devotional developments as a dilution of the teachings of Buddhism, but others view them as the inevitable result of applying these teachings to special situations that require elaborate adaptation.

And yet, in spite of its diversity and its evolution into so many distinct offshoots, there is still a unifying element in Buddhism, namely, the *story* about the Buddha himself, his adventurous quest for enlightenment, and his eventual arrival after a long and difficult journey at the peace and bliss of *nirvana*. Just as the story of Jesus still places an umbrella of common persuasion over the many kinds of Christianity, or as the story of Muhammad unifies the diverse factions of Islam, the main lines of the story of the Buddha provide a thread of continuity pulling together the widely distinct types of Buddhism. All strands of Buddhism share the story about the Buddha himself. And it is in great measure the retelling of this story, centering on the Buddha's moment of "enlightenment" and entrance into *nirvana*, that gives an overall unity to Buddhist religious traditions.

Religions are inseparable from stories. It is especially by sharing a common story that traditions are born and people welded into community. Participating in stories of heroes and events that lie at the origins of a tradition gives one a sense of identity, confidence, solidarity with others, and purpose to life. In accounts of the Buddha's own life and enlightenment countless millions of people have for centuries been attracted to a certain possibility of human existence that could not have been communicated to them in any other form than that of a heroic story of struggle, perseverance and victory. Partaking of this story has given them the courage to bear their own suffering. And, like religious myth in general, it has fashioned them into a people with a shared memory, destiny and identity. Thus the story of Gautama Siddhartha, who became the Buddha, a term which means "the Enlightened One," is quite possibly the most important religious aspect of Buddhism.

Conclusion

Ironically, Buddhism eventually almost disappeared from India, the place where it was born, but it had little difficulty finding domicile elsewhere in Asia. The more austere Theravada Buddhism moved into Sri Lanka, Thailand, Burma, Cambodia and Laos. Mahayana Buddhism, on the other hand, spread mainly to China and Japan, where one of its types is called Zen. And in Tibet, Tantric Buddhism, the most exotic type of all, took root. The renowned Dalai Lama is today the exiled spiritual leader of Tibetan Buddhism.

Buddhism has become more and more fascinating to Westerners ever since the nineteenth century German philosopher Friedrich Schopenhauer took up a serious study of its teachings. Schopenhauer himself often confused it with aspects of Hinduism. But today it has become the object of immense scholarly expertise, and we now have more precise interpretations of it. Westerners have become increasingly exposed to its wonders, and many have been attracted to aspects of its teachings.

Buddhism is a "world religion" that can easily blend with other religious ways. Remarkably tolerant and non-polemical, it appeals immediately to many searchers who have become disillusioned with the dogmatism, arrogance and hostility that may be found at times in the religious life

THE BUDDHA—THE AWAKENED

He whose conquest cannot be conquered again, into whose conquest no one in this world enters, by what track can you lead him, the Awakened, the Omniscient, the trackless?

He whom no desire with its snares and poisons can lead astray, by what track can you lead him, the Awakened, the Omniscient, the trackless?

Even the gods envy those who are awakened and not forgetful, who are given to meditation, who are wise, and who delight in the repose of retirement from the world.

Difficult to obtain is birth in human form, difficult is the life of mortals, difficult is the hearing of the True Law, difficult is the attainment of Buddhahood.

Not to commit any sin, to do good, and to purify one's mind, that is the teaching of all the Awakened.

The Awakened call patience the highest penance, longsuffering the highest Nirvana; for he is not an anchorite who oppresses others, he is not an ascetic who insults others.

Not to blame, not to strike, to live restrained under the law, to be moderate in eating, to sleep and sit alone, and to dwell on the highest thoughts—this is the teaching of the Awakened.

There is no satisfying lusts, even by a shower of gold pieces; he who knows that lusts have a short taste and cause pain, he is wise; even in heavenly pleasures he finds no satisfaction; the disciple who is fully awakened delights only in the destruction of all desires.

Men, driven by fear, go to many a refuge—to mountains and forests, to groves and sacred trees.

But that is not a safe refuge, that is not the best refuge; a man is not delivered from all pains after having gone to that refuge.

He who takes refuge with Buddha, the law, and the Order—he who, with clear understanding, sees the Four Holy Truths: pain, the origin of pain, the destruction of pain, and the Eightfold Holy Way that leads to the quieting of pain—that is the safe refuge, that is the best refuge; having gone to that refuge, a man is delivered from all pain.

A Buddha is not easily found: he is not born everywhere. Wherever such a sage is born, that race prospers.

Happy is the birth of the Awakened, happy is the teaching of the

True Law, happy is peace in the Order, happy is the devotion of those who are at peace.

He who pays homage to those who deserve homage, whether the Awakened [Buddhas] or their disciples, those who have overcome the host of evils and crossed the flood of sorrow—he who pays homage to such as have found deliverance and know no fear, his merit can never be measured by anyone.

Dhammapada XIV quoted in *The Sacred Books of the East*, edited by Max Müller, Oxford: Clarendon Press, 1897.

of other traditions. Above all, its emphasis on silence can be made a part of all religious life. Silence, we shall see later, is an essential moment within the unfolding of any authentic religious awareness. In religion there is a need for silence as well as symbols. And probably no religion has made this point more explicitly than Buddhism.

4.

Prophetic Religion

There is another type of "axial" religion that takes a radically different approach to the problem of suffering from either Hinduism or Buddhism. And it offers a correspondingly unique interpretation of the mystery to which religions point. This type is represented by the Near Eastern traditions that originated in association with a man known as Abraham. These traditions are Judaism, Christianity and Islam. They all claim Abraham as their father, and this common ancestry is of utmost significance in shaping their distinctive character.

The name of Abraham is inseparable from the theme of divine promise for a glorious future, a doctrine held by all three traditions. The claim to Abraham by Judaism, Christianity and Islam binds them together in a shared vision of hope for the future. They all have a special relationship to the theme of *promise*. And because of the prominence in these three traditions of the figure of the "prophet" who proclaims the divine promise, they may be called *prophetic* religions.

The Meaning of Promise

In a broad sense, it seems, most religion is characterized by the anticipation of "salvation," fulfillment or liberation. Because of the universal experience of guilt, suffering and death, people have naturally sought deliverance from their sorrow. And religions have captured people's attention because they provide "ultimate" ways to freedom from suffering. But they have not all portrayed the passage to liberation in the same way. The "way of union" typified by the *Upanishads*, for example, is not the same as the "way of renunciation" taught by the Buddha, or the "way of sacrifice" prevalent in early religion. And in the "prophetic" religions going back to Abraham there is yet another way. We may call it the "way of *hope*."

Some kind of "longing" for deliverance is a feature of other religious types also. The kind of yearning we find in Abrahamic religions, however, opens up an aspect of mystery barely noticeable in many other traditions. This new dimension is that of the "future." And an intuition of the "futurity" of the sacred sets these religions apart from prehistoric religion and, to some extent at least, from the Asian traditions. Prehistoric religion was captivated by the cycle of seasons. Its proximity to the animals and the earth filled its religious life with a symbolic and mythic consciousness based on the regularities of nature. The axial religions of Asia and China also maintained a close connection to nature's rhythms and cycles. The prophetic religions, on the other hand, represent a departure from nature-oriented religion. Fueled by unprecedented hope in a future fulfillment, they move from nature out into *history* as the sphere in which liberation may be sought. Not that they abandon nature altogether, for their followers still cultivate the earth and remain grateful for its abundance. But their God is primarily a God of historical happenings, one who holds out fulfillment in the future, who calls for trust in the divine *promise*.

The response to suffering in this religious type lies especially in the hope for future deliverance. Such looking toward the future has been called *eschatology*, and so Judaism, Christianity and Islam are also known as eschatological religions. They have all been influenced at least indirectly by another ancient eschatological religion, Zoroastrianism. The term "eschatological" comes from the Greek word *eschaton*, meaning final or last. And "eschatology" strictly speaking implies a concern about the "last things," such as death, the end of the world, and immortality. But in the broader meaning given here, eschatology designates simply the hopeful looking forward to a future salvation.

To people whose consciousness has been steeped in eschatology the answer to suffering lies in a *hope* that the future will bring deliverance. This hope for a future salvation takes the finality out of present suffering and makes it bearable. Without such hope pain might indeed be intolerable, and for that reason eschatological religions provide their followers with a rich variety of images of a future salvation. The mystery of reality here is pictured as a personal, caring God intent not only upon delivering people from suffering, but also establishing for them a realm of fulfillment and enjoyment surpassing all their present expectations. This idea of God diverts the religious instinct from its tendency to seek fulfillment in union with nature alone, and directs it toward a less secure, but ultimately more satisfying horizon of an unknown historical future. For this kind of religion the liberation sought by humans may be anticipated by hope in the future, because it is in the realm of the future that God's reality most fully resides. The God of promissory religion has "future as his very essence." (Moltmann, 1967, 16)

The religions of promise have no illusion that the ways of liberation they set forth will be easy, and they know that people will not readily take the risk of trusting in an uncertain future. This kind of religion does not appeal to the human instinct for security. Nestling down in the sureness of nature's rhythms and regularities, or escaping from history into some "other world," might provide more immediate refuge from the hazards of living on this earth. Nature and the "next world" might provide a haven from the "terrors of history." But Abrahamic religions are not content with this clinging to the security of predictable natural rhythms, or with religious escapism. Instead they embrace the more uncertain realm of history and its future as their proper terrain.

Abraham

It is hardly a coincidence that this promissory vision of existence began in the dreams of a semi-nomadic people. Semi-nomads are required by seasonal changes to move their herds and families constantly in order to find water and food. Abraham, the father of prophetic religion, was a "wandering Aramean" who made his livelihood by transferring family and livestock from one place to another in search of sustenance. In the consciousness of such a wanderer there is never any final settling down securely into one spatially limited location. The nomadic life breeds a spirit of restlessness, stirring families and tribes from place to place in quest of greener pastures. In such a context the future becomes the dominant focus of attention. And in such a setting the religious "way of hope" was born.

As the story goes, there was a man from Ur of Chaldea (in Mesopotamia) named Abram who lived in the early part of the second millennium B.C.E. He apparently travelled along the caravan routes linking Ur, Haran, Damascus, Shechem, Hebron and Egypt, in what has been called "the Fertile Crescent." According to the biblical accounts Abram experienced a summons from God to leave his ancestral home and go forth to a new life of promise. We do not know exactly what happened, for the biblical stories are colored over with the hopes and ideals of later periods of Israel's history. But it is hardly stretching things historically to assume that Abram felt the mystery of life as a future promise beckoning him to an adventure into the uncertainty of a whole new way of existing. The calling and the promise are put this way in the book of *Genesis:*

Now the Lord said to Abram, "Go from your country and your kindred and your father's house to the land that I will show you. And I will make of you a great nation, and I will bless you, and make your name great, so that you will be a blessing. I will bless those who bless you, and him who curses you I will curse; and by you the families of the earth shall bless themselves. (*Genesis* 12: 1–3)

In the course of his long life, according to biblical portraits, the promise of God to Abram was repeated over and over. "To your descendants I will give this land." (12:7) "All the land which you see I will give to you and to your descendants forever." (13:15) "Look toward heaven, and number the stars, if you are able to number them. So shall your descendants be." (15:5) "Behold my covenant is with you, and you shall be the father of a multitude of nations." (17:4) And when Abram was ninety-nine years old, to signify the transformation of his life into one of fidelity to the promise, his God bestowed on him a new name:

"No longer shall your name be Abram, but your name shall be Abraham; for I have made you the father of a multitude of nations. I will make you exceedingly fruitful; and I will make nations of you, and kings shall come forth from you. And I will establish my covenant between me and you and your descendants after you throughout their generations for an everlasting covenant, to be God to you and to your descendants after you. And I will give to you, and to your descendants after you, the land of your sojournings, all the land of Canaan, for an everlasting possession; and I will be their God." (17:5–8)

We do not have to attribute all of these promissory experiences literally to the historical Abram, since they sometimes express the sentiments of later stages in the history of Israel. The point here is to notice the distinct quality of the kind of religion expressed in these passages. What stands out is the promise of *future* fulfillment, and this is the essence of the religious "way of hope." This is the emblem of "prophetic" religion.

If we keep before us the extravagance and utter gratuity of the divine promises made to Abraham, we will begin to gain some insight into the specific character of prophetic religion. It is one shaped from its very origin by the invitation to adventure, to trust, to open oneself to the mystery of the future. Like the Buddha, Abraham was invited to risk all for the sake of finding his goal. He had to leave his ancestral home and journey into unknown parts. Abraham, too, followed a "path of renunciation," but one colored over by promise and hope.

Ultimate reality according to Abrahamic religion is conceived of not simply as the ultimate One behind appearances (like the Hindus' *Brahman*), nor as a *nirvana* that extinguishes desire (as in Buddhism). Ultimate reality is thought of as a personal God who makes and keeps promises. Abraham did absolutely nothing to merit the promise that came to him. It arrived out of the blue, completely unanticipated, bestowed as sheer gift, without conditions. Later theology has called this abundance by the name "grace" (from the same root as "gratuitous," implying completely free, with no strings attached). And it has given the name "revelation" to the events and verbal interpretations that unfold this promise. Revelation is not the transmission of "information" from heaven to earth, but something much less frivolous. It is simply the gift of God's future, made vivid in the sense of promise and the many images of hope that abound in prophetic religion.

In response to God's promise of a glorious future all Abraham is expected to do is to remain "faithful." That is, he must continue to believe, trust or hope in the fulfillment of the promise. Trust in God's promise, after the model of Abraham, is the core of authentic religion in Judaism, Christianity and Islam.

We saw in our brief look at Buddhism that the story of Gautama provides an exemplar of persistence on the path toward final freedom from suffering. Such a story communicates enormous courage to his followers. Likewise for Jews, Christians and Muslims Abraham's enduring faith in God's promise is a model of endurance. Like Gautama with his temptations to cease struggling for ultimate peace, Abraham had many reasons not to continue his own adventure. For example, the infertility of his own wife Sarah hardly boded well for one who was promised so many descendants. But Abraham continued to trust, even when his own character flaws and the hostilities of others seemed to stand in the way.

His faith received its severest challenge when he was commanded, by the same God who had given him the promise of enormous progeny, to sacrifice his own son Isaac. In spite of the irrationality of such a demand, Abraham kept faith. He was about to comply with the horrifying directive to slaughter his own son when he was suddenly relieved of the obligation. The point of the story will be missed if we focus on what to us is the obvious barbarity of child sacrifice (just as we miss the point of the Buddha's "renunciation" if we dwell only on his "irresponsible" abandonment of wife and child). The story intends simply to show the ruggedness of Abraham's trust, that God remains faithful to the promise no matter how absurd the circumstances, and that no frustrations may legitimately cause us to lose heart either. As such, this baffling story expresses the very soul of prophetic religion.

1. Judaism

Sometime between 1750 and 1250 B.C.E. a people known as the Hebrews lived in slavery in Egypt. Toward the end of this period a man called Moses rose up in their midst and led a revolt against the pharaoh's regime. Crossing over the "Sea of Reeds," he brought a band of followers into the Sinai desert, and from there they made their way to the land of Canaan. There they merged with the inhabitants and eventually became the biblical people of Judah and Israel. Moses himself never reached the "promised land," but his liberating efforts and his fidelity to the "promise" have made him the central ancestral figure in the religion known today as Judaism.

Exodus. Judaism traces its existence as a distinct nation or people not only to the remote figure of Abraham, but more immediately to the events surrounding the life of Moses. Judaism looks back again and again to the event of deliverance from Egypt known as the "Exodus." (This term comes from the Greek *ex*= out and *hodos*= way; once again we see how the metaphor "way" or "path" lies at the heart of a religion.) Accounts of this deliverance are given in the biblical book of *Exodus*. As in all religious narratives they appear highly exaggerated if we view them simply in terms of historical standards. Actually there may have been only a small group of people summoned to a new land and a new life of promise, but the book of *Exodus* makes it into a cast of thousands. It would be misreading the meaning of *Exodus*, though, if we concentrated only on the question, "did it actually happen that way?" For the book's purpose is to arouse trust in the future, and it looks back to the past liberation of the Hebrew people in order to provide a basis for our hoping here and now.

Having made their escape, Moses and his followers gave thanks to the deity who had brought them to freedom. Their name for this divine liberator was *Yahweh*. At the time of the Exodus (approximately 1250–1220 B.C.E.) the religious consciousness of the Hebrew people had not yet developed the axial period's intolerance of a multiplicity of deities, and so we cannot assume that "Yahweh" was originally the "one and only" transcendent being that he was later to become. Initially Yahweh was possibly the name of a tribal deity adopted by the Hebrews. But as their religious consciousness became transformed during the tumultuous centuries that followed in Israel and Judah, the name "Yahweh" took on a more comprehensive character. And finally, during the axial period, Yahweh became for the children of Moses not only the liberator who fashioned them as a distinct people, but also the creator, savior and ruler of the entire world. Strict monotheism, intolerant of the existence of a plurality of deities, came into being in the history of Israel probably somewhere around the sixth century B.C.E.

Sinai and the Covenant. The book of *Exodus* tells of how, after the deliverance from Egypt, Moses and his people continued their relationship with the God of promise. In the desert, at Mount Sinai, Yahweh made a covenant with them. Once again the theme was that of promise. Yahweh offered the Hebrews a new life in a new land, and the Hebrews on their part were expected only to trust in the future fulfillment of this promise. They would express their trust by turning away from idols, which were incapable of giving them freedom, and placing their faith in Yahweh alone. The "Ten Commandments" given at Sinai as part of the covenant agreement are simply the unfolding of what it means to turn away from slavery to idols and toward a life based on the hope for future fulfillment.

As the Exodus journey continued, the Hebrews "murmured" in the desert, despairing of the promise and allowing their original trust to sag. They fell back into idolatry and gave up the dream of freedom. Moses struggled to have them remain faithful to the promise, but the people longed to return to Egypt, even to be slaves again, because in slavery there is a kind of security, while the call to freedom and the unknown future is full of risk. But in the end they reached their destiny, the promised land.

The Prophets. And after that the struggle against idolatry continued. The people consorted with the gods of nature and fertility. The fulfillment of history's promise always seemed too far off, whereas the gods of nature provided immediate satisfaction. But *prophets* rose up, individuals who spoke authoritatively on behalf of the God of Abraham and Moses, challenging the people to trust in the promise without hesitation. In the heat of their allegiance to Yahweh the prophets protested any flirtation with gods of nature, and they questioned the establishment of a monarchy that would tempt people to settle down in the false security of political power. For the prophets religion was anything but a rule of safety. Rather it was the quest for a perfection too grand to be contained in the present moment, a vision that only the uncertain future is adequate to hold.

The prophets called for a continual widening of what it means to be a

THE TEN COMMANDMENTS

And God spoke all these words, saying,

"I am the LORD your God, who brought you out of the land of Egypt, out of the house of bondage.

"You shall have no other gods before me.

"You shall not make for yourself a graven image, or any likeness of anything that is in heaven above, or that is in the earth beneath, or that is in the water under the earth; you shall not bow down to them or serve them; for I the LORD your God am a jealous God, visiting the iniquity of the fathers upon the children to the third and the fourth generation of those who hate me, but showing steadfast love to thousands of those who love me and keep my commandments.

"You shall not take the name of the LORD your God in vain; for the LORD will not hold him guiltless who takes his name in vain.

"Remember the sabbath day, to keep it holy. Six days you shall labor, and do all your work; but the seventh day is a sabbath to the LORD your God; in it you shall not do any work, you, or your son, or your daughter, your manservant, or your maidservant, or your cattle, or the sojourner who is within your gates; for in six days the LORD made heaven and earth, the sea, and all that is in them, and rested the seventh day; therefore the LORD blessed the sabbath day and hallowed it.

"Honor your father and your mother, that your days may be long in the land which the LORD your God gives you.

"You shall not kill.

"You shall not commit adultery.

"You shall not steal.

"You shall not bear false witness against your neighbor.

"You shall not covet your neighbor's house; you shall not covet your neighbor's wife, or his manservant, or his maidservant, or his ox, or his ass, or anything that is your neighbor's."

Exodus 20: 1–17, *Revised Standard Version.*

community of hope by not allowing people to forget the poor and society's outcasts. Societies that exclude certain groups for the sake of homogeneity would lose their vitality, and so the prophets forbade such narrowing of social consciousness. They refused to let the children of Abraham forget the dark side of history, the forgotten sufferings of the past, the poverty of their own origins. The figure of the prophet stands out most clearly in its representation of the ideal of *justice*.

In the eighth century B.C.E., a young herdsman named Amos from the southern kingdom of Judah (which by that time had split off politically from the northern kingdom of Israel) experienced a "calling" to journey to Israel and speak out in the name of his God about the social injustice that had become rampant at the time. He considered himself only a humble farmer and had not sought the burdensome life of a prophet. But he was grasped by a compulsion for justice that he could not resist, and he must have concluded that nothing less than Yahweh himself could be the basis of his hatred of injustice. His words rang out with such divine authority that they were gathered by his followers and eventually recorded in the biblical book of *Amos*.

The prophet Amos observed that the Israelites "trample the head of the poor into the dust of the earth, and turn aside the way of the afflicted." (2:7) He harangued them for presuming that their election by God amounted to a guarantee of safety. They had failed to keep their side of the Sinai agreement, and as a consequence the promised "Day of Yahweh" (one of many Israelite symbols of future fulfillment) would be for them a day of doom rather than joy. The divine promises made to Abraham and Moses were not to be taken lightly. They required that the people adopt the same concern for the needy as Yahweh had done in choosing Abraham and the Hebrews in the first place. But the people of Israel had failed to follow the encompassing and deepening implications of the election and covenant, and had greedily turned back onto themselves. Their neglect of justice had been a serious violation of the religious heritage of hope.

In Amos' prophetic outcries we see another instance of "axial" religion's critique of a piety based exclusively on ritual and sacrifice. About the same time that the *Upanishads* were growing weary of the Vedic rites, and the Buddha was reforming religion in India, the prophets of Judah and Israel were lamenting the superficial religiosity that warmed people's hearts without having anything to do with overthrowing social, political and economic evils. Perhaps nowhere in the classic sources of religion is there a more thunderous indictment of ineffective religiosity than in the book of Amos. Amos' God reproaches the people whose religious life revolved mainly around sacrificial rituals:

I hate, I despise your feasts, and I take no delight in your solemn assemblies. Even though you offer me your burnt offerings and cereal offerings, I will not accept them, and the peace offerings of your fatted beasts I will not look upon. Take away from me the noise of your songs; to the melody of your harps I will not listen. But let justice roll down like waters, and righteousness like an ever-flowing stream. (*Amos* 5: 21–24)

Prophetic religion cannot separate worship of God from concern for the needy. Hope for the future must include the dreams of all, not just the aspirations of an elite minority. In the prophetic concern for justice we witness a standard that has been cherished by Judaism, Christianity and Islam. At the same time, though, we are forced to wonder how well the followers of these traditions have lived up to this ideal.

2. Christianity

From among the long line of prophetic figures in Israel's history, one in particular has had special significance for Christianity. His name is Jesus of Nazareth, and although there are many different ways of approaching him, here we situate him among the company of the prophets. For he too was a son of Abraham and Moses. He dwelt within the horizon of a religious consciousness molded by the sense of promise. In his ruminations on the idea of a God of promise he reached radical conclusions about the depth of this God's justice and compassion. After what appears to have been a long struggle (represented as a "desert experience" in the Christian scriptures), he arrived at his own version of "enlightenment." For Jesus it took the form of a vision of ultimate mystery as "loving father." The Aramaic term he used in reference to God was "abba," a term of endearment and deep familiarity. So intimate did this expression and Jesus' talk about God appear that it seemed to some of his contemporaries to be blasphemy.

In the tradition of the prophets Jesus interpreted God's love as all-inclusive, and to make his convictions known he consorted freely with the outcasts of society, with lepers, prostitutes and tax-collectors. Partly because his conduct and ideas offended those in power, and partly as the result of a complex set of social and political circumstances, he was eventually executed as a common criminal. Christians, however, have interpreted his death by crucifixion, the most potent symbol of a failed life available at the time, as their own way to salvation. Jesus' death (the "way" of the cross) is their access to freedom.

The Gospels portray Jesus as one who spoke to all, including the poor and the outcasts, about his conviction that they are cared for in an unimaginably loving way by the mystery of God. He put his conviction of God's unwavering fidelity to humans into the form of "parables" in order to startle his listeners into his novel frame of reference. Such stories communicated the content of his religious sentiments in a way that no other medium could. One of the most familiar is the parable of the "Prodigal Son":

> There was a man who had two sons; and the younger of them said to his father, 'Father, give me the share of property that falls to me.' And he divided his living between them. Not many days later, the younger son gathered all he had and took his journey into a far country, and there he squandered his property in loose living. And when he had spent everything, a great famine arose in that country, and he began to be in want. So he went and joined himself to one of the citizens of that country, who sent him into his fields to feed swine. And he would gladly have fed on the pods that the swine ate; and no one gave him anything. But when he came to himself he said, 'How many of my father's hired servants have bread enough and to spare, but I perish here with hunger! I will arise and go to my father, and I will say to him, "Father, I have sinned against heaven and before you; I am no longer worthy to be called your son; treat me as one of your hired servants." ' And he arose and came to his father. But while he was yet at a distance, his father saw him and had compassion, and ran and embraced him and kissed him. And the son said to him, 'Father, I have sinned against heaven and before you; I am no longer worthy to be called your son.' But the father said to his servants, 'Bring quickly the best robe, and put it on him; and put a ring on his hand, and shoes on his feet; and bring the fatted calf and kill it, and let us eat and make merry; for this my son was dead, and is alive again; he was lost, and is found.' And they began to make merry.
>
> Now his elder son was in the field; and as he came and drew near to the house, he heard music and dancing. And he called one of the servants and asked what this meant. And he said to him, 'Your brother has come and your father has killed the fatted calf, because he has received him safe and sound.' But he was angry and refused to go in. His father came out and entreated him, but he answered his father. 'Lo, these many years I have

served you, and I never disobeyed your command; yet you never gave me a kid, that I might make merry with my friends. But when this son of yours came, who has devoured your living with harlots, you killed for him the fatted calf!' And he said to him, 'Son, you are always with me, and all that is mine is yours. It was fitting to make merry and be glad, for this your brother was dead, and is alive; he was lost, and is found.' (*Luke* 15:11–32)

Though this parable is well known, it is worth pointing out its continuity with the theme of divine extravagance and inclusiveness that we see in the story of Abraham and the prophets. It was impossible to sink any lower in society than to be a swine-herd and want to eat with the pigs. But the father in the parable is utterly non-judgmental toward the son whose life had disintegrated as the result of "unethical" behavior; the father even goes out to embrace the deviant son while the latter is "yet at a distance." In Jesus' teaching the "Kingdom of God" strains to the breaking point the boundaries of social reality in order to incorporate those elements that we normally exclude. The elder son represents an exclusivity at odds with Jesus' prophetic message. The father, however, embraces the lost son without conditions, requiring no apology and no expiation, and refusing to let him grovel in self-hatred. In this parable Jesus is apparently attempting to give his listeners a vivid sense of the nature of ultimate mystery as all-inclusive love.

Christology. Christians, like Jews, believe that God has been disclosed to them by way of a *word* of promise that makes possible for them a

Christ, the All-Sovereign. Mosaic from the Church of the Dormition in Daphni, Greece.

life of hope. The obvious difference is that for Christians the person and
life of Jesus are the decisive manifestation of God's promise. The Christian, then, cannot appropriately conceive of God without thinking of the
man Jesus. Because of this religious requirement a complex theology,
called "Christology," has emerged within the Christian religion. Christology looks upon Jesus as the Christ, the "anointed of God" (hence the name
"Christianity"). Jesus, according to Christian teaching, *is* the "Word of
God," the "Son of God," the fulfillment of the hope of all the ages. In the
life and person of Jesus Christians perceive the very revelation of God's
own being. Hence they speak of the "divinity" of Christ.

Resurrection. For Christians the death of Jesus is not a reason to
despair but the beginning of a new hope. This hope is given expression in
the accounts of Jesus' appearances to his followers after his death. The
stories of these "appearances" in the *New Testament* (which together with
the Jewish scriptures, the so-called "Old Testament," constitute the sacred
writings of the Christian faith) are similar in style to the manifestations of
God that we read about in the Jewish scriptures. That is, like God's
appearances to Abraham and Moses, they are *promissory* in essence, opening up the sense of a new future for all who trust in the power of God to
conquer even the threat of death. The Exodus from Egypt through the
Reed Sea and into a new land is for Jews the perennial landmark on which
they build their hope for the future. Christians add to this set of events the
"exodus" of Jesus through death to new life as the basis of their hope.

3. Islam

In the seventh century after the birth of Jesus, the youngest of the
world's great religious traditions, Islam, was born. It sprang from the same
eschatological hope in the future that we have already seen in Judaism and
Christianity. And though it is in serious conflict with them on some major
doctrinal issues, it is linked to both by its adherence to the spirit of
promise that goes back to Abraham. Its continuity with the great patriarch
is traced through Abraham's son Ishmael rather than Isaac, but it is still
the same Abraham, the one who remained faithful to God's promises.
Thus Islam also exemplifies the religious "way of hope" and falls under the
heading "prophetic religion."

Islam (which means "surrender" to God) developed as a reaction to
the animism and polytheism that prevailed in the tribal existence of seventh century Arabia. As is often the case in tribal societies, the individual's

uniqueness was submerged in the identity of the tribe, and kinship ties overrode considerations of justice and the dignity of personality. Moreover, such a situation made for bitter conflict between and among the various kinship groups competing with each other in commerce. In the territories around Mecca ethnic and racial self-exaltation, slavery, greed and other forms of injustice prevailed. This chaotic situation awakened a prophetic figure named Muhammad (born around 570). And at the age of forty, after receiving revelations from his God, Allah, he dedicated the rest of his life to protest what he considered to be the source of the chaos, namely, idolatry.

Idolatry is the raising of something finite to the status of the infinite. In Arabic it is called *shirk* (=association). This term designates the act of "associating" two or more things with each other, placing them on the same level, when in reality they do not belong together. Muhammad observed that his contemporaries at Mecca had raised kinship, wealth and other specifically cultural factors to the status of utmost importance in their lives. Devising thereby to secure their existence, their idolatry had only produced a pathetic enslavement of individuals and unnecessary conflict among the various tribes. After his revelations Muhammad publicly proposed a "way" that would provide lasting freedom from the anguish that results whenever people define themselves in terms of superficial ethnic and economic criteria. He taught that the solution to this suffering lies in belief in the One God, Allah, who rules all of history. Only in commitment to Allah could there be freedom from all the obligations to idols invented by popular religious piety.

Like Yahweh of the Hebrews, Allah had originally been one tribal deity among many others, but in Muhammad's religious revelation Allah is given the status of universal Creator and Lord of all. It is hard for us to fathom how radical Muhammad's monotheism must have appeared to his contemporaries, for it announced nothing less than a complete social and religious revolution. By challenging the status of various deities it undermined the authority of tribal leaders and the ways of life that had been legitimated by their gods. Muhammad's prophecy that there was only *one* God, Allah, proved in fact to be too innovative. And as a result of his revolutionary message he was forced to flee from Mecca, with his newly established community of believers, to Medina, about two hundred and fifty miles to the north. Here he hoped to receive more favorable treatment. His famous flight from Mecca to Medina is known as the *Hegira*. It took place on September 24 in 622, the first year of the Muslim calendar.

At Medina things did not go as smoothly as expected. But with patient endurance as well as some use of military force, after a considerable struggle Muhammad triumphed over his enemies, took control of Medina, and eventually returned to Mecca and conquered it for Islam. He purified the city's shrines of their idolatry, declared an amnesty for those who had resisted him, and returned to Medina, where he died in 632. As in the other great traditions, the story of Muhammad's struggles, disappointments and eventual victory is the source of great strength and rejoicing to his followers in their own life journeys.

The Five Pillars of Islam. The deposit of Allah's revelations to Muhammad and Islam is recorded in the Qur'an, a book of recitations approximately the size of the Christian *New Testament*. The Qur'an unfolds what it means to be a true believer. Much of the appeal of Islam, like that of Buddhism with its four Noble Truths and Eightfold Path, is the relatively uncomplicated nature of the directives it sets forth in its "Five Pillars." The Qur'an indicates, without considerable detail, that the religious life of Muslims takes shape around five easy to learn (though not necessarily easy to follow) articles: faith, prayer, fasting, almsgiving and pilgrimage.

I. **Faith.** The true believer is one who can say in complete trust: "There is no God but Allah, and Muhammad is His prophet." The daily repetition of this formula binds one to the community of other true believers, and it provides constant protection against the temptation to idolatry.

II. **Prayer.** There are no priests in Islam, so the individual's prayer provides the primary access to God. At least five times a day a Muslim (the name given to a follower of Islam) turns toward Mecca in prayer of gratitude and petition. This gesture provides not only a sense of intimacy with God, but also a feeling of oneness with fellow believers who in prayer are all oriented geographically toward the same location. The life of prayer, of course, is not limited to these five occasions, and there is an enormous body of devotional writings that Muslims can draw upon in order to intensify their communion with Allah. Like the other traditions we have seen, Islam has developed significant mystical and meditative ways to promote the sense of mystery.

III. **Fasting.** During *Ramadan,* the ninth month of the Islamic calendar, the Qur'an prescribes a fast in honor of the revelations of Muhammad and his battle against idolatry. As a reminder of the plight of the poor, and as a way of purifying desire, all healthy adults are required during this month to abstain from food, drink and sexual activity from sunrise until dark. Such fasting might easily be interpreted as unnecessary self-punishment, but this discipline has a positive meaning for Muslims who see it as a "way" through unnecessary distractions, and toward a deeper union with God and suffering humanity.

IV. **Almsgiving.** In gratitude for God's gifts, the Muslim is instructed to give generously to the welfare of others. Islam considers care of the needy central to authentic religion. As in the other prophetic religions the ideal of justice is given expression in the special concern for the down-trodden that comes through clearly in the Qur'an and other Islamic texts.

V. **Pilgrimage.** Travelling to sacred shrines is characteristic of religions everywhere. Indeed even non-religious people often feel a need to visit cities and monuments that embody their ideals. Such places possess a special power to renew our lives. Among the great traditions probably none has made pilgrimage so special as has Islam. The Muslim is encouraged, if at all possible, to make a pilgrimage to the holy city of Mecca at least once in a lifetime. Such an extraordinary act would solidify one's identity with Islam in a profound way.

ALLAH

He is God;
There is no God but He.
He is the knower of the unseen and the Visible;
He is the All-merciful, the All-compassionate.
He is God;
There is no God but He.
He is the King, the All-holy, the All-peaceable.
the All-faithful, the All-preserver,
the All-mighty, the All-compeller,
the All-sublime.
Glory be to God, above that they associate!
He is God;
the Creator, the Maker, the Shaper.
To Him belong the Names Most Beautiful.
All that is in the heavens and the earth magnifies Him;
He is the All-mighty, the All-wise.

The Qur'an, LIX 23–25, reprinted from *The Koran Interpreted*, translated by A. J. Arberry, Allen & Unwin, 1955.

Conclusion

Judaism, Christianity and Islam are all "prophetic" religions. In the traditions descended from Abraham the figure of the prophet holds the prominent place that the shaman or priest had in earlier religion, or that the "teacher" or "seer" has had in shaping Asian religions. Not that the prophet is the sole religious authority, for there are still priests, kings, rabbis and other divinely sanctioned dignitaries. But in these three traditions the prophet stands out distinctly as the chief spokesperson for God. The prophet has the special function of summoning people to trust in God's promise and live in conformity with hope.

In prophetic religion the authentic life of trust requires a special commitment to the ideal of justice. Moses, Jesus and Muhammad all invite their followers to trust in the promise that they are cared for by God, that they have a future. Such trust, if it is sincere, has the effect of liberating people from self-preoccupation. And in the trust that they are already cared for, people can be free to live for others. So in the prophetic traditions there is the constant conviction that true religion comes to expression in concern for the social well-being of one's fellows. Sacrificial offerings to God are less important than a life offered to the promotion of the good of others. "For I desire steadfast love and not sacrifice, the knowledge of God, rather than burnt offerings." (*Hosea* 6:6) "Religion that is pure and undefiled before God and the Father is this: to visit orphans and widows in their affliction . . ." (*James* 1:26) And the Qur'an states: "Didn't [God] find you as an orphan and shelter [you], find you in need and make you rich? Therefore you shall not do violence to the orphan, nor shall you assault the beggar." (Sura 93, 6–9; in Küng, *et al.* 1986, 9)

In remaining faithful to the divine promise prophetic religion adopts an outlook that never allows it to take the past or present as prescribing the limits of reality. Hope in a promise opens reality out toward the novelty and complexity of a wider fulfillment than has yet been attained. This hope is touchingly expressed in a rabbinic expectation of the Messiah: "Even though he tarry, yet shall I wait for him." It comes out in the eucharistic prayer of Christians: "We hope to enjoy forever the vision of Your Glory." And it is manifest in the Qur'an's vivid picture of the life to come: "Therein they shall hear . . . only the saying 'Peace, Peace!' (56:25)

PART II

Ways of Religion

5.

Sacramentalism

Religions seek to overcome human suffering by guiding their participants toward ultimate fulfillment. In order to do so they formulate "ways" through the most unyielding limits on life. But these ways are not all alike. To understand religion then we must distinguish and relate several of the most prominent ways religions have set forth for the purpose of orienting us toward mystery.

We can immediately grasp the distinctiveness of these ways if we highlight a dominant trait from each of the previous four chapters and place it side by side with the others: the *symbolic* consciousness that prevails in "primitive" religion; the *mystical* quest for union that reaches such a high pitch of intensity in Hinduism; the return to *silence* that gives Buddhism its distinctive character; and the exhortation to *action* that becomes so explicit in prophetic religion. Each of these emphases teaches us something significant about religion. Religion is a synthesis of these four elements, and if any of them drops out of the picture, then religion has lost an essential ingredient. As we shall see later, various forms of escapism and skepticism result from the excision of any of the four elements.

Religion then is symbolic, mystical, silent and active. And each of these qualities suggests a distinct "way" of being religious. Specifically: 1. "Primitive" religion follows a predominantly symbolic or "sacramental way" toward mystery. 2. Hinduism exemplifies the "mystical way." 3. Buddhism illustrates the "way of silence." 4. And Judaism, Christianity and Islam emphasize the "way of action."

Each of our four elements is related to the others, and religion, as we shall understand it here, has to maintain elements of each way in order to keep its identity. But there is an accent in each of our four descriptions that we may now isolate and configure into a specific religious "way." *Sacramen-*

talism, mysticism, silence and *action* are four diverse shadings of human religious life and awareness. Or, to use a musical analogy, they are four different keys in which religion is played. Religion is most integral when it blends all four ways harmoniously. And if it is to maintain its integrity it needs to entertain aspects of all four ways. Religion begins to disintegrate into something other than religion whenever any of the four paths is isolated from contact with the others. In the concrete world of religious life such splitting of one aspect off from the others is not unusual. But when this splintering occurs, religion rapidly decays into magic, obsession with esoteric teachings, cynicism or vacuous activism. For religion to maintain its "religiousness" it requires all four aspects, even though one way is usually emphasized more than the others.

Each of our four ways also gives rise to a distinct type of religious official or personage. Sacramental religion is closely associated early with the figure of the "shaman" and later with the institution known as "priesthood." Mystical religion is cultivated most explicitly by the "contemplative." The "way of silence and renunciation" is most formally practiced in "monasticism," by monks and nuns. And activist religion is nurtured most intensely by the "prophet." The mass of religious people do not identify clearly with these roles. But these four types have been most responsible for cultivating the content of religious traditions. It is in them that our four ways are embodied most explicitly.

Any one person may at times participate in all four modes. The activist may also be a priest, contemplative and ascetic. But often the activist exists in tension with the other three types. The latter have at times looked negatively upon the activist whose life is devoted to betterment of the socio-political world. And the activist is sometimes critical of the priest, contemplative and ascetic for not getting sufficiently involved in the process of political and economic renewal of the social world. Sometimes the priestly or mystical representatives of religion have questioned whether the life of an activist is sufficiently oriented toward sacred mystery to qualify as religious. But activist religion, as we shall see later, gives the life of social involvement a thoroughly religious meaning, and it even makes such acts as taking care of the needy the very core of authentic religion.

Each of our four styles of religious awareness also has its characteristic way of interpreting the world of "secular" reality. Sacramental religion's posture toward the world, for example, is one of *enjoyment*. Mystical religion, in its quest for the One beyond the many, exemplifies best the religious *relativization* of all particular items in the world. Silent or "apophatic" religion, especially in the Buddhist renunciation of clinging, is significant for its *letting be* of the world. And finally, activist religion seeks to *transform* the world.

These approaches are not in contradiction to one another, and they may even be combined in a balanced way by exceptional religious persons. Aspects of all four are found in all the major religious traditions. But most of the time they are distinct emphases in the lives of religious persons or communities. Individual human beings lean dominantly toward one or another of these styles in their religious lives. It is not impossible to be priest, mystic, ascetic and activist all at the same time. But since this balance is rare we may speak separately about the sacramental, mystical, silent and activist religious ways, even though actual religious life involves constant oscillation back and forth along this spectrum of types.

Moreover, each type is associated with a distinct setting or "environment." The primary setting of sacramental religion is nature or the cosmos; mysticism's ambience is that of the soul and its quest for God; apophatic religion emerges against the backdrop of an "abyss," a "void" or an "emptiness"; and activist religion's context is history with its future possibilities.

Finally, each of our four types has its own peculiar temptation. Religion in any of its four main manifestations has inclinations which, if not held in check, can lead to a posture hostile to religion in its fullness. For example, sacramentalism may, and often does, degenerate into *idolatry* and *ritualism* as an escape from the demands of social existence. Mysticism can lose touch with nature and history by turning into *escapism*. The way of silence and renunciation can lead to *nihilism* (the view that nothing has any truth or value) if it is not carefully qualified. And activism can easily break its ties with any sense of the transcendent, as in the case of Marxism, for example. In that case it becomes indistinguishable from *secular humanism*. In general, these temptations can be overcome only if each of our four religious types allows itself to be influenced by the other three.

The four ways of religion are not at root incompatible with one another. Rather they are varying expressions, at the level of religious existence, of four distinct ways of being human. Some people, for example, are more sensitive to the multifarious colors and varieties of phenomena in the world than are others. They are especially attracted to enjoyment of particular things, and so they might be called the "sacramentalists." Some are more restless to find in all this variety a deep underlying unity, and such individuals might correspond to the "mystics" among us. Some of us are by nature reluctant to disturb the serenity of life with too many words. These are the "hesychasts," those given to silence. And still others understand life as the opportunity to do something. These are the "activists." Each of us has aspects of all of these traits, but one tendency may stand out more emphatically than the others. And so in religious life some persons may identify themselves more closely with one tendency than another.

Given the various inclinations of different personality types we should not be surprised that religion would unfold in such diverse ways also. In this and the following three chapters we shall explore our four religious "ways" in more detail.

Sacramentalism

Our first religious "way" may be called "sacramentalism." The sacramental way, like all religion, seeks to transcend the limits on life, but it does so in a manner distinct from that of religious mysticism, silence and action. Sacramental religion finds mystery manifest in symbols or "sacraments" derived especially from the human encounter with *nature*. The "sacramental way" looks toward mystery, but not nakedly. It senses the presence of mystery only through the medium of symbols, myths, rituals and sacrifices associated especially with our natural environment.

As an example we may think of the sacrament of baptism or of the ritual washings that are present in many religions. Here the pouring of water, one of the most natural of phenomena, symbolizes the power of a "sacred" reality, hidden in the depths of nature, to bring about spiritual renewal. Because we are bodily, natural beings, sacramental religion generally employs the physical aspects of nature in order to symbolize the dramatic occurrences in the world of the sacred.

Religion	"Way"	Approach to Mystery	Approach to the World	Social Role
"Primitive"	Sacrifice	symbolism	enjoyment	shaman or priest
Hinduism	Union	mysticism	relativization	contemplative
Buddhism	Renunciation	silence	"letting be"	ascetic
Judaism, Christianity, Islam	Hope	action	transformation	activist

The sacramental religion of preliterate peoples perceives sacred mystery in concrete aspects of the physical world. Mystery is transparent in the sun, the sky, the earth, rivers, oceans, seasons, animals, fertility, floods, storms, etc. Human sexuality in particular is one of the most numinously charged "natural" realities in sacramental religion. This most powerful human experience has often been interpreted by sacramentalism as the vital link between humanity and the sacred. Today we have lost much of this sacramental sentiment concerning sexuality. Sex has been secularized to a great extent today, but in the story of religion the phallus or the breasts are often prominent symbols of the power of the sacred. And there are still disguised sexual themes present even in the most puritanical and ascetical of religions.

By interpreting natural phenomena as symbols of the sacred, sacramental religion gives them a value beyond their mere matter-of-factness. It transfigures the natural world with a "thou" quality that connects it more intimately to human life. In the case of "primitive" human experience, for example, the world appears

> . . .neither inanimate nor empty but redundant with life; and life
> has individuality, in man and beast and plant, and in every phe-
> nomenon which confronts man—the thunderclap, the sudden
> shadow, the eerie and unknown clearing in the wood, the stone
> which suddenly hurts him when he stumbles while on a hunting
> trip. Any phenomenon may at any time face him, not as 'It', but
> as 'Thou'. (Frankfort, *et al.*, 14)

Thus aspects of nature which to our modern sensitivities may seem to be completely impersonal can symbolically mediate a "personal" presence to the sacramental mind.

Sacramental aspects persist in all religious traditions up to our own time. It is doubtful whether religion can exist without some aspect of sacramentalism. As religion has developed in the post-axial period, the realm of mystery has been perceived as more and more distinct from nature. The major religions emphasize that there can be no adequate naturalistic or human representation of this mystery. But at the same time symbols remain necessary. All religious reference is symbolic. Ultimate reality cannot be encountered or talked about at all apart from some symbolic elements derived from our immediate world. If we are to become aware of the divine at all it can only be by way of the various aspects of our "cosmic" experience. Natural objects, persons and events in our lives bring to awareness a sacred world that is embodied in but at the same time distinct from them. Nature manifests itself to sacramental religion as an array of symbols or sacraments pointing beyond itself to a deeper presence incarnate in, but simultaneously outreaching, the cosmos.

This symbolic nature of sacramental religion implies therefore that sacred mystery will be understood as "something like" the symbols that interpret it for us. Another way of putting this is to say that sacramental language about the divine employs *analogy*. Sacramental religion has a premonition that ultimate mystery is infinitely beyond, but also somewhat akin or analogous to things, persons and events that we experience in everyday life. For example, the energy of divine creativity is "something like" the experience of human fertility. Or the love of God for the world is "something like" our experience of a mother's care for her children. In sacramental religion the nature of mystery cannot be captured except by way of analogy with our "natural" experience.

This means that the entire enterprise of religion rests upon the plausibility of symbolic or analogous expression. Today we live in an intellectual climate where there is a strong demand for clear and literal language. If our ideas cannot be stated directly and distinctly, then we are suspected of being obscure or covering something up. The language of analogy, however, cannot say exactly or clearly what something is. It can only imply that something is "like" or "akin to" something else. Symbol and analogy cannot bring into view the totality to which they are pointing. And since religion has to resort to symbolic and analogous discourse today's skeptics find this failure a sign of religion's inadequacy to put us in touch with reality.

We shall discuss skepticism at greater length later on. For now it is important only to observe that the sacramental mind would vigorously protest any quest for complete clarity about the mystery it perceives in religious symbols. If religious symbols were reduced to literal clarity then that which is most vital to religion would be lost, namely, the sense of an incomprehensible mystery. It is of the essence of religion to resist the reduction of reality to what can be mastered by the mind and its quest for clarity.

Attitude Toward the World

The distinctive mark of the sacramental way is *enjoyment* of the goods of the earth. It might seem peculiar for us to associate religion so closely with enjoyment. For many people religion seems anything but enjoyable, and so they have lost interest in it. But such colorless and joyless religiosity has not always been the norm. And sacramentalism, from the time of its remote historical origins, has been intimately connected with the human capacity for joy. Even burial or initiation rites, in spite of the pain and sorrow accompanying them, intend the recovery of our enjoyment of life. They are not carried out just for the dead or the initiates but also for the whole living tribe or people. Religious ritual, which we associate primarily with sacramental religion, is concerned with deepening our sense of sharing life and its joys with others.

Sacramental religion invites its devotees to feel their connection to the rest of life, to plants, animals, sun, moon, stars and the totality of cosmic reality. It places a high value on the cosmos. It does not despise the world or seek to escape it. Instead it finds the universe good and "enjoyable." In fact, it is the delightfulness of things that elicits in sacramental piety a longing for more, even infinitely more, enjoyment. There is an unquenchable thirst for enjoyment in the human spirit, and this longing quite naturally turns first toward the world of immediate experience in order to find satisfaction. Sacramental religion seeks to extract as much from nature as it can in order to satisfy this craving. But as it does so it becomes increasingly aware of the human need for an inexhaustible "depth" of significance beneath all specific natural objects. And so it eventually begins to read nature as *symbolic* of an infinite mystery. The notion of "God" and other religious ideas of transcendence stem from this intuition.

Sacramentalism rejoices in nature, in other persons, in human community, in food, sexuality and all the goods of the earth. These are "blessings" which need not be renounced, as they often are in other religious ways. Yet sacramental piety does not become completely fixated on the things themselves. It interprets them as a foretaste of wider and more intense enjoyment. It sees them as gifts originating in a more encompassing domain of mystery. In the sacramental vision worldly objects become transparent to the deeper and more alluring divine depths manifest in them. Christians, for example, perceive in the simple elements of bread and wine of the Eucharistic ritual a rich set of meanings connecting them to an ultimate mystery of divine goodness. And ancient Egyptians saw in the Nile River a mysterious meaning that allowed them to trust in an ultimate order. Similarly, most of the world's religions have transfigured ordinary aspects of their immediate environment with intimations of a wider, sacral order. Later we shall have occasion to wonder, though, how such a way of reading the world can in any sense be considered realistic.

Gratitude

Accepting and enjoying the various aspects of the world as symbolic media pointing to an inexhaustible sacred abundance—this is the main feature of the sacramental vision. Sacramental religion is therefore quite understandably suffused with *gratitude*. In the manner appropriate to the accepting of a gift, it relishes the world with an almost childlike delight. And eventually it may even turn its focus from the gift itself to the idea of a possible Giver. As the sacramental motif of preliterate religion is taken up into later religious developments the overflowing feeling of gratitude for immediate things blossoms more and more explicitly into the concept of a distinct divine creative principle transcending the world. The enjoyability of the world, a conviction of its utter goodness, sooner or later leads sacramental religion toward rites of praise and sacrifice to an intimated source or "creator" of the world's grandeur. The theme of divine creativity then becomes a central theological implication of sacramental religion. The many stories of creation in oral and written religious traditions are fashioned out of a feeling of wonder and gratitude at the gift of the world.

The Beginning of the World
An Omaha Indian Explanation

"At the beginning," said the Omaha, "all things were in the mind of Wakonda. All creatures, including man, were spirits. They moved about in space between the earth and the stars (the heavens). They were seeking a place where they could come into bodily existence. They ascended to the sun, but the sun was not fitted for their abode. They moved on to the moon and found that it also was not good for their home. Then they descended to the earth. They saw it was covered with water. They floated through the air to the north, the east, the south, and the west, and found no dry land. They were sorely grieved. Suddenly from the midst of the water uprose a great rock. It burst into flames and the waters floated into the air in clouds. Dry land appeared; the grasses and the trees grew. The hosts of the spirits descended and became flesh and blood. They fed on the seeds of the grasses and the fruits of the trees, and the land vibrated with their expressions of joy and gratitude to Wakonda, the maker of all things."

Quoted in Fletcher and La Flesche, "The Omaha Tribe," in the *Annual Report* of the Bureau of American Ethnology, 1911.

The Survival of Sacramentalism

Partly as the result of modernity's affair with science and technology, but partly also because of religious developments that occurred during the axial period, the sacramental side of religion has a less prominent place today than it did in the earliest period of religious history. Mystical, silent and prophetic religion all contain emphases that assisted the process of its demotion. For example, prophetic religion seems at times almost to drain "mystery" out of the natural world. For the prophets mystery resides primarily in the realm of history whose God cannot be tied down to nature. If the God of history alone is holy, then nature is not. Nature is mere matter-of fact "stuff" and not something to be worshipped. The cosmos loses much of its symbolic character, and then strict sacramentalism becomes questionable as the only approach to mystery. In its bias toward "radical monotheism" prophetic religion itself seems to have contributed in some way to the decline of sacramentalism.

Suspicion of sacramentalism in the great teachings is a result of the axial protest against idolatry. The axial religions that emerged around the middle of the first millennium B.C.E. were afraid that our linking spirituality too closely to sensual delight in natural objects might lead us to substitute these objects for the transcendent mystery they symbolize. In the case of Buddhism there was the conviction that clinging to things would lead to further suffering. Buddhists and Vedantic mystics, as well as the prophets, were keenly aware of the temptation to "clinging" that always accompanies sacramental religion.

However, if we look at the history of religion we observe an interesting paradox. No matter how lofty and "pure" the teachings about the transcendence and unity of God became during the axial age, popular or "folk" religion has endured anyway, often with a pronounced tendency toward polytheism. No matter how much the great teachers of Vedanta, of Theravada Buddhism, of prophetic Yahwism, of Islam and classical theism cautioned against multiplication of images of the sacred, most of the actual religious life of people has found this demand to be too austere. And so religion in the actual world is often a sort of rebellion against the "purity" of mystics, prophets and theologians. It is a luxuriant body of undergrowth often almost choking out the "essential" theological insights concerning the ultimate unity or radical transcendence of God. It seems more at home with diversity, color and variety. Popular religion resists the mystical and prophetic protests against images and idols. Without necessarily being idolatrous itself, it often comes dangerously close. Its veneration of saints, of holy men and women, its attachment to statues, pictures, medals, fetishes and sacrifices seems to border on animism and polytheism at times.

One might be tempted to scorn the extravagant multiplication of "gods" or other elaborations accompanying popular religion. Not only skeptics, but also the most important religious figures, have been disturbed by the excesses in popular religion. They have often looked upon sacramental extravagance as a deviation from pure devotion to an absolutely transcendent mystery. In the teachings of Moses, the prophets of Israel, Buddha, Jesus, Paul, Augustine, Muhammad, Shankara, Luther and numerous others there is a degree of revulsion toward any excessive complicating of piety. For some religious teachers the fear of idolatry has become almost an obsession since the axial age, and at times their consternation has cleansed religion of some of its most colorful aspects. And yet, folk religion still thrives with its endless multiplication of sacraments, feasts, processions, saints, demons, novenas, relics, perfumes, etc. that may seem initially to have very little to do with the heart of religious awareness as understood by its most famous instructors.

How are we to account for this irrepressible florescence of popular religious devotion? How can we explain the sometimes virtual ignoring of the reforms proposed by the *Upanishads*, or by the likes of Moses, Buddha, Jesus or Muhammad? Is there any explanation for the opaqueness of the average person to the lofty ideals of theology and spirituality? Can we simply attribute it to our idolatrous tendencies, or to our childishness, weakness and escapism? Perhaps to some degree, at least. It would not be surprising, given what we know about human nature, that a certain level of immaturity always accompanies human spiritual devotion.

But such an answer is too easy, and certainly misleading. It is more likely that alongside the motivations arising from our immaturity and weakness, there is a vital and wholesome need to inject beauty and enjoyment into religious life. Perhaps we have been too one-sided in our depiction of religion up to this point. Have we not overlooked the simple fact that we are human beings? Most of us are not saints or mystics, but ordinary people. Most people are not very literate even in terms of their own religious traditions. Very few have the luxury of spending their lives in meditation or in perusing sacred writings in order to arrive at some "universal" or "essential" meaning beyond the particularity of their sacramental modes of expression. Most of religion in the concrete is a far cry from that taught by the seers, prophets and theologians. It is not highly conceptual or deeply reflective. Rather it is spontaneous and richly symbolic.

The fundamental language of religion is symbol. It has been so since the beginning, and it is safe to say that it will always be so. Therefore, it would be misleading to conclude that religion is richly symbolic simply because of the lack of intellectual and spiritual sophistication on the part of most believers. A sacramental-symbolic base undergirds religious mysticism, silence and action also. Even for those religious geniuses who have been sensitive to the propensity of symbols to degenerate into idols, religious devotion is still connected in some way with sacraments. Without some aspect of symbolism there would simply be no such thing as religion.

Like most other aspects of prehistoric religion, sacramentalism has never been completely forsaken. It still survives not only in pre-literate religions but also as an indispensable layer of the major religious traditions. In the latter it does not exist independently of mysticism, silence and action, but it is still identifiable as a distinct dimension. In Roman Catholicism and some other forms of Christianity, for example, participation in the "sacraments" is considered essential to the religious life of their members. In these sacraments natural realities like water, or substances close to nature like bread, wine and oil, or the natural processes of becoming an adult, mating and dying, are given a religious meaning (in such rites as baptism, eucharist, marriage, confirmation and anointing). It is important to note, however, that these Christian sacraments, closely linked to nature as they may be, are also overlaid with deep historical meaning. They signify not only the divine closeness to the cosmos but also to history. For example, the sacrament of marriage which focuses on the natural mystery of sexuality also signifies the central historical theme in prophetic religion, God's fidelity to the Promise. The example of two individuals faithful in marriage is one way in which many believers gain a tangible awareness of the faithfulness of God in human history.

The Significance of Sacramentalism

In some phases of the history of religion, the sacramental attitude has been submerged. Mystical, silent and active religious ways have often been suspicious of it. One obvious example is the Protestant reformers' hesitations about Catholic sacramental practice. Another is the Brahmanistic critique of Vedic religion. Still another is Muhammad's polemic against the idolatrous religious practices of seventh century Arabia. And perhaps the best example of all is the Buddha's suspicion of the rich symbolic piety of popular forms of Hinduism. These critiques represent the axial intuition that sacramental religion can easily succumb to magic, superstition, ritualism and idolatry.

At the same time, though, most religious thinkers today insist that the suppression of sacramentalism would be disastrous both for religion and human well-being as such. This point is made especially by those sensitive to environmental issues. Their argument is that we need an attitude of reverence for nature and life, as well as an enduring impression of our kinship with the rest of the universe. A renewed sacramental piety, many think, is perhaps the best way to foster this enrapturement.

In sacramental religion aspects of nature are charged with a numinous quality that we no longer feel very powerfully in a scientific age. To us nature is often nothing more than mere "matter." It has apparently lost its former symbolic function of connecting our consciousness to a sacred mystery. Our technological power over nature has demoted the physical universe to the status of intrinsically valueless particles or mechanisms to be transformed into humanly meaningful creations by our own ingenuity. To the secularized consciousness of the West nature seldom evokes the reverential attitude that we find, for example, in the sentiments of many native Americans. How many of us, for example, could share very deeply their piety toward the sky, the mountains, the wind, the sun and other aspects of our natural environment? Could we sincerely address the earth as our mother, or the winds as our grandfathers?

Sacramentalism stubbornly resists the subjection of nature to human control. A great deal of modern thought has divested the natural world of any intrinsic meaning, often to the point of explicitly stating the universe to be purposeless. It has at times enshrined the human will as supreme over the universe. The results of this self-exaltation have been calamitous whenever we have taken it upon ourselves to destroy the beauty of nature for the sake of our own ambitions. Thus many religious thinkers argue today that a recovery of the sacramental vision, in some form or other, may play a significant role in the restoration of our environment.

However, some scholars observe that the decline of a sacramental view of nature has not been entirely unbeneficial. Its decline, they argue, has contributed to the emergence of science. According to this hypothesis the "disenchantment" of the world, divesting it of its "apparent" divinity, has opened the previously forbidding world of nature to the investiture of scientific control. (Cox, 21–24) As long as our ancestors approached nature with religious awe they were hesitant to analyze it scientifically or to exploit it technologically. If the cosmos is experienced as the sacramental embodiment of an inexhaustible mystery, people might be afraid to turn it into material for human mastery. But if it is made to seem ordinary, then it invites our exploring, and exploiting, it without fear.

In order to be subject to our scientific and technological domination nature needs first to be stripped of its forbiddingly sacral demeanor. And the process of secularization, whereby the sense of the sacred becomes increasingly lost to consciousness, has expelled the gods and spirits from the forests, waters, and lands of the earth, opening them up to science and human domination. By stripping nature of its sacramental countenance modern secularized consciousness has been less reluctant to manipulate and exploit it than our shamanistic ancestors were. And this "desacralization" of the cosmos has allowed the invasion of science into territory previously held captive by the gods. (Cox, 21–24)

Hence the loss of sacramentalism seems to have contributed to the origins and advance of science. Some thinkers applaud the demise of a sacral view of the cosmos, holding that it provides the opportunity for humans to become more aware of their own power and creativity than ever before. Others lament the disenchantment of nature, giving many examples of how it opens up the possibility of abuse. Desacralizing nature may have prepared the way for science, but according to many experts it has also led to the disastrous ecological conditions that threaten human existence today.

But is it possible for us now to return to a pre-scientific understanding of the world? Many would argue that such a return is neither possible nor appropriate at this point in history. It would be "unnatural" for us to suppress our need for exploration, including the kind that science undertakes. However, human exploration and creativity do not have to mean conquest or subjection. They may be carried out in more responsible ways than in the past. Scientists are now becoming more aware of our dependence on a whole hierarchy of life systems whose survival is essential for our own. One way to promote responsibility for sustaining this essential environment is to become aware of the intrinsic value of nature. It is in this respect that we might ask about the significance even today of a sacramental vision of the cosmos.

Thomas Berry, an environmentally sensitive religious scholar, writes that we need to recapture a sacramental "mystique" of nature in our own post-scientific context. This sacramental vision has been lost in modern times, and the results have been the destruction of our natural habitat, the deaths of thousands of species, the pollution of our rivers and lakes. Berry discovers the roots of this bitter experience in the dream of "progress" derived from the "prophetic" strain of our religious heritage. Our environmental problems result not just from scientism, but also from a religious striving that has lost touch with sacramentalism. According to Berry, activist-prophetic religion (our fourth type) itself contributes to our environmental problems. Its obsession with progress and transformation of the world has, he thinks, justified an anti-environmental attitude. It has led people to destroy nature for the sake of dubious notions of human fulfillment. (Berry, 1988, 207)

However, it is not prophetic religion as such that is to blame. Rather, it is the activist or transformative aspects of prophetic religion that have lost touch with their sacramental roots. The perversions of religion occur whenever one of our four ways strays off from its primordial connection to the other three. In this case it is the isolated activist or progressivist tendencies, and not prophetic religion itself, that have led to the present environmental crisis. Once they pulled themselves away from the sacramental aspects of religion certain activist and visionary aspects of biblical religion have indeed launched tendencies toward "progress" that have been slanted toward environmental recklessness.

Sacrament and Revelation

Sacraments "reveal" mystery. *Revelation* is a theological term designating the symbolic disclosure of mystery to religious participants. All four religious ways contribute to a doctrine of revelation in one form or another. In mystical religion, for example, the mystery of divine unity and love is "revealed" to the mystic in a more immediate and less symbolically rich manner than in sacramental religion, though even in mystical experience there is often a subordinate sacramental component. In "silent" religion paradoxically the ultimate mystery is disclosed or revealed by way of the very removal of words and images, and in the ensuing "emptiness" of silence itself. Silence becomes the "medium" of revelation. Finally, in prophetic religion the primary medium of revelation is the spoken "word." The three prophetic religions make a great deal of God's "speaking" through the prophets.

However, in sacramental religion revelation means the *symbolic* manifestation of mystery. Symbols, myths and rituals are bridges to an ultimate reality. They are the media through which an ultimate mystery insinuates itself into the lives of religious people, thus giving them a reason for trusting in spite of the negativities of life. To the sincerely religious, symbols are *revelatory* of the transcendent mystery encompassing their lives. Symbols are themselves the "way" through the limits on life.

The Sacramental Temptation

As we have already noted, mysticism, silence and activism, the other three religious ways, are somewhat suspicious of sacramental religion's attachment to nature. They are afraid that it will become too attached to the symbols themselves and thereby lose touch with the mystery to which the symbols are pointing. In other words, they are suspicious that sacramentalism can easily deviate into "idolatry." Each religious way loses its specifically religious character whenever it becomes isolated from the other three. The "religiousness" of each way requires an abiding contact with the others. In the case of the sacramental way, the "enjoyability" of the symbol can become so seductive that the "mystical" or transcendent meaning is lost. Religious awareness then narrows itself down to an obsession with the symbol and a suppression of that to which the symbol is pointing. This reduction is what is known in theology as idolatry.

Idolatry is indeed the characteristic temptation of sacramental religion. It is possible for us to become so entranced by the symbol itself that we gradually lose awareness of its transparent character. We then enshrine the symbol as our ultimate concern and lose consciousness of the mystery it symbolizes. For that reason sacramental religion needs also to hold onto the mystical, silent and active aspects of religion. These other ways work against the tendency to reduce religion to infatuation with specific aspects of the world. Mysticism would oppose the latent "naturalism" or "secularism" present in all types of idolatry. The way of silence, as we shall see later, would seek to widen the symbolic base of religion, preventing a fixation on only one or a few symbols. And by emphasizing the need for religion to make a difference in our social existence, the way of action would resist the decay of sacramentalism into empty ritualism. The key to preserving the fullness of religion lies in a balancing of all four ways.

6.

Mysticism

For reasons that no one knows for certain, some people are more sensitive than others to the presence of "mystery." They are sometimes called "mystics." For most of us, mystery remains somewhat vague, even to the point of our questioning whether it is there at all. For others its reality is fragmentarily grasped by way of sacraments and symbols. For example, in beholding the beauties of nature we may have a faint intuition of an even more perfect beauty that lies behind and shines through the natural world. But for a few exceptional individuals mystery has been seen, tasted and felt in such an immediate and palpable manner that we may speak in their case of the distinct mode of religion known as *mysticism*.

We cannot draw absolutely clear lines between or among our four types. They are distinct but related modes whose roots in the depths of religious life are richly entangled. But sometimes they generate separate shoots above ground level. And this differentiated sprouting allows us to distinguish, but never to isolate, them from one another. Thus a tendency toward mysticism may be part of all religious experience. Mysticism stands out as a distinct religious way, but its foundations are so intertwined with the other three ways that any separate treatment of it will quite likely miss important connections essential to understanding it.

What is mysticism? The answer to this question is not easy, for the term is used in so many different ways by religious thinkers and authors. At times it is defined so broadly that it almost loses any distinctive meaning, and it becomes almost the equivalent of "religion." It is used by skeptics, for example, as a derogatory term referring to anything religious, and therefore having nothing at all to do with "reality." Accordingly, a "mystic" is one who has lost touch with the "real" world and surrendered to nonsense. But at the opposite extreme mysticism is understood by some religious thinkers as the only appropriate path to reality, and any mode of consciousness other than the mystical is judged to be an imperfect and distortive rendition of reality.

In between these extremes mysticism has been given a whole range of evaluations and connotations, such that it has at times become almost a useless term because of its referential vagueness. We cannot avoid talking about it in any discussion of religion, but in order for it to signify anything of interest for us we must restrict its meaning somewhat.

Once we attempt to define it, however, we begin to wonder if mysticism differs from other religious ways in any manner other than the intensity and immediacy of its awareness of mystery. There is a mystical aspect to all religious experience, insofar as religion means the state of being grasped in some way by mystery. Therefore, mysticism cannot signify something absolutely distinguishable from religion in its other modes. Human awareness of mystery lies along a spectrum ranging from inexplicit to explicit, from weak to strong, from tentative to certain. But there are no logically strict dividing lines separating mysticism from the rest of religion. For that reason it may be more accurate to speak of mysticism as a dimension, rather than a separate type, of religion.

Nevertheless, Evelyn Underhill (1911) and other experts on mysticism have noticed that some individuals have made the quest for union with mystery such an explicit theme in their religious lives that mystical preoccupation becomes a virtually distinct religious phenomenon. And so we may follow here the custom of setting it aside for special consideration, keeping in mind that the reality of religious life is never so neat as our theoretical clarifications seem to make it.

Although admittedly the term "mysticism" has additional connotations for other authors, I shall employ it here simply as the exceptionally vivid intuition of one's *union* with ultimate reality. A mystic is one who has become exceptionally aware of how estranged our ordinary existence appears to be from the ultimate "ground" of being and has successfully sought to overcome this intolerable feeling of isolation. After sometimes many years of careful preparations, having followed closely the discipline of a traditional spirituality, the mystic eventually begins to have episodic experiences of complete union with mystery. This mystery may be interpreted in both theistic and non-theistic ways, depending on the tradition and language in which the mystic has been nurtured.

Many people set out to have such an experience and never seem to reach their goal. The mystic, however, is one who succeeds, though not simply because of his or her own efforts. In the proper sense, then, the "mystic" may be understood here as one who occasionally experiences in a *conscious* way the ecstasy of being encompassed by and intimately united with a divine mystery. In this experience the "normal" sense of being separated in some way from one's ultimate destiny is conquered by the more vivid experience of being completely tied into it, at least momentarily. Bernadette Roberts' account of her own mystic journey is a good illustration:

> I went to the mountains to learn how to live a new type of existence, an existence without time, without thought, without emotions, feelings and energies of the self. . . . Not for a single day had I ever lived before. Without a doubt I was in the Great Flow, so totally at one with it that every notion of ecstasy, bliss, love, and joy, pale by comparison to the extraordinary simplicity, clarity, and oneness of such an existence. (Roberts, 33)

Meister Eckhart, a thirteenth-century Christian mystic, describes mystical experience as the suspension of the ordinary sense of being a separate self, and a clear impression of the "soul" becoming one with God.

> For though [the soul] sink all sinking in the oneness of divinity, she never touches bottom. For it is of the very essence of the soul that she is powerless to plumb the depths of her creator. And here one cannot speak of the soul any more, for she has lost her nature yonder in the oneness of divine essence. There she is no more called soul, but is called immeasurable being.

> The knower and the known are one. Simple people imagine that they should see God, as if He stood there and they here. This is not so. God and I, we are one in knowledge. (cited by Huxley, 1970, 12)

The Marks of Mysticism

Can we state more clearly the characteristics that make mysticism a seemingly distinct religious phenomenon? Some religious writers note the presence of love as the inner core of mystical experience. It is undeniable that the intense feeling of love and being loved is a vital aspect of mystical experience. However, by identifying it too closely with love there is a tendency to dilute the specific meaning of mysticism. Love gives much of religion its substance and authenticity, so it may not take us very far to make it the distinguishing mark of mysticism. Love, as the great mystics themselves know from personal experience, is often enshrouded in darkness and permeated by the feeling of separation from or even abandonment by God. Love may be present even when a sense of union (which is the essential aspect of mystical experience) is absent.

For our purposes it is preferable to understand mystical religion not simply as the loving quest for mystery, but as the consciously ecstatic experience of union with ultimate reality. The practice of selfless love is an aspect of all the religious modes. It is no less present in sacramental, apophatic and activist religion than in mysticism. Mystical experience itself is generally fleeting and occasional, whereas love may be constant even in the experience of desolation and seeming abandonment by God. Most mystics would agree with this, since for them the actual mystical experience itself is not the result of their quest for God but rather a free and completely undeserved gift, the origin of which none of their strivings is able fully to explain. The fifteenth-century English mystic, Julian of Norwich, for example, insists that her mystical visions are not the result of her being morally better or more loving than the "least soul." "I am certain there are full many who never had [mystical visions] . . . and who love God better than I." (Reynolds, ed., 16) Hence taking love as the defining mark of mysticism is questionable.

What then are its distinctive marks? A standard attempt to outline the main characteristics of mystical experience is given in a famous discussion of religion, *The Varieties of Religious Experience*, by the renowned American philosopher William James. Some critics of James have complained that the marks he finds in mysticism also apply to experience other than mystical, and so they do not serve well to set mysticism apart as a distinct religious phenomenon. However, there simply may not be any absolutely crisp demarcation between mysticism and ordinary human experience of a world enshrouded in the oneness of mystery. Perhaps mysticism is simply a very intense concentration of ingredients latent in *all* human experience, rather than a totally different kind of experience. If that is so, then the same logical marks found in general human experience may be attributed in an eminent way to mysticism. We need only keep in mind that in the case of mysticism we may be dealing with a highly concentrated exemplification of, rather than a complete exception to, them. Thus even though James' treatment of mysticism may in many respects be inadequate, his designations are still useful. (James, 299–336)

The first mark of mystical experience, James says, is its *ineffability*, its quality of being extremely difficult to explain to others. This is an aspect, to one degree or another, of all human experience. None of us can ever communicate to another exactly what it is like to have any experience, but we struggle to find words to do so, never quite succeeding. The mystical experience is so compelling that the mystic often cannot refrain from telling others about it, or seeking to share it with them by writing it down. But in the final analysis the mystical experience itself is incommunicable, only more so than other experiences. The terms "mystery" and "mysticism" both come from the same Greek root, *muein*= "to close (the eyes or mouth)." No words or images can capture the mystery. And as much as the mystic tries to divulge the content of the mystical experience to others, there is always a sensation of falling infinitely short. At times this impression of failure becomes so acute that the mystic falls into utter silence. And at this point mysticism shows its affiliation with the "way of silence," which we shall look at more closely in the next chapter.

The second mark of mysticism is its *noetic quality*. By this expression James means that the mystical rapture is not just a vague feeling, but an exceptionally sharp insight into reality, serving as the basis for a whole new understanding of oneself and the world. Even though the skeptic will continue to suspect that there is projection and wishful thinking at the root of the experience, the mystic is *absolutely certain* that the experience was no illusion. And in light of the mystical insight ordinary and scientific consciousness now appear deficient. Moreover, the transient mystical perception has a staying power in the consciousness of the mystic. Even after its vividness has been lost, the mystic remains certain that something very enduring has happened. And we read about people who, having had such mystical moments only once or twice, find such isolated occasions sufficient to readjust for a whole lifetime their convictions about the horizons of the real world. To them, at least, there is no doubt whatsoever about the veracity of what they have seen or felt. In summary, then, "noetic quality" means that the mystical experience simply cannot be discarded by the mystic as a passing fancy. It becomes the foundation for a deeper appreciation of the mystery of reality.

The third characteristic mark of mysticism is *transiency*. That is, the experience does not last for long. The temporal span of most mystical experiences ranges from only a few moments to a couple of hours at the most. And then, James says, the experience fades. We notice from the testimony of mystics that their ecstasy does not survive for extended periods. But after returning to the everyday world some memory of the experience still lingers. And even if the mystical raptures are only occasional, they can fill the mystic's life with the continuity of an abiding meaning. Knowing that such heightened experiences of mystery are even possible makes existence significant and reality completely trustworthy.

In the fourth place, according to James' analysis, mystical experience has the quality of *passivity*.

Although the oncoming of mystical states may be facilitated by preliminary voluntary operations, as by fixing the attention, or going through certain bodily performances, or in other ways which manuals of mysticism prescribe; yet when the characteristic sort of consciousness once has set in, the mystic feels as if his own will were in abeyance, and indeed sometimes as if he were grasped and held by a superior power. (James, 300)

Mystical experience, in other words, comes as a gift and not as the predictable outcome of human effort. Some individuals can labor intensely and fruitlessly to have such moments, whereas others may find them occurring unannounced and uninvited. Usually, though, some sort of discipline is required by the religions in preparation for mystical intimacy with God. In Eastern traditions mystical experience is generally prepared for by various types of yoga or meditation, whereas in the West mysticism often falls in the context of a highly regimented life of prayer, action and contemplation.

Those religions are called mystical in which a high degree of deliberate attention is devoted to the attainment of mystical states of consciousness. Thus we may say that Eastern religions are generally more mystical than Western religions are. In prophetic religion the most important expression of one's devotional life lies in actions of charity undertaken on behalf of one's neighbor, not in "enlightenment" or whatever exceptional states of consciousness religious life might happen to bring with it. It is easy to comprehend, then, why mystical experience has not generally been as highly esteemed in the West as in the East. Recently, however, Western religious scholars have begun to pay much more attention than before to the rich traditions of mysticism present in Judaism, Christianity and Islam.

Is Mysticism Religious?

There is considerable controversy among scholars as to whether mysticism is distinctively religious. The controversy arises in part because the ecstatic experiences of "ultimate" unity, in which the individuality of the participant is momentarily caught up into a transcending bliss-bestowing totality, has parallels in the experience of some individuals who otherwise have no formal interest in religion. And on top of this there are a number of thoroughly "secular" individuals who have experimented with LSD or other hallucinogens and whose reports of the results seem, at least on the surface, to differ little from the accounts of the mystical encounter with God given by holy men and women. William James himself experienced the "mystical" results of inhaling nitrous oxide:

Depth beyond depth of truth seems revealed to the inhaler. This
truth fades out, however, or escapes, at the moment of coming
to; and if any words remain over in which it seemed to clothe
itself, they prove to be the veriest nonsense. Nevertheless, the
sense of a profound meaning having been there persists; and I
know more than one person who is persuaded that in the nitrous
oxide trance we have a genuine mystical revelation. (305)

Since James wrote these words in 1902 there have been countless
similar testimonies to the "cosmic consciousness" resulting from ingesting
LSD, mescaline or other psychedelic substances. The most famous of such
testimonies is given by Aldous Huxley in his book, *The Doors of Perception*
(1954). Here he questions whether there is any fundamental difference
between the mystical experience of famous religious persons and the drug-
induced ecstasy of ordinary people. But Huxley's association of hallucino-
genic experience with religious mysticism is vehemently excoriated by R.
C. Zaehner in *Mysticism, Sacred and Profane* (1961).

Several of my students have told me of their own experiments with
LSD. One of them found that a single drug-induced ecstatic experience of
his unity with the mystery of the universe induced in him the strong desire
to seek through traditional religious meditation a similar experience not
subject to the disastrous effects of taking chemical substances. And another wrote the following in a paper at the end of a course dealing with the
question of cosmic purpose:

I find the mechanistic approach [which denies the existence of
cosmic purpose and the truth-value of any religious experience]
very difficult to accept or deal with, due mainly to the fact that I
have personally experienced the overwhelming purposiveness of
nature on several occasions while sitting alone in the middle of a
pasture in Florida on a moonlit summer night ingesting hallucino-
genic mushrooms. That may sound strange, but the feeling of
unity with my environment, the clarity with which I perceived
my universe, was something I shall never forget and will never
deny to myself. Perhaps Monod [a mechanist who repudiates all
religious experience as illusory] could benefit from a similar experience. (written in the Spring of 1982)

Such statements hardly sound so foreign anymore, but they still raise
troubling questions about the specifically "religious" nature of mystical
experience. Can intoxicants really bring about religious experience? All the

major traditions require a life of contemplation, discipline or charity as the sign of authentic relation to the transcendent. So how could anything as easy as falling into an hallucinatory state be dignified with the adjective "religious"?

Or is it possible that, even though artificially altered consciousness might not itself qualify as religious, nonetheless drugs and other intoxicants are so tantalizing precisely because they awaken religious propensities in us that normally lie dormant? Opinions vary, though William James, speaking of the attractions of our most popular intoxicant says this:

The sway of alcohol over mankind is unquestionably due to its power to stimulate the mystical faculties of human nature, usually crushed to earth by the cold facts and dry criticism of the sober hour. Sobriety diminishes, discriminates and says no; drunkenness expands, unites, and says yes. It is in fact the great exciter of the *Yes* function in man. It brings its votary from the chill periphery of things to the radiant core. It makes him for the moment one with truth. Not through mere perversity do men run after it. To the poor and the unlettered it stands in the place of the symphony concerts and of literature; and it is part of the deeper mystery and tragedy of life that whiffs and gleams of something that we immediately recognize as excellent should be vouchsafed to so many of us only in the fleeting earlier phases of what in its totality is so degrading a poisoning. The drunken consciousness is one bit of the mystic consciousness, and our total opinion of it must find its place in our opinion of the larger whole. (304–05)

James thinks that we have to revise our understanding of the nature of reality and of human consciousness in the light of drugged experience:

. . . our normal waking consciousness, rational consciousness as we call it, is but one special type of consciousness, whilst all about it, parted from it by the filmiest of screens, there lie potential forms of consciousness entirely different. We may go through life without suspecting their existence; but apply the requisite stimulus, and at a touch they are all there in all their completeness, definite types of mentality which probably somewhere have their field of application and adaptation. No account of the universe in its totality can be final which leaves these other forms of consciousness quite disregarded. (303)

But can we call such experiences religious if they often occur outside of any devotional framework? One group of respondents to this problem replies that mysticism is not specifically religious and should not be taken seriously as one of the central aspects of religion. According to this critical position mystical experience itself may even be regressive and childish, by no means the heart and soul of religion. If mystical experience were crucial to religion then faith would come too cheaply. And religious faith would be especially trivialized if its highest moments could be induced by the mere consumption of certain pharmacological substances. Furthermore, religion would seem elitist and esoteric if we identified it too closely even with the more conventional kind of mystical experience available only to the few religious persons who have the time or the talent to cultivate their mystical faculties.

A quite different response to our question is to admit that mysticism is religious but to redefine mysticism in rather vague and general terms. By this reckoning, the essence of mysticism is love, and since genuine love is not easy to achieve, its eventual attainment raises mysticism to a sufficiently high status to merit being called "religious." But it is not very helpful to define mysticism so broadly. Of course people are certainly free to define their terms as they like, but the latter approach evades the problem of whether mystical *states of consciousness* are properly called religious. Perhaps the life of genuine love is the most noble and difficult to come by. And maybe, as Friedrich Heiler has written, the "way of love" is the heart of all the great religions. (1959) But we are still left with our question about mystical states of consciousness and whether they are or are not genuinely religious.

The poet William Blake wrote that if the doors of perception were cleansed we would see everything as it is—infinite. He was alluding to the fact that our ordinary way of perceiving the world is predominantly a filtering out of most of reality. Human perception can take in the complex stream of sensations only by blocking out most of the world that surrounds us, including the dimension of mystery. If we took in everything, we would be so overloaded with information that we could not process any of it. Psychology books may marvel at how sensitive we are to the world around us, but they often overlook the fact that our perceptive apparatus is so effective also because it can be so restrictive. Perceptivity is selectivity. Our senses actually shield us from *most* of the bombardment of our being by the incredibly complex universe in which we live. They refine this enigmatic maze of material, narrowing it down into the more manageable data of ordinary experience.

What would happen, though, if the "doors of perception" were cleansed? And does it matter whether this "cleansing" is accomplished in the superficial way of artificially altering the chemistry of our central nervous system or in the more rigorous manner of the religious mystic who for years prepares arduously for the experience of union with God, through a life of prayer, humility and charity?

Such questions are still very much under discussion. However, the consensus of most religious scholars seems to be that genuine religious existence would be better represented by a *bodhisattva* than by a Timothy Leary. We may recall that the exemplary human type in Mahayana Buddhism, the *bodhisattva*, hesitated on the threshold of ultimate bliss and turned back to suffering humanity, renouncing the attainment of *nirvana* until all living beings could also partake of it. Having had a brief taste of ecstasy, the *bodhisattva* then reaches out to include all others in the visionary experience and refuses to rest until all living beings are participants. In the thinking of most religious men and women this renunciation of private ecstasy for the sake of a wider, all-inclusive vision of peace would be more representative of authentic religious life.

We have to ask whether such compassionate inclusiveness is present in the experience of those who have taken up the "psychedelic way." If such compassion is lacking, and if there is little willingness to abandon the shortcut to bliss, or to renounce private rapture for the sake of promoting the good of the rest of humanity, then such a path seems to fall short of the religious quest for ultimate reality, at least as it has been proposed by the great traditions. The addiction that often accompanies artificially induced ecstasy seems to token an unwillingness to abandon the easy road to bliss. It fails to live up to the ideal of concern for others that would render it truly religious.

One of my students, a sensitive and bright young man, who had experienced the opening of his "doors of perception" once or twice by way of LSD disclosed to me his conviction that it did not feel "right" for him to repeat such an experience or to make it pivotal in his life. Instead he came to the conclusion that the meaning of his life lay in journeying together with others through darkness and shadows toward the light that would illuminate all. To seek the light without the shadows would banish the contrast that gives fullness to a human life. Though it is useful to know about the mystical experiences of others, and as James said, necessary to alter our metaphysical views accordingly, the premature acquiescence in or absolutization of mystical states of consciousness would be a suffocation of humanity's religious adventure.

Mysticism and the Other Three Ways

Mystical experience differs from sacramental religion in that it does not always need to rely so heavily upon the mediation of symbols. Or at least symbols play a less prominent role than in ordinary religious experience. Mystics speak of an *immediate* losing of themselves in a divine or cosmic mystery, and they often testify that they are able to leave behind the images most religious people rely upon in their prayer. While images and symbols may be needed to bring the mystic to a certain point of religious awareness, there comes a juncture at which they may be put aside in favor of a more direct encounter with the One. However, even in the most mystical of religious moments, symbols are still operative at a certain level of the mystic's experience. In other words, a stratum of sacramentality is still functioning, more quietly perhaps, in the mystical type. On the other hand, there is also a dimension of mysticism operative in sacramental piety, silence and religious activism.

Mysticism is closely related to, but nonetheless distinct from, the way of silence, such as we find in Buddhism. Although in actual religious experience the silent and mystical moments are often both present at the same time, they are not logically identical. They are often confused with each other, but they are quite distinct aspects of the more complex kind of religious style of life known as "contemplation." Contemplation is actually a mixed mode of religious existence, integrating in a meditative way elements of all four of our types, but especially mysticism and silence. Mysticism, as I am using the term here, is not identical with silence, but refers specifically to the quest for and experience of the *oneness* of all things in mystery. It has a distinct content to it, namely, transcendent unity, whereas apophatic (silent) religion does not necessarily seek any specific content at all. (For that reason Buddhism, at least in the form of Theravada, might better be called an apophatic, rather than a mystical religion.)

Moreover, mysticism is distinct in that it has an ambiguous relation to the ideal of detachment associated with our third type, the way of silence. Though the practice of silence and detachment from desire often accompany the mystical quest for the One, they are not an absolute requirement. Some religious writers suspect that any mystical experience not preceded by the way of renunciation is quite likely a pseudo-mysticism, but this may be too severe a requirement. Such authors insist that the path of "purgation," a long process of purification of the senses and the spirit must be undertaken to prepare one for the mystical reception of God. For example, St. John of the Cross, perhaps the best known of the Christian mystics, spoke about a "dark night of the senses" followed by a "dark night of the soul" as part of the journey to mystical ecstasy. In these phases of the mystic's quest there is typically a feeling of desolation and even separation from God. These seemingly depressive episodes are interpreted by the mystics as part of the process of detachment readying the spirit for a deeper implantation of divine love. Mystics of many traditions generally emphasize the need for some sort of discipline and renunciation as ways of emptying oneself for the full experience of God's presence in mystical union.

However, even though renunciation or detachment is often judged to be essential preparation for mystical union, renunciation is not the same as mystical union. And there is no inevitability that the way of detachment will lead to mystical ecstasy. In fact, it may very well lead to illness and even psychosis if it is not animated by trust and intimation of a deeper and wider enjoyment. Religion, especially in its sacramental mode, is essentially tied to enjoyment, and when it becomes divorced from the deep human longing for wider attainment of joy, it loses its vitality. If renunciation is emphasized independently of the promise of joy it becomes the occasion for despair. Much damage has been done to innocent people by promoting an asceticism devoid of the promise of joy.

Furthermore, it is not absolutely certain that genuine mystical experience requires asceticism or renunciation as a pre-condition. Though this is a highly controversial issue, it is quite possible that mystical experience can occur at the pinnacle of the enjoyment we have associated with sacramental religion. The opinion of some that mysticism must always be preceded by a rigorous path of purgation of the senses seems excessively stringent. It almost insinuates that the mystical vision somehow has to be earned or paid for. But such a rigid requirement runs counter to the theology of grace found in the mainstream of the great traditions.

Mystical experience can occur, for example, concomitantly with the delights of sensual experience. Many have testified to having had unsurpassed union with God in moments of sexual union or while listening to a great musical composition, or while beholding the beauties of nature. In the context of such pleasurable experience there is often such an effusion of gratitude for the gift of life and enjoyment that the event may be the occasion for an absolutely certain conviction of being in loving union with the mysterious depths of reality. Such experiences can be called mystical even though they are not preceded by an arduous period of asceticism. Still, perhaps the test of their authenticity is a subsequent willingness to live a life of concern for others. In such cases renunciation and detachment may follow rather than precede mystical experience.

The religious integrity of mystical experience may be measured also by the degree to which it is open to the transformation of social life that we are associating especially with the "active" way. Although the two ways are not identical, many of the great mystics are also effective reformers as well. Contrary to common misconceptions, religious mysticism does not promote passivity and social conformism. At its highest points it follows the style of the *bodhisattvas* who renounced even their own ecstasy and devoted their lives to the expression of compassion for the mass of suffering beings.

Though it is vitally connected to the other three modes, mysticism is characterized by a more vividly conscious awareness of immediate intimacy with ultimate reality. It might be said that we are all "mystics" in an unconscious way. For at some level mystery always impinges upon our existence, even though we may not be explicitly conscious of it. The axial religions all maintain that the divine has already united us to itself. According to *Vedanta*, we are already at one with *Brahman*, but we generally remain ignorant of this unity. And prophetic religions likewise maintain that God has already embraced us with the divine promise, but "sin" prevents us from acknowledging that we are so loved.

In the same sense that a mother's love always enfolds the wayward child, even though the child is not aware of it, prophetic religion asserts that from God's perspective we are unceasingly encompassed by divine love. In the properly mystical moments of religion, however, one becomes *conscious* of this union in such a striking way that the reality of being completely enfolded by divine love is absolutely unquestionable. To the mystic there is no doubt whatsoever of the reality of God or of being in communion with the ultimate dimension of reality. And the mystic is amazed that people in general are oblivious to the divine. As the Christian mystic Hans Denk expresses it:

> O my God how does it happen in this poor old world that Thou art so great and yet nobody finds Thee, that Thou callest so loudly and nobody hears Thee, that Thou art so near and nobody feels Thee, that Thou givest Thyself to everybody and nobody knows Thy name? (cited in Huxley, 1970, 13)

The Mystical Attitude Toward the World

What is the attitude of mysticism toward secular reality and how does it compare to that of the other three ways? We have already noted that sacramental religion rejoices in the world, even to the extent of employing elements thereof as symbols of God. Its attitude to the world is one of gratitude for the gifts of life and the abundance of the earth. As sacramental religion develops out of the fundamental posture of enjoyment and gratitude it begins to move more and more explicitly toward the idea of a transcendent giver of gifts. In the earliest historical phases of sacramental religion the hints of such a distinct source were probably not sharply defined. But as the internal logic latent in enjoyment and gratitude unfolded, the conscious conviction of a divine creator began to emerge more explicitly in many regions of the earth.

Mystical religion is an intensification of this looking beyond the gifts and goods of life in order to pay more focal attention to the mystery, or creative goodness, out of which they come into being. Mysticism is less preoccupied with things of nature and secular reality than with the mystery out of which these are born. Its attitude toward the world, therefore, is one of *relativization*. It is so concerned with the one mystery in which the world is grounded that the many items in the world itself begin to lose some of their significance. To relativize something means to put it into a perspective relative to what is considered absolute. Mysticism puts the world of multiplicity and appearance into a perspective relative to that of the One beyond or within the many. Genuine mysticism still enjoys and appreciates the world, but it is often more reserved in its attachment than is sacramental piety. It is more sensitive than sacramental religion to the possibility of idolatrous infatuation with the fragmentary beauties of the world, and to how we can thereby become distracted from an ultimate beauty beyond our discrete enjoyments. It does not renounce enjoyment, but seeks instead a wider and more inclusive one.

The Mystical Temptation

Relativization of the world is both the glory and the risk of the mystical attitude. Relativizing something without depriving it of its value is a very delicate procedure. For such an attitude can be subtly transformed into one of rejection and condemnation, and this is one of the main temptations of the mystical way. Although its posture of relativization is indispensable to the true enjoyment of things, the history of mysticism provides numerous instances where it has degenerated into a *despising* of the world. And it is not uncommon for this rejection of the world to be followed up by attempts to escape from nature and history altogether. *Escapism* is the characteristic temptation of mysticism. Sometimes this escapism takes the form of *gnosticism*. Gnosticism is the belief that encounter with mystery takes place only by acquiring a secret knowledge (in Greek, "gnosis"). Gnosticism is especially appealing to those who have tired of sacramental, silent and active aspects of religion, and who wish to attain salvation by "knowledge" alone.

Mysticism may be protected from the temptation to escapism by

THE MYSTICS SPEAK

Disease is not cured by pronouncing the name of medicine, but by taking medicine. Deliverance is not achieved by repeating the word "Brahman," but by directly experiencing Brahman. . . Caste, creed, family and lineage do not exist in Brahman. Brahman has neither name nor form, transcends merit and demerit, is beyond time, space and the objects of sense-experience. Such is Brahman, and "Thou art that." Meditate upon this truth within your consciousness.

SHANKARA

Who is God? I can think of no better answer than, He who is. Nothing is more appropriate to the eternity which God is. If you call God good, or great, or blessed, or wise, or anything else of this sort, it is included in these words, namely, He is.

ST. BERNARD

It was from the Nameless that Heaven and Earth sprang; The named is but the mother that rears the ten thousand creatures, each after its kind.

Truly, "Only he that rids himself forever of desire can see the Secret Essences."

He that has never rid himself of desire can see only the Outcomes.

LAO TZU

When I came out of the Godhead into multiplicity, then all things proclaimed, "There is a God" (the personal Creator). Now this cannot make me blessed, for hereby I realize myself as creature. But in the breaking through I am more than all creatures; I am neither God nor creature; I am that which I was and shall remain, now and for ever more. There I receive a thrust which carries me above all angels. By this thrust I become so rich that God is not sufficient for me, in so far as He is only God in his divine works. For in thus breaking through, I perceive what God and I are in common. There I am what I was. There I neither increase or decrease. For there I am the immovable which moves all things. Here man has won again what he is eternally and ever shall be. Here God is received into the soul.

ECKHART

Goodness needeth not to enter into the soul, for it is there already, only it is unperceived.

THEOLOGIA GERMANICA

When the Ten Thousand things are viewed in their oneness, we return to the Origin and remain where we have always been.

SEN T'SEN

The Beloved is all in all; the lover merely veils Him;
The Beloved is all that lives, the lover a dead thing.

RUMI

Behold but One in all things; it is the second that leads you astray.

KABIR

My Me is God, nor do I recognize any other Me except my God Himself.

ST. CATHERINE OF GENOA

In those respects in which the soul is unlike God, it is also unlike itself.

ST. BERNARD

Thy spirit is mingled in my spirit,
  even as wine is mingled with pure water.
When anything touches thee it touches me.
  Lo in every case thou art I!
I am he whom I love, and he whom I love is I:
We are two spirits dwelling in one body.
If thou seest me, thou seest him,
And if thou seest him, thou seest us both.

HALLAJ

All citations except the last are from Huxley, 1970. *Hallaj* quote cited by R. A. Nicholson, *The Mystics of Islam* (Cambridge: Cambridge University Press, 1930), p. 151.

maintaining a living connection with the other three ways. First, the sacramental way sustains the particularity, diversity, color and nuance that add contrast to mystical unity and prevent unity from overriding multiplicity. At the same time it emphasizes the goodness and enjoyableness of the world, holding in check the mystical tendency toward relativization, keep-

ing it from negating the world. Secondly, the way of silence is suspicious of
any specific content in the mystical vision, thus combating the constant
temptation in all religion toward defining God in terms of human desire
and imagination. The apophatic disdain for images and concepts of ultimate reality, we shall see in the next chapter, seeks to preserve mystery
from confinement in specific concepts or images. For that reason the way
of union links up with the way of silence in most cases of contemplative
religion. And finally, the mystical way is protected from a "gnostic" escapism by staying close to the way of transformative social action. It is worth
pointing out once again that according to many experts religious mysticism
exhibits its authenticity most explicitly when it provides the grounds for
human involvement in the task of transforming history and society into a
more just world.

7.

Silence

During the axial period in China a most impressive development occurred in religious thought. Today it is called Taoism (pronounced "dowism"), after the word *tao*, which appears in the title of a small book of wise sayings, the *Tao Te Ching*, containing the kernel of Taoist thought. This important work is usually associated with a seer named Lao Tzu who also probably lived sometime around the sixth century B.C.E.

The word *tao* means the invisible "way," "power" or "truth." It points to the mystery that quietly and unobtrusively underlies and shapes the universe. It is a great unknown and cannot be spoken about directly. "The Tao that can be spoken is not the real Tao." These are the opening words of the *Tao te Ching*, and they bespeak the "apophatic" character of Taoism. That is, they express the conviction that the deepest mystery of the universe lies beyond human words and thoughts. "The name that can be given is not the name itself. The unnameable is the source of the universe." (Chung-yuan, 3)

> Gaze at it, there is nothing to see.
> It is called the formless.
> Heed it; there is nothing to hear.
> It is called the soundless.
>
> Invisible, it cannot be called by any name.
> It returns again to nothingness.
> Thus we call it the form of the formless
> The image of the imageless.
> It is the evasive.

Approach it; you cannot see its face.
Go after it; you cannot see its back. (Chung-yuan, 43)

To those who become truly sensitive to the presence of this great mystery, only silence seems appropriate:

One who is aware does not talk.
One who talks is not aware. (154)

This theme of the "ineffability" or unspeakability of ultimate mystery, with its corresponding exhortation to silence on the part of the worshipper, is not peculiar to Taoism. It is present to one degree or another in all the religious traditions. They unanimously agree that no words or symbolic expressions can ever adequately communicate the content of the mystery encountered in religious experience. In mystical experience especially, words fail more than in any other area of human life. But the sacramental and activist styles of religion also become so sensitive to the inadequacy of images and language about ultimate reality that they lead back into silence as well.

The very multiplicity of symbols that we find in sacramental religion is already an indication that none of them by itself quite fits the unknown and unnameable mystery. A sure sign of the liveliness of religion is its awareness of the inadequacy of any particular representation of mystery, and its willingness to experiment with a wide variety of metaphors. But in addition to the proliferation of images and symbols religions have often developed a more direct way of acknowledging the unspeakability of God—namely, by assuming the posture of pure silence. The penchant for silence is part of the very definition of religion as a movement into mystery. Like sacramentalism and mysticism, silence is an aspect of all religion. And at times the "apophatic" disposition virtually stands out as a distinct religious "way."

One of the most familiar examples of religion's collapse into silence may be found in the biblical book of *Job*. There Job is presented as a man who enjoys the complete favor of God. He enjoys a prosperous life, with a healthy family, land and livestock. What is more, he is a good and righteous individual whose ethical integrity seems to merit such an opulent existence. But suddenly everything is taken away—children, land and cattle. Job even loses his health and is left covered with boils, abandoned to utter misery. His friends tell him to repent of his misdeeds and everything will be restored. But he adamantly maintains his innocence, heatedly protesting the injustice of his suffering. And after lengthy, verbose discussions, lamentations and complaints about the unfairness of his plight, he

can still find no answer to why he should have to suffer so. His outcries
against his predicament are unrelenting:

> Perish the day when I was born,
> and the night which said, 'A man is conceived'!
> May that day turn to darkness; may God above not look for it,
> nor light of dawn shine on it. (*Job* 3:3–4)

> Why should the sufferer be born to see the light?
> Why is life given to men who find it so bitter? (3:20)

> One man, I tell you, dies crowned with success,
> lapped in security and comfort,
> his loins full of vigour
> and the marrow juicy in his bones;
> another dies in bitterness of soul
> and never tastes prosperity;
> side by side they are laid in earth,
> and worms are the shroud of both. (21:23–26)

Chapter after chapter of the *Book of Job* is filled with such understandable grievance against the horrors of an innocent man's suffering and the
inequities of life in general. Suddenly, however, the voice of God appears
out of the whirlwind:

> Who is this whose ignorant words
> cloud my design in darkness?
> Brace yourself and stand up like a man;
> I will ask questions, and you shall answer.
> Where were you when I laid the earth's foundations?
> Tell me if you know and understand.
> Who settled its dimensions? Surely you should know. (38:1–4)

> Have you comprehended the vast expanse of the world? (38:18)

> Did you proclaim the rules that govern the heavens,
> or determine the laws of nature on earth? (38:33) (*New English
>   Bible*)

The author of this classic religious text portrays the divine mystery as
so far beyond our comprehension that we simply do not have the perspective to challenge it with our paltry understanding. We may be tempted at

times to judge life unfair and not worth living, but in the final analysis who are we to make such blanket judgments? Although dialogue, words, petitions and even complaints are part of the encounter of humanity with God, eventually we, like Job, are reduced to silence. God invites Job to respond, but Job hesitates:

> What reply can I give thee, I who carry no weight?
> I put my finger to my lips.
> I have spoken once and now will not answer again;
> twice have I spoken, and I will do so no more. (40:3–5)

This account illustrates well the "apophatic" disposition of religion. The deliberate move away from words, images and symbols and into utter silence is a distinct religious "way" of approaching mystery. Resorting to silence after all words and ideas have exhibited their limitations signals religion's willingness to admit that there is an infinitely wider perspective challenging the narrow boundaries of our finite perception of the world. Moving into silence at the end of a process of religious groping displays a willingness to break out of the monotony of the restrictive frame of reference bounded by our ignorance. The way to make this breakthrough is, occasionally at least, to cease our obsessive verbalizing or imagining what ultimate reality is like and to allow the dimension of mystery to be itself, independently of our always inadequate symbolic impressions of it. The way of silence becomes the opening to an ever deeper sense of mystery.

The "Negative" Approach to Mystery

Silence, according to this third way, is the most appropriate response to "mystery," a term which, it is worth being reminded once again, comes from the Greek *muo* which means "to close" (the eyes or mouth). Anything we might say about mystery will inevitably fall short. Words and images, necessary as they are to draw us into it, will finally end up shrinking the inexhaustible depth of reality if we bind our impression of mystery too closely to them. Might it not be religiously more suitable simply to keep our mouths closed and our visionary and imaginative faculties from getting too excited? Like Job we might best press our fingers to our lips and refrain from saying anything at all about the mystery that encompasses our lives. Perhaps mystery reveals itself most fully not through finite sacramental symbols, or in our good works, but through the unrestricted "emptiness" of serene silence. Perhaps we have a better chance of experiencing the divine, or allowing God to break through to us, if we empty ourselves as much as possible of all words and images of the ultimate. This at least is the perspective of apophatic religion.

In Buddhism we have seen this emphasis on silence elevated to the status of a distinct world religion. The Buddha thought it most wise not even to talk about God. But other religious traditions also share with Buddhism a reserve about religious talk. There is an apophatic strand, an acknowledgement of the futility of too much God-talk, in the traditions of Hinduism, Taoism, Judaism, Christianity, and Islam as well. And in their coming together on the plain of stillness, where all parties have reached the point in their religious development where only silence seems appropriate, these very diverse traditions exhibit a profound convergence and communality. Their common attraction to silence makes doctrinal differences and disputes almost fade into insignificance, at least for as long as the silence lasts. In the apophatic way we have perhaps the most obvious basis for positing a deep unity underlying all of the world's religious experience.

This "way of silence" generates a distinct kind of theology, or reflection on mystery, known as the *via negativa,* the "negative way" or the "way of negation." The sacramental, activist and, to some extent at least, the mystical styles of religion follow the *via positiva,* the *"positive way,"* according to which it is essential to speak analogously or symbolically about ultimate mystery. According to the *via positiva* human beings require positive images, such as loving father, caring mother, faithful lover, friend or spouse, mighty warrior, rock, liberator, refuge, ground etc. in order to indicate in a fragmentary manner what ultimate reality is like. And all religions, including Buddhism, employ at least some imagery, since human consciousness cannot exist independently of the imagination. However, the *via negativa* of apophatic religion relinquishes its hold on the customary images, concepts and words about God, just as it renounces our propensity to cling to anything whatsoever. In doing so it moves the religious person's sensibilities toward a state of "emptiness" which can then be filled more completely with the mystery that is only partially and inadequately revealed through words and sacraments.

Thus in some of its most interesting and authentic moments religion seems almost to cast aside the very images that attract people to it in the first place. In Christianity, for example, this occurs in a body of spiritual writings called "hesychasm" (from the Greek word for silence). These writings are inspired especially by the ideas of a sixth-century writer known as Dionysius the Areopagite. The latter maintained that we cannot talk directly about God. If we speak of God at all it can only be indirectly, by *denying* in the Deity those qualities that characterize all finite beings. If the things of our ordinary experience are all finite, then God must be *in-* finite, that is, "not finite." If finite beings are temporal, then God must be *e*-ternal, "not temporal." Whereas finite beings are capable of suffering and dying, God must be *im*-passible, and *im*-mortal. And while finite beings are related to one another, God must be "absolute," that is, free of the confinement of relatedness to other entities. According to this influential tradition we can suitably speak about God only negatively. Every positive thing we say about God will be too belittling to the divine majesty. Therefore, it might be better not to talk about mystery in positive terms at all.

Ordinarily religion and theology employ the *via positiva,* or the *via eminentiae* (= the way of eminence) as the typical mode of God-language. This positive way of referring to mystery involves three steps: (1) first it observes the positive experiences in everyday life, especially that of being loved and cared for by others, or the experience of beauty, courage, power, stature, truth, wisdom, freedom, etc. (2) Second, it imaginatively and conceptually "stretches" these positive characteristics to their maximum

---

BUDDHIST SILENCE

Bear always in mind what it is that I have not elucidated, and what it is that I have elucidated. And what have I not elucidated? I have not elucidated that the world is eternal; I have not elucidated that the world is finite; I have not elucidated that the world is infinite; I have not elucidated that the soul and body are identical; I have not elucidated that the monk who has attained [the arhat] exists after death; I have not elucidated that the arhat does not exist after death; I have not elucidated that the arhat both exists and does not exist after death; I have not elucidated that the arhat neither exists nor does not exist after death. And why have I not elucidated this? Because this profit not, nor has to do with the fundamentals of religion, therefore I have not elucidated this.

And what have I elucidated? Misery have I elucidated; the origin of misery have I elucidated; and the path leading to the cessation of misery have I elucidated. And why have I elucidated this? Because this does profit, has to do with the fundamentals of religion, and tends to absence of passion, to knowledge, supreme wisdom, and Nirvana.

Majjhima Nikaya 63 from *Buddhism in Translation,* Henry C. Warren, Harvard University Press, 1922.

imaginable degree of intensity. That is, it conceives of an "eminent" or highest degree of love, beauty, power, truth, wisdom or freedom, etc. (3) And finally, it applies or attributes the eminent rank of these qualities to God, as for example when the Qur'an calls Allah the "All-Compassionate" or Charles Wesley speaks of God as "Pure Unbounded Love." God is thus conceptualized as the highest or most excellent embodiment of all the positive, life-promoting aspects of human experience. This speaking of ultimate reality by positive analogy is the dominant method in the theology of most religious traditions.

But for apophatic religion this *via eminentiae* is inadequate. The central intuition of the way of silence is that mystery lies far beyond anything of which we can think, even if we conjure up the supreme degree of any value. In the end, therefore, the only adequate God-talk is no talk at all. The only way to imagine the divine is to abandon all images of God. The only adequate way to think about mystery is not to think at all.

In the late *Upanishads*, for example, *Brahman* is said to have no describable attributes (*Nirguna Brahman*). Anything one says of ultimate reality must be qualified by the refrain, *neti, neti,* "not this, not that." No matter how subtle our attempts to grasp the ultimate, words are insufficient. This restraint is even more emphatic in the teachings of the Buddha, who of all religious figures is perhaps the most given to silence. He would never allow himself to be pressed into saying anything theologically either positive or negative, even about *nirvana.*

Noting the Buddha's spurning of God-talk, some Western interpreters have been led to classify Buddhist silence as a kind of atheism. They construe Gautama's disillusionment regarding the extravagant sacramentality and ineffectual theological speculations of Hindu religion as an outright rejection of the transcendent. But it is possible also to interpret his silence as a protection of mystery. Silence may safeguard mystery from the omnipresent threat of vulgarization by human language and desire. The Buddha's apparent reduction of religion to the compassionate pragmatic alleviation of suffering (a movement away from the sacramental to the activist mode of religion) is not a denial of mystery, but simply a disapproval of the fruitlessness of a religious life so preoccupied with curiosity about the nature of an ultimate environment that it neglects the suffering in our immediate one. Buddhism and other representatives of hesychasm may be interpreted as witnesses to, rather than deniers of, an ultimate dimension of mystery.

In any case, the *via negativa* acts as a check upon the possible excesses of sacramental, mystical and activist religion. Its main function may be that of shielding mystery from diminishment by popular religion and "positive" theology. In the wider story of religion the main concern of the way of silence is to let God be God, to avoid the distortion of mystery that occurs by way of our filtering it through words, thoughts and images until it has been rendered all too familiar. The objective of apophatic religion is to remove the obstacles that hide mystery from us in its absolute otherness. Even though human consciousness cannot untie itself completely from images, words and ideas, it can come to the point of acknowledging the insufficiency of these mediating elements. The apophatic way seeks to quiet our minds and imaginations so that our consciousness might experience itself as enfolded by or entering into mystery. Mystery invites us into itself, and to those who deeply experience the invitation, silence often seems the most appropriate posture to assume. We do not shout in cathedrals and temples, nor does the mystic verbalize excessively about the experience of intimacy with God. In such restraint there seems to be a mature desire to avoid reducing mystery to the triviality of the mundane.

Scholars sometimes note that in its apophatic moments religion displays an effort toward realism that rivals anything we might find in science or philosophy. Hesychasm exhibits a yearning to be utterly honest about the idea of God. Thomas Merton once wrote that our images and ideas of God usually tell us more about ourselves than about God anyway. We simply cannot have a perfectly pure, thoroughly "objective" image of ultimate reality. The apophatic aspect of religion humbly accepts this fact and tries to provide a "method," including a distinct style of prayer, for removing the illusory aspects of religion. Apophatic religion is above all concerned that we allow mystery to maintain its status of incomprehensibility. It is aware of the ever present possibility of illusion, and so it seeks to break through our customary projections. Or rather, it promotes an attitude in us that would permit mystery to break through our religious deceptions.

The Prayer of Silence

However, does not this kind of religion make prayer to God impossible or pointless? If God cannot be adequately imagined, talked about or thought about, then is prayer realizable? Is conversation with God conceivable, as is apparently the case in the other three modes of religion?

The hesychasts would insist that their approach offers the possibility of the purest and most honest prayer possible. Apophatic prayer, consistent with the theology of silence, involves the gradual "letting go" of images, words and thoughts. And at the stage where these are abandoned one has attained the highest form of prayer. The ideal of Buddhist meditation, for example, is to purify one's mind of all distractions, including any thoughts about *nirvana*. Nirvana, it will be recalled, means "extinguishing," removing the thirst or desire that causes us to cling to images of one sort or another, including religious ones. This cleansing the mind of thoughts and images may be facilitated by such meditative techniques as focusing on a single item, like one's breathing, or in the recitation of a *mantra* (a single word or phrase repeated over and over in order to relax the mind and remove distractions).

To Westerners this style of prayer may initially seem quite remote from the kind of address to God or attending to the word of God and responding to it such as we find in the Qur'an, the Psalms or the "Our Father" taught by Jesus. Prophetic traditions see prayer as a dialogical, I-Thou encounter between God and humans, or as a direct address of thanksgiving and petition to the divine liberator and creator. In the sacred scriptures of Jews, Christians and Muslims there appears to be very little of the pure apophatic style of prayer we find in Buddhism. But even in the prophetic traditions there is a strong theological suspicion of images. Muslims, for example, do not allow pictorial representations of Allah. And so their religious art has been highly abstract, largely consisting of beautifully intricate geometrical patterns instead of anthropomorphic images. We might interpret this rejection of all human likenesses of God as an apophatic quality of Islam. And in biblical religion there are prominent apophatic strains: Yahweh's refusal to give His name to Moses, telling him "I will be who I will be"; Moses' wrath at his fellow Hebrews' worshipping the golden calf; the prophets' protest against the establishment of a monarchy in which the king would be too easily identified as an image of divine rule; the prophetic suspicion of a priestly, temple-centered cult whose ritualism could diminish the sense of Yahweh's justice and transcendence. It seems that some degree of the apophatic is essential to many of the world's religions.

Furthermore, where prophetic religions have come under the spell of Platonic and neo-Platonic thought the apophatic aspect has been even further amplified. Dionysius the Areopagite, for example, was under the spell of Platonism when he prescribed the *via negativa* in theology. And Christianity has inherited from him and his followers an influential tradition of praying in silence. Dionysius writes:

> Do thou, then, in the intent practice of mystical contemplation, leave behind the senses and the operations of the intellect . . . and strain upwards in unknowing, as far as may be, towards the union with Him Who is above all things and knowledge. For by unceasing and absolute withdrawal from thyself and all things in purity, abandoning all and set free from all, thou shalt be borne

up to the ray of divine darkness that surpasseth all being. (Johnston, trans. 1973, 26)

The writings of Dionysius have inspired a strong tradition of hesychasm in Eastern Christianity. And in the West their influence is nowhere more evident than in a work on how to pray composed by an unknown English contemplative during the fourteenth century. It is entitled appropriately *The Cloud of Unknowing*. Writing to a disciple its author prescribes a method of prayer that clearly illustrates the apophatic way:

> Now you say, "How shall I proceed to think of God as he is in himself?" To this I can only reply, "I do not know."
> With this question you bring me into the very darkness and *cloud of unknowing* that I want you to enter. A man may know completely and ponder thoroughly every created thing and its works, yes, and God's works, too, but not God himself. Thought cannot comprehend God. And so, I prefer to abandon all I can know, choosing rather to love him whom I cannot know. Though we cannot know him we can love him. By love he may be touched and embraced, never by thought. Of course, we do well at times to ponder God's majesty or kindness for the insights these meditations may bring. But in the real contemplative work you must set all this aside and cover it over with a *cloud of forgetting*. Then let your loving desire, gracious and devout, step bravely and joyfully beyond it and reach out to pierce the darkness above. Yes, beat upon that thick *cloud of unknowing* with the dart of your loving desire and do not cease come what may. (Johnston, 54–55)

And in another work, *The Book of Privy Counseling*, this same writer is even more explicit:

> When you go apart to be alone for prayer, put from your mind everything you have been doing or plan to do. Reject all thoughts, be they good or be they evil. Do not pray with words. . . . See that nothing remains in your conscious mind save a naked intent stretching out toward God. Leave it stripped of every particular idea *about* God (what he is like in himself or in his works) and keep only the simple awareness *that he is as he is*. Let him be thus, I pray you, and force him not to be otherwise. Search into him no further . . . (Johnston 149–50)

Usually apophatic prayer begins by pondering the many positive images or stories about God given in the sacramental, mystical or prophetic layers of religion. But at a certain point the images recede, and one is carried off into the "cloud of unknowing." Necessary as they are, images or symbols from the *via positiva* are often accompanied by distortions and illusions that suppress the sense of the divine. The prayer of silence, whether that of the Buddha or of Dionysius and his Christian disciples, or of Hindu, Jewish and Islamic contemplatives, is an attempt to find a way through the illusions and self-deceptions of religious life.

Both Buddhist and Christian prayer of silence yearns to tame our ordinary desires that give rise to illusions. Buddhism sees desire as the cause of all our suffering and disappointment; and so its various types of meditation seek to rise above it in order to attain the state of *nirvana*. And in a somewhat different vein Christian apophatic prayer seeks a state of "emptiness," a consciousness void of desire, not in order to eliminate desire altogether, but so that a person's consciousness may be filled with what it *really* desires in its depths. Too often we go after what we merely "wish" for rather than what we desire at the most fundamental levels of our being. And so we remain disappointed with our lives and loves. A famous Spanish mystic and follower of Dionysius, St. John of the Cross (1542–91), wrote that in praying one has to proceed more by unknowing than by knowing. And he offers this advice for those who want to approach God in prayer:

> In order to arrive at having pleasure in everything,
>   Desire to have pleasure in nothing.
> In order to arrive at possessing everything,
>   Desire to possess nothing.
> In order to arrive at being everything,
>   Desire to be nothing.
> In order to arrive at that wherein thou hast no pleasure,
>   Thou must go by a way wherein thou hast no pleasure.
> In order to arrive at that which thou knowest not,
>   Thou must go by a way that thou knowest not.
> In order to arrive at that which thou possessest not,
>   Thou must go by a way that thou possessest not.
> In order to arrive at that which thou art not,
>   Thou must go through that which thou art not. (Quoted by Leech, 1985, 185–86)

This is the apophatic way, the way of unknowing, of not possessing, of not wanting anything short of what we *really* want. If we are to reach

God, we need to proceed by not understanding, that is, by a "process of blinding." "Obscurity is the essence of faith." The famous Carmelite explains why:

> . . . the excessive light that is given in faith is thick darkness for the soul, because the greater overwhelms and eclipses the lesser. The light of the sun overwhelms all other lights so that they do not seem to be lights at all when it shines and overwhelms our power of vision. It blinds the eyes and deprives them of sight because its light is excessive and beyond all proportion to the faculty of vision. In like manner, the light of faith, by reason of the excessive intensity, oppresses and overwhelms the light of the intellect, which of its own power extends only to natural knowledge . . . (186)

Apophatic religion approaches mystery in the humble posture of *docta ignorantia,* that is, "learned ignorance." Having renounced the will to subject all reality to the control and criteria of human reason, it enters into the cloud of unknowing without any pretense of being able to comprehend it. Employing a disposition called "faith" (and what the author of *The Cloud of Unknowing* calls "love") apophatic religion and prayer testify to the incomprehensibility and inexhaustibility of mystery.

Apophatic devotion arises, perhaps more directly than any of the other three ways, from a distaste and even revulsion for monotony. It seems to be concerned primarily with protecting religion from reduction to the banality of the overly familiar. By putting our words, images and thoughts aside it demonstrates its openness to the radically new and surprising aspects of mystery. In its "not this, not that" it seems to be exposing our sensitivities to the widest dimensions of the unknown and incomprehensible. Such a "clearing operation" is indispensable if we are to feel the refreshing openness of an inexhaustible religious frontier.

Attitude Toward the World

The apophatic attitude toward God is that of "letting be," of not intruding into the sphere of mystery with instruments of cognition, or with names, concepts and symbols, for these may not be adequate or applicable. Likewise, the apophatic attitude toward the world might best be understood also as one of "letting be." It is a posture that can well be captured in the words "waiting" and "patience." Waiting is an essential attitude of those who cultivate the *via negativa*. Unlike the activist moments of religion it is not concerned with an immediate transformation of the world. It seeks the desert or places where it can lie fallow and hibernate until the time is ripe for action and language. Like water, "it is always at rest in humble places that people dislike. Thus it is close to Tao." (Chung-yuan, 27) Such patience, painful as it is, eventually widens our impressions of reality and deepens the sense of mystery. The sacramental, mystical and activist types of religion may all succumb to impatience, but the apophatic way is willing to accept the experience of emptiness and frustration as opening to an infinitely wider enjoyment, the full taste of which may have to be put off for now. "In order to arrive at possessing everything, desire to possess nothing. In order to arrive at being everything, desire to be nothing."

Apophatic religion suffers the dark night of the senses as a corrective to exaggerated sacramentalism. And it opens itself to a dark night of the soul as a check on exuberant mystical longing for premature union. *Asceticism* is the name of the attitude toward the world generally associated with apophatic religion. The *via negativa* of apophatic theology is often accompanied by a spirituality advising renunciation of the world and its delights. This renunciation is not necessarily a despising of the world. Rather it can be an acknowledgement of how easy it is for the human spirit to cling to an inadequate base of security when its true home is an inexhaustible mystery. In order to direct us toward a solid and inviolable destiny the way of silence invites us not to denounce the world but to let go of it, to let it be.

This doctrine may be hard for Westerners to accept, especially since it seems at times to devalue the world which biblical religion, in particular, sees to be intrinsically good. But we must be careful not to allow verbal conflicts and contradictions to obscure the possible agreements Buddhism may have with theistic religions at a deeper than linguistic level. (Ward, 1987) Above all, we must recognize that most religious traditions advocate an attitude of non-clinging as the way to freedom. The Buddhist tradition does this by rejecting the notion of fixed substances, such as the self and God. But its objective is not to make absolutist metaphysical claims. Rather it is attempting to formulate a language about existence that will prevent people from tying themselves down to the monotony of an abstract and frozen world.

The attitude of letting the world be itself is also exhibited in the sabbath theology of Judaism. "When people celebrate the sabbath they perceive the world as God's creation, for in the sabbath quiet it is God's creation that they are permitting the world to be." (Moltmann, 1985, 321) The meaning of the sabbath is not simply that people should rest from their labors, but that they should let the world be itself. The sabbath stillness is another instance of the religious need to provide a time for quiet. It establishes within the life of the Jewish people a "space" in which God can be God and the world can be world.

This meaning of the sabbath has been lost to a great extent in the busyness of our contemporary world. And the meaning of the sabbath obligation is hardly captured in the Christian precept to attend church services on Sunday. It is much more serious than that. It is the imperative to refrain, occasionally at least, from the activist enterprise of labor in order to contemplate the world as a divine gift and not just as material for human transformation. It is a call to establish a time for silence so that both God and the world will appear in their otherness, distinct from our human projects.

The Apophatic Temptation

Silent or apophatic religion abandons talk and images of ultimate reality since any such representations will inevitably be inadequate or irrelevant. By its refusal to speak of or imagine God at all this radical religious posture effectively combats the narrowness of our symbolic and mystical language. It advocates a patience that forces us to widen indefi-nitely our sense of God and the world. But in doing so it exhibits a "leaning" toward the view that reality is perched over a void. It is not inaccurate to say that the specific temptation of apophatic religion is *icono-clasm*, the view that no images have any value. And such an attitude may not be far removed from *nihilism*, the view that nothing has value.

In other words, the danger of an exaggerated renunciation is cyni-cism. The asceticism that often accompanies apophatic religion is an essen-tial aspect of any adventurous religious movement. However, asceticism may so de-value the world at times that it leads to the feeling that life with its little enjoyments is meaningless. The ascetic, if not checked, can be-come an ungrateful cynic, despising rather than rejoicing in the world. The history of religion is full of examples of asceticism gone sour. Such a temptation may be avoided if the way of renunciation stays connected in some way to the theme of enjoyment in sacramental religion, the sense of an ultimate *ground* of being in mystical religion, and the valuation of this-worldly affairs in the prophetic-activist religious way.

Precisely because it risks the abandonment of all content, the way of silence may succumb to *nihilism*. Nihilism is the view that only nothing-ness underlies reality and our lives, and that there is no ultimate basis for trust or values. Insofar as it is religious, of course, the way of silence would reject nihilism. Hesychasm does not deny God, only the validity of our references to God. It does not deny that the world is good, only that it is an ultimate good to be clung to. But this style of religiousness can sometimes come perilously close to undermining the very possibility of *any* talk of mystery. It may forget that it is being silent about *something* or *someone*. And its asceticism, if it becomes excessive, can lead to a cynical repudiation of the intrinsic value of the world and its gifts.

Religious people are usually first introduced to mystery by way of images, stories and religious doctrines about the divine. Even in Buddhism they are told the story of the Buddha and his quest for enlightenment. One of the things that keeps Buddhism within the camp of religion is that it has not completely forsaken its sacramental, mystical and activist aspects, and these continue to feed it, even if at times only in the form of the timeless and symbol-saturated narrative of the Buddha's own quest for *nirvana*. What would happen if religious people ever lost touch with such initial mediating narrative elements? Good psychology and common sense, as well as the teachings of most of the religions, indicate that we can never completely dispense with the sacramental, mythic and linguistic aspects of religion. And most advocates of the way of silence would agree. They themselves do not reject images, they merely relativize them.

However, as we shall examine in more detail later, much that goes under the heading of nihilistic "atheism" may be understood as an exaggerated development of the apophatic strain of religion which has lost contact with the sacramental, active and mystical aspects of religion. If apophatic religion forsakes altogether the positive references to the divine provided by the other ways of religion, it becomes indistinguishable from nihilism. This extreme does not occur in the lives of religious people devoted to silence, but it is a "leaning" inherent in apophatic religion, and if not carefully qualified it may become indistinguishable from the most radical form of atheism. Especially when the way of silence loses touch with its sacramental base it forfeits its substance. If its reluctance, for religious reasons, to speak of God ever became completely uprooted from its natural entanglement with the *via positiva* the result would be nihilism. Perhaps it is the intuition of such a prospect that helps explain the seemingly reactionary sacramental extravagance of so much popular religion.

8.

Action

"Religion that is pure and undefiled . . . is this: to visit orphans and widows in their affliction . . ."

These words are taken from the *Epistle of James* in the *New Testament*. (1:22–27) They capture plainly the spirit of our fourth religious way, namely, that genuine religion is inseparable from transformative action in the world. Religion requires as an essential component the performance of good deeds to improve the lot of the disadvantaged. According to this way, the substance of religion is the willingness to give oneself on behalf of others. Symbols and rituals, contemplation and silence, fastings and renunciations, prayers and sacrifices—all of these are insufficient. "If I have not charity," another famous early Christian writer remarks, then "I am a noisy gong and a clanging cymbal." (St. Paul, in 1 *Corinthians* 13:1)

Those of us who are familiar with the religions of Moses, Jesus and Muhammad will not be surprised at this close association of religion with charitable doings. Prophetic religion has always kept the dimension of action very close to the heart of its vision. But lest we give the wrong impression, the way of loving action toward one's fellows is taught by the other religions as well. In fact, in all the major traditions the true test of one's religious sincerity is the willingness to put one's actions and even one's life on the line in service to others. Therefore, it is risky for interpreters of religion to make comparisons, maintaining that one tradition is more concerned with charity, compassion and right action than another might be. For we can find no end of evidence from the teachings of all the major religions that a life of love and compassion is the height of authentic human existence.

We might recall, for example, how the Buddha renounced what he considered fruitless theological speculations and turned the focus of his creed toward the immediate alleviation of suffering. Compassion is the very essence of religious life, not something incidental to it. And this compassion extends beyond humans to all living beings. For the *bodhisattva* the salvation of other living beings is more important than personal enlightenment. This attitude is similar to one proposed by the medieval Christian mystical theologian, Meister Eckhart. He declared that if in the heights of religious ecstasy you noticed a sick person in need of food, it would be more genuinely religious to forsake your rapture and provide sustenance to the one in need than to remain in your state of contemplative fervor. Furthermore, in Buddhism, as in other religions, participation in and support for the *sangha* (the community of fellow devotees) is essential for the full actualization of religious life. There is a deeply social side to Buddhist and Hindu religion that our stereotypes of solitary ascetics often overlook.

The word for "action" in Hinduism is *karma*. And Hinduism has developed a type of devotional life called *karma yoga* which teaches one how to conduct a life of action in the world. In the *Bhagavadgita, karma yoga* is given an exalted religious meaning. Krishna explains there that not just any action is religiously acceptable. In fact, a great many of our actions keep us tied to the cycle of rebirth. Sometimes it seems that it would be better for us not to do anything at all if our actions generally have such a severe outcome. But the message of the *Gita* is that we can bring a religiously purified attitude to our actions, and especially to our work, that will eventually liberate us from *samsara*. This attitude is the one suggested to Arjuna by Krishna: act without concern for the fruits of your labor. Surrendering all the consequences of your actions to God, and not seeking to promote selfish interests—this will lead to *moksha,* to awareness of union with *Brahman,* to an end of suffering and the fear of death.

Charity

The post-axial religions all emphasize the religious importance of the self-giving, self-forgetful kind of action which we know by the word "charity." It is not an exclusively Christian ideal. We could multiply examples of the emphasis on charitable action, including love of one's enemy, present in non-Christian religion. Few scholars have made this point as emphatically as Friedrich Heiler:

> Confucianism, Taoism, Brahmanism, Buddhism, Hinduism, Mazdaism, Islam, and Christianity all preach brotherly love.

. . . The early Christian writer Tertullian asserted that the love of the enemy was an exclusive characteristic of Christianity. In this he was profoundly mistaken. All high religions of the earth, not only the Eastern religions of redemption but the pre-Christian religions of the West know the commandment to love the enemy. And the Chinese *Liki* (Book of Ceremonies) says, "By returning hatred with goodness, human concern is exercised toward one's own person." The wise Laotse emphatically demands the "reply to adversity with mercy and goodness." Loving the enemy has been commanded in India since the earliest times. We read in the heroic epic *Mahābarāta*, "Even an enemy must be afforded appropriate hospitality when he enters the house; a tree does not withhold its shade even from those who come to cut it down." In the other epic, *Rāmāyana*, we read: "The nobleman must protect with his life an enemy who is in distress . . ." (1959, 146–48)

There are numerous illustrations of the ideal of love of enemy in Buddhist literature. For example, there is the story of the king who before being executed admonished his son: "Enmity is not pacified by enmity; enmity is pacified by peaceableness." And there is the case of the prince whose eyes were torn out by the wife of a king after her romantic overtures had been rejected: ". . . I do not feel the fire of wrath. My heart bears only love for her who had my eyes torn out." Such examples are no less powerful than Jesus' preachings about the necessity of loving our enemy.

Heiler comments:

The spreading of the concept of loving the enemy in pre-Christian times proves the validity of Lessing's statement, "Christianity existed before evangelists and apostles had written." But also post-Christian saints, Jews as well as Muslims, have preached and lived the love of the enemy. The Sufist Ibn Imad says: "The perfect man shall render good to his enemies; for they do not know what they do. Thus he will be clothed with the qualities of God, for God always does good to his enemies even though they do not know him." (148f.)

And finally, the Jewish religion also teaches love of enemy:

In humility, the pious believer shall not return evil for evil, but forgive those who hate and persecute him, and also love sinners. He shall say to himself, that in the eyes of God the sinner counts as much as he himself. How can one hate him whom God loves? (Paul Levertoff, as quoted by Heiler, 1959, 149)

Justice

It is important for our understanding of religion that we remain aware of the widespread teaching of the precept of neighborly love, as well as love of enemy, in the religions of the world. Nevertheless, after making this point, it may still be correct to say that the project of transforming history is closer to the center of the prophetic type of religion than of any other. Generally speaking, non-prophetic traditions have not placed as much religious emphasis on history, and on the virtue of performing social *justice* in order to change history, as have the prophetic.

This is not at all an argument for the religious superiority of one tradition over the other. Such comparisons are fruitless in any case. Rather it is a simple observation about the distinctive orientation of a certain body of religious teachings. And this does not mean that societies in the world influenced by Abrahamic religions are in fact any closer to realizing the virtue of justice than other social situations not so influenced. One could find many instances in Jewish, Christian and Islamic cultures, for example, where the grossest forms of injustice reign. Rather, what we are talking about here is a distinct inclination in the *teachings* of prophetic religions. We are not speaking of the actual practices of their followers.

In the writings of the prophets, and in the teachings of Moses, Jesus and Muhammad, the task of making this world and its history a more just situation in which to live is central, and by no means incidental, to being religious. Not that such an emphasis is absent elsewhere, but broadly speaking it is not as close to the center of religious life as it is with the biblical prophets. There are clear exceptions to this, especially in modern times. For example, Mahatma Gandhi interpreted the Asian teaching of non-violence (*ahimsa*) in such a way as to improve the general lot of people (though Gandhi was also influenced by Christianity as well). And we may recall the Buddhist monks who immolated themselves in protest of the war in Vietnam. Recently Buddhist monks have become more involved in political protest movements in Burma, Tibet and elsewhere. And Buddhist history contains other examples of deep involvement in political and social life. Such activism indicates a profound desire to make this a better world.

Buddhism has its powerful doctrine of compassion for living beings, including animals, that would put to shame the life-ethic of many Christians, Jews and Muslims. But it also teaches a strong doctrine of world-renunciation. Such a doctrine, according to many critics, can be easily interpreted in such a way that the social or economic state of affairs in this world seems to be of little consequence. The quest for enlightenment can go on even in the midst of human misery, and without necessarily taking actions to change the political, legal and social structures that uphold the situation of poverty. Prophetic spirituality, however, cannot in any way separate religion from what is going on in the social, economic and political orders.

Hindu piety is also filled with reverence for life, and its theologians have taught the importance of love and compassion. At the same time, however, Hindu religion and theology have been tolerant of a caste system, involving the exclusion of the poorest poor. Such stratification of society is quite acceptable to many devout Hindus. In their thinking it is quite compatible with, and even demanded by, the ideas of *karma* and reincarnation. But such a system would surely have scandalized the biblical prophets. They would have judged such discrimination as incompatible with God's will. Much biblical scholarship has concluded that the biblical deity even has a "preferential" disposition toward the poor. Though in fact people living in prophetic cultures have practiced a virtual caste system of their own, for example, by promoting racism or economic policies that marginalize masses of people, there can be no religious support for or tolerance of such a situation in the social teachings of the prophets.

Much indifference to the ills of society goes hand in hand with a religious mysticism that has lost touch with the secular world. Excessive other-worldliness can easily lead to a disregard for "this world." In general, the biblical prophets were not interested in the "other world," but concentrated on the need to change society and history to correspond with what they took to be God's will.

However, the religions that have come down from the prophets have themselves also become quite other-worldly at times. Christianity, for example, under the influence of Platonic and dualistic ideas has proclaimed, throughout much of its history, that the present world is of little importance and that we should put our hope only in the next one. Its own doctrines of renunciation of the world have condoned present injustice to an extent that the biblical prophets would also have found abominable. While the doctrine of renunciation of the world provides a certain type of consolation by giving individuals another world to hope for, it often privatizes religion and disengages it from temporal affairs. And when religion becomes a matter of purely private feelings of consolation, it easily ends up tolerating and legitimating the most horrendous social, political and economic arrangements. A secluded individualistic piety based on the rejection of this world implies that if the next world is the only important one then we may neglect the task of caring for the present one. Ironically, then, in practice Christians are often much more world-denying than are compassionate Buddhists. When Christianity is reduced to this style of world-denial, however, it has certainly lost touch with its prophetic ancestry.

As a result of being cut off from the social concern of their biblical roots, Christians have often passively tolerated destructive political, economic, racial, gender and environmental policies. One of the central questions for Christians to ponder today, for example, is how the so-called Holocaust, the slaughter of millions of Jews and other minorities by Hitler, occurred with so little opposition from Christians. Part of the answer seems to lie in the classic Christian instruction that placed so strong an emphasis on the "other world" that affairs in "this world" were taken to be of little significance. When religion builds too heavily on a doctrine of renunciation, and forgets its active and sacramental elements, it can eventually end up fleeing from all responsibility for the affairs of earth. This, as we have already seen, is one of the great temptations of mystical and apophatic religions.

However, if we return to the biblical sources of prophetic religion we find no desire there to escape the world or responsibility for it. Rather we discover that the longing to make this a better world, rather than something to be renounced, is central to its teachings. The God of prophetic religion is not one who demands of people that they withdraw from the world into some Platonic heaven. The Hebrews did not even have a concept of survival after death. Abraham, the father of the Hebrew nation, was given the promise of a new land, not a paradise after death. His sons and daughters placed their hope not in a heaven beyond time, but in a thisworldly future where they would achieve status among the nations and where peace would reign on earth.

Moses made a covenant with Yahweh in which the Hebrew people were promised the blessings of a new land and a new life on the plane of history, not a refuge in the hereafter. The theme of the "land" has been preeminent in Israel's self-understanding. Ideas about life beyond death and a separate realm of souls were quite foreign to the early phases of Israelite religion. And it was not that its followers were unfamiliar with notions of survival beyond death. After all, at least some of their number had made contact with the Egyptians and other peoples who were much preoccupied with death and the beyond. Renunciation of this present life and its enjoyments could not have been further from the Mosaic mind. According to the Bible, the God of Israel was intent upon having his people enjoy the blessings of creation, provided only that they spread the joy around and not leave anyone out of the social picture. Their rather "secular" hope for a home of abundance overflowing with milk and honey represents the spirit of early Israelite piety.

Israel's famous prophets, Amos, Hosea, Micah, Isaiah, Jeremiah, Ezekiel—none of them wanted us to withdraw from this world and escape from responsibility for it. But they did insist on the fair and all-inclusive distribution of the blessings of life. For them the very essence of religion is the doing of justice. The words of *Micah* epitomize the prophets' concern. Not without reason have they been called the "Magna Carta" of prophetic religion:

> With what shall I come before the Lord and bow myself before God on high? Shall I come before him with burnt offerings, with calves a year old? Will the Lord be pleased with thousands of rams, with ten thousands of rivers of oil? Shall I give my first-born for my transgression, the fruit of my body for the sin of my soul?" He has showed you, O man, what is good; and what does the Lord require of you but to do justice, and to love kindness, and to walk humbly with your God? (6:6–8)

The prophets were all devout believers in the God who had promised a great future to Abraham and Moses. But they did not interpret this promise in an other-worldly way. They were no less filled with religious energy than the authors of the *Upanishads,* but they channeled it into a concern to "do justice and to love kindness." Their religion was directed toward changing the social, political and economic landscape so that it might more closely correspond to God's plan and promise. In a very real sense prophetic religion is quite worldly in its thinking.

Those who have acquired the other-worldly mood of later religious developments, especially in Christianity, sometimes have a hard time understanding the prophets. But so also do secularistic thinkers. On the one hand lovers of the "other world" cannot always appreciate the urgent need for doing justice in "this world." They do good works, it is true, but often out of the extrinsic motivation of making themselves and others deserving of eternal life, not so much to improve the general quality of life in "this world." On the other hand, secularists may have no problem with the prophets' desire to make this a better world, but they see no need to relate such a concern to the notion of a transcendent, promising and commanding God of justice. Why root the demand for justice in a divine reality?

The biblical prophets avoided both extremes. Their compassion for the downtrodden could not let them postpone compensation to some world hereafter. Thus they insisted on the need to overturn social injustice here and now. But they could never have gotten the energy for their social concern without feeling deeply that it arises out of a relationship to transcendent mystery. One might even say that it was the *mystical* side of their religion that fired their activism on behalf of the disadvantaged. God for them was not an assurance of eternal life in the hereafter (though they never rejected this idea), but instead a present and future power with a plan for history, motivating them out of some deep interior infusion of hope to condemn any social situation devoid of the practice of justice. Amos, the farmer from Judah, chastises the transgressions of those who "oppress the poor, who crush the needy." (*Amos* 4:1) And this includes the people of Israel,

> . . . because they sell the righteous for silver, and the needy for a pair of shoes—they that trample the head of the poor into the dust of the earth, and turn aside the way of the afflicted . . . (2:6–7)

"Justice" has a deeper meaning for the prophets than our English word is capable of communicating. The biblical ideal of justice (*sedeqah*) means not just a vague sense of fairness, but "fidelity to the demands of a relationship." (Donahue, 69–76) According to biblical religion the practice of justice is itself the key to understanding the nature of God. Without the doing of justice the mystery of God remains hidden from us. Our own practice of justice is a necessary condition for God's becoming manifest in historical and social existence. In the context of prophetic religion therefore justice is a religious and not just an ethical ideal. The prophets would insist, if they were here, that for us to experience the mystery of God today we must also experience and practice justice in the social sphere of our existence. To the extent that justice does not yet reign, the mystery of God is still obscured. Thus the doing of justice is not just morality. It is religion. The prophets would argue that the main obstacle to our believing in the God of justice is the present reign of injustice in the world. The apparent "implausibility" of the idea of God to modernity is not so much the result of religion's uncongeniality to "science," but a result of the untransformed and unjust nature of our social world.

Strange as it may sometimes seem to Christians today, the teachings of Jesus of Nazareth are also best understood if they are situated within this prophetic tradition with its concern for justice. Jesus was not obsessed with the theme of other-worldly salvation any more than the classical prophets were. A key theme in his teaching was that the time is now ripe for the coming of the "Reign of God." In fact, biblical scholars today find overwhelming evidence that the coming of the Reign of God was the very heart of his teachings. All of his parables and ethical teachings were concerned with this theme. Jesus, it must be remembered, stood within a religious tradition dominated by the theme of promise. Like his fellow

Jews he hoped for a climactic fulfillment of the promise first communicated to Abraham. This hope for the future was embodied especially in the theme of the coming Reign of God which would bring liberation and peace. And the Reign of God was to be established "on *earth* as in heaven."

Like the prophets before him Jesus taught love of neighbor and one's enemies as the authentic religious way. Ritual must always take a back seat to caring for others. Jesus proposed that we should leave our gifts at the altar and first be reconciled with our brothers and sisters. Such acts of reconciliation are not incidental to his religion. They are its very substance. Ritualistic observance of the Sabbath is not as important as healing people of their miseries. The narrow exclusivity of a religion overly concerned with rites of purification must give way to one in which all people, including the unclean and defiled, are made to feel that they belong. Like the Buddha, Jesus taught that true piety begins with caring for others. His teachings were all centered on the coming Reign of God, but this was not some ethereal, other-worldly, far off dream. It was a present reality, now dawning in and transforming our present history. Kenneth Leech writes:

> It is quite impossible to read the prophets and fail to see the way in which, in their thought, the spiritual and the social were united. Equally it is impossible to make any sense of the ministry of Jesus without taking account of the Old Testament background to his teaching, for he came to fulfill the Law and the Prophets. The view, commonly expressed today, that the Church has been traditionally concerned with the condition of the inward soul, and has recently begun to deal with matters of social justice, is utterly incorrect. Orthodox Christianity has never taken such a narrow and purely inward view of religion. We need therefore a 'return to Biblical Christianity' if we are to move away from the false spirituality which is gaining popularity, and if we are to recover the centrality of the divine justice. (380)

Several prominent theological movements have sprung up in the past two decades attempting this "return to Biblical Christianity." One of them is associated especially with situations of poverty and oppression in the so-called developing nations. It is known as "liberation theology," and its central concern, like that of the biblical prophets, is with the theme of justice. It arises out of extremely oppressive conditions, such as those of much of Latin America, where a very small percentage of the population contains ninety percent or more of the wealth, or where a tiny minority possesses most of the arable land. According to liberation theologians this is the sort of derangement of social life that Moses, Amos, Hosea, Micah, Isaiah and Jesus would have found absolutely opposed to God's will.

Liberation theology addresses itself to this situation. So desperate are the lives of the people it serves that, like the prophets, it feels called to accentuate transformative socio-political action ahead of all other religious concerns. Liberation theology does not reject the sacramental, mystical and apophatic aspects of religion, as many of its critics have accused it of doing. It cherishes them while at the same time giving greater emphasis to action than would other styles of religion and theology. It does not find this emphasis at all irreligious. In fact it sees a need to keep its transformative impulse closely connected to the other three religious modes. If it did not do so it would become indistinguishable from secular humanism. Like the *Epistle of James*, however, it cannot divorce religion from caring for the needy. Religion is essentially about the doing of justice.

Because of its emphasis on action liberation theology has been severely chastised by those who have made sacramentalism, mysticism or renunciation the privileged ways of religion. But there is nothing new in such conflicts. Such controversies have always been a part of religious history. And on the whole they seem to be healthy for the general state of religion, for they keep alive the tensions without which a splintering into the various misshapings of religion might readily occur. Many of its critics hold that liberation theology has lost its religious depth. But the original proponents of liberation theology are mostly Roman Catholic priests who have their spiritual roots in sacramental and contemplative religion. Like any of our four types of religion, action has its own bias that could potentially lead it away from its relation with the other three ways. But it would be hard to prove that this has clearly happened in the case of contemporary liberation theology.

Finally, it should be emphasized also that the religion of Islam is also unintelligible outside of the tradition of prophecy. Islam even refers to Muhammad primarily as a prophet, one who speaks on behalf of God. And one of the five pillars of Islamic faith is the giving of alms to take care of the poor. Concern for social justice is part of the substance of Islam. It is also a motivating factor in the intense missionary zeal that moves Islam to the status of a world religion.

Action and Mystery

Religion seeks to relate us to mystery. It is easy enough to acknowledge this in the case of its sacramental, mystical, and apophatic facets. But how can *action* on behalf of good causes be considered a passage into mystery? Usually we relate action to the sphere of the profane or the secular? How can it be distinctively religious? How can doing justice be the very substance of religion, rather than merely something that religious people do in the secular sphere?

The answer given by the prophets is quite simple. Action for the sake of bringing about a just world is itself a response to the *mystery of promise* which is the very foundation of the prophetic religious sensibility. Religious action is animated by a hope that is kept alive only by a relationship to the *future*, which in prophetic religion is the primary place where mystery dwells. According to the religion of the prophets the future *is* the great domain of mystery. For out of the future new life comes into being and impossible things become possible. The future is an inexhaustible, incomprehensible reservoir of limitless possibilities. It is the arena where God dwells and out of which God "makes all things new." Prophetic religion is rooted in mystery no less than any other tradition, but it is in the future that it glimpses the mysterious shape of something for which to hope unconditionally.

Hence, the prophets felt secure in their conviction that an activist movement into the mysterious future by way of doing justice is itself worship of divine mystery, and deserves to be called religion. Doing works of justice to transform the world is not just a preparation for heaven, not simply preliminary effort after doing which one then encounters God. Rather, doing justice is already a movement into the mystery of the future.

We have inherited in popular religion the view that God abides somewhere "up there," vertically situated "above" the world. But in biblical religion the transcendent One dwells essentially in the future. The Bible may even be said to have opened up to human consciousness a radically new way of experiencing transcendence, namely as "essentially future." (Moltmann, 1967, 16) It allows for a new type of mysticism, one that might be called a "mysticism of the future."

The Question of the Afterlife

But if the way of action has such a this-worldly concern, then how do we account for the fact that many of the traditional teachings associated with the prophetic religions put so much stress on life beyond death? Does not the doctrine of immortality, in which the soul is said to have its true home in "heaven" above earth and history, distract people from the emphasis the prophets have placed on doing justice here and now? Can we reconcile belief in heaven with the strong commitment of activist religion to the present alleviation of suffering and injustice? This is the question that Karl Marx and many others have raised in modern times.

Islam, Christianity and some types of post-exilic Judaism have all accepted the doctrine of life beyond the grave. But within the context of prophetic religion the teaching of survival does not mean the same thing as in Plato or Brahmanism or Egyptian religion. Rather it is a doctrine that itself flows out of the themes of justice and promise that dominate prophetic religion. The doctrine of immortality is appropriately biblical only to the extent that it is a carrying out of the prophetic theme of hope for future fulfillment. Such hope would simply be an extension of prophetic religion's idea of a God who creates new life out of impossible situations, in this case death. For many theologians today the doctrine of immortality (or better, "resurrection") is a doctrinal development consistent with the prophetic trust in a God whose character is that of creative fidelity. Belief in a God who is a promise-keeper and who cares in a special way for the poor is also the foundation of prophetic religion's belief in life beyond death.

Greek philosophy, especially that of Plato, offered to Jewish, Islamic and Christian thinkers a ready-made doctrine of immortality of the soul. This belief in immortality has been grafted onto, and at times substituted for, the biblical theme of hope in a new creation. And it has also often replaced the New Testament hope for resurrection of the *body*. The biblical view, however, can support the idea of life beyond death only in the context of its basic theme of a creative and liberative God who is faithful to the promise of justice for the poor and oppressed. The state in which all people die, after all, is one in which justice has not yet reigned. Death is itself a symbol of the enslavement, impossibility, hopelessness, injustice and oppression that exist in the absence of the Reign of God. Death is the final expression of a basic "existential" poverty characteristic of all living beings. It is in the context of vanquishing this ultimate forlornness that the God of the prophets, who always promises new life to the poor, is understood by theologians as victorious over death as well. Suffering and death, the universal emblems of injustice, do not have a legitimate place in the divine plan for human existence. Therefore, belief in life beyond the present world seems consistent with biblical religion provided that it emanates from the hope for justice and new creation nurtured by the prophets.

The viewpoint of much recent theology is that the plausibility of life after death cannot be meaningfully established on the basis of logical or scientific proofs, any more than can the reality of God. (Küng, 1984) In the context of prophetic religion God can be "known" only by those who have trusted in the divine promise. So too any genuine religious "contact" with the hereafter can occur only in the risk-taking context of trust and hope. The idea of life beyond death apparently cannot be made a matter of mathematical certitude. If immortality is interpreted in the animist, Platonic or Egyptian way, as an automatic migration of the soul to another land, then prophetic religion would be unable to accommodate such an idea. However, if it is a belief growing out of trust in the God who can accomplish what is humanly speaking "impossible," then it can easily be fit into the fabric of biblical faith.

The Activist Temptation

There is a point where each religious way along our continuum of types begins to depart from a full openness to mystery. It is especially at this point of slippage that the other three types would express their disapproval. But when they do so a severe strain begins to appear within the religious world. The continuum of types can break apart into divergent and conflicting trails, and this splintering causes many violent disputes in the history of religion. Priests are attacked by mystics, ascetics and activists. Religious activists and prophets are lampooned as mere secularists by priests and contemplatives. Contemplatives and ascetics are charged with escapism by activists, and so forth. And today, as we shall see later, skepticism or atheism enters the fray with the accusation that all of religion is obsolete.

Activist religion seeks to alter and renew the world by bringing fresh forms of order and justice into it. It thrives on the conviction that there is a mysterious region of the future seeking to interrupt the monotony of the present. But religious activism also contains a certain bias that can lead it to slip away from its intrinsic openness to the novelty of mystery. It may be tempted at times to what we may call, for lack of a better term, *impatience*. Activists dream about the reconstruction of history, but when the fulfillment of their dreams seems too remote from realization, they are tempted to force history and society into their restrictive and hastily construed schemes. Purely human planning may then be substituted for what the prophets saw as a divine plan. Activism then becomes indistinguishable from secular humanism. A narrowly human sketch takes the place of the mysteriously whole divine plan discerned by the prophets.

The compulsive impatience of a purely secular activism can lead at times to social disasters, war and slaughter of those who do not "fit" the activist's visions. If activism loses its sacramental, mystical and apophatic religious base, the question arises as to how it will sustain the energy to be patient and tolerant. Can activism indefinitely continue the struggle for justice, knowing that fulfillment of its dreams may lie far beyond the

THE WAY OF COMPASSION

May creatures all abound in weal and peace; may all
be blessed with peace always;
all creatures weak or strong,
all creatures great and small;
creatures unseen or seen,
dwelling afar or near,
born or awaiting birth,
—may all be blessed with peace!

Let none cajole or flout
his fellow anywhere;
let none wish others harm
in dudgeon or in hate.

Just as with her own life
a mother shields from hurt
her own, her only, child,—
let all-embracing thoughts
for all that lives be thine,

—an all-embracing love
for all the universe
in all its heights and depths
and breadth, unstinted love,
unmarred by hate within,
not rousing enmity.

So, as you stand or walk,
or sit, or lie, reflect
with all your might on this;
—'tis deemed 'a state divine.'

SUTTA-NIPATA

A Buddhist hymn to love. From E. A. Burtt, *The Teachings of the Compassion-ate Buddha* (New York: New American Library, 1982).

13 If I speak in the tongues of men and of angels, but have not love, I am a noisy gong or a clanging cymbal. [2]And if I have prophetic powers, and understand all mysteries and all knowledge, and if I have all faith, so as to remove mountains, but have not love, I

am nothing. [3]If I give away all I have, and if I deliver my body to be burned, but have not love, I gain nothing.

4 Love is patient and kind; love is not jealous or boastful; [5]it is not arrogant or rude. Love does not insist on its own way; it is not irritable or resentful; [6]it does not rejoice at wrong, but rejoices in the right. [7]Love bears all things, believes all things, hopes all things, endures all things.

8 Love never ends; as for prophecies, they will pass away; as for tongues, they will cease; as for knowledge, it will pass away. [9]For our knowledge is imperfect and our prophecy is imperfect; [10]but when the perfect comes, the imperfect will pass away. [11]When I was a child, I spoke like a child, I thought like a child, I reasoned like a child; when I became a man, I gave up childish ways. [12]For now we see in a mirror dimly, but then face to face. Now I know in part; then I shall understand fully, even as I have been fully understood. [13]So faith, hope, love abide, these three; but the greatest of these is love.

ST. PAUL, 1 CORINTHIANS 13:1–13, *REVISED STANDARD VERSION*

Righteousness does not consist in whether you face towards the east or towards the west. The righteous man is he who believes in Allah and the Last Day, in the angels, and the Scriptures and the prophets; who for the love of Allah gives his wealth to his kinsfolk, to the orphans, to the needy, to the wayfarers and to the beggars, and for the redemption of captives; who attends to his prayers and pays the alms-tax; who is true to his promises and steadfast in trial and adversity and in times of war. Such are the true believers; such are the God-fearing.

QU'RAN, 2, 172 (Pelican Tr.)

lifespan of an individual or even a generation? Can it effectively survive the loss of a sense of the eternal? History is full of instances of the horror wrought by impatient activists and social visionaries who are unwilling to practice the apophatic virtue of silent waiting.

PART III

Aims of Religion

9.

Reassurance

In Part I we glanced at several brief chapters of the religious story. There we looked at religion from a *descriptive* point of view. And in Part II we examined four corresponding "ways" of being religious. In doing so we employed a *typological* approach, organizing the data of religion in terms of distinct "ways" that can be placed side by side for purposes of comparison. Although the range of data we have surveyed is very limited, it is nevertheless representative enough for us to undertake, here in Part III, a more *theoretical* examination of religion. At this point we shall seek to understand why people "do religion" and how religion fits into the context of human life and consciousness. Then in Part IV we shall turn to a *critical* examination of religion and inquire whether it is really important and, above all, truthful.

Our theoretical look at religion must also be a limited one. It is impossible for us to cover all the important aspects of religion in a text such as this. Nevertheless, we can gain some understanding of religion if we observe how it links up with our "natural" existence. We shall begin by paying close attention to four common aspects of our human nature, and then we shall attempt to discern how religion is related to them. The first is our natural tendency to trust. The second is our enchantment with the "unknown." The third is our longing for some sort of fulfillment or meaning, the other side of which is the experience of dissatisfaction and disillusionment. And the fourth is our aspiration to morality. These traits are not themselves necessarily religious. For they are present in the lives of people who have nothing to do with specific religions. But religion is intimately related to them, and we can understand what is specific to religion if we dig down into the roots it has in these universal elements of human experience.

Stated briefly, therefore, religion may be understood in the following four ways. (1) In relation to trust, religion is *ultimate reassurance;* (2) in relation to our attraction to the unknown, religion is openness to *ultimate mystery;* (3) in connection with our expectation of fulfillment and our experience of what Buddhism calls the "unsatisfactoriness" of life, religion is the affirmation of an *ultimate perfection;* and (4) as it relates to our moral impulses, religion is the articulation of an *ultimate goodness.*

We may associate each of these respectively with the four religious ways we reviewed in the previous section. The aspect of reassurance is presented to the religious person primarily through symbols such as we find in sacramental religion. The openness to mystery is brought out most explicitly in mysticism. The quest for perfection is expressed especially well in the *via negativa* or the way of silence. And finally, the association of religion with "goodness" is most vivid in the way of action.

Trust

It is safe to say that religion has a great deal to do with the disposition of *trust*. At the heart of religion there lies an attitude of confidence and assurance. Religion is not in the same category of understanding as, for example, knowledge of the multiplication table. It hardly possesses that kind of clarity and distinctness. People do not become religious simply by performing automatic operations of logic. Religion instead is closer to interpersonal kinds of experience and knowledge. The latter require that we *risk* ourselves by going out to people in acts of trust. If we are to know another person intimately we have to go beyond the detached methods of reason or science. There are certain kinds of knowledge, indeed the ones that are most significant to us, that we can acquire only if we take a trusting "leap," sometimes before all the facts are in and before we see things clearly. Religion falls into this genre of awareness. It is an interpretation of reality that cannot occur apart from the posture of trust.

We are brought into this world with at least some capacity to trust. Trusting is as natural as our capacity to smile. Our very nature "programs" us to place our confidence both in others and in the world as such. This potential for "basic trust" has been identified by modern psychology as the indispensable foundation upon which our very growth as persons depends. Trust is essential to our being. Without it we would be unable to relate meaningfully to others or to develop into functional adults. Basic trust is at least an aptitude given with our existence, even if it is at times buried beneath layers of mistrust. Religion, we shall see, fits into human existence in the general area of our spontaneous, natural propensity to trust. Religion is not identical with the natural tendency to trust, but it has a close relationship to it.

Sociologist Peter Berger has shown that there is a basic trust at the root of such everyday gestures as ordering, playing and laughing. If you were to put into words the core conviction that underlies such mundane activities as these, it might be something to the effect that "the universe is trustworthy," or "reality fundamentally makes sense." If, on the other hand, you were absolutely convinced that reality is completely untrustworthy, then you would be unable to put order into your life, to play or to laugh. Such ordinary activities of everyday life are built upon a foundation of "basic trust." And so is religion.

However, spontaneous expressions of confidence can well up even in those who have had no explicit contact with religious expressions of trust. Berger invites us to look, for example, at one of the most fundamental expressions of trust that we find in human life, namely, a mother's reassurance of an anxious child:

> A child wakes up in the night, perhaps from a bad dream, and finds himself surrounded by darkness, alone, beset by nameless threats. At such a moment the contours of trusted reality are blurred or invisible, and in the terror of incipient chaos the child cries out for his mother. . . . She will turn on a lamp, perhaps, which will encircle the scene with a warm glow of reassuring light. She will speak or sing to the child, and the content of this communication will invariably be the same—"Don't be afraid— everything is in order, everything is all right." If all goes well, the child will be reassured, and in this trust he will return to sleep. (Berger, 1970, 54–55)

The mother's "everything is all right" is a commonplace expression of human trust, but Berger sees deep significance in it:

> All this, of course, belongs to the most routine experiences of life and does not depend upon any religious preconceptions. Yet this common scene raises a far from ordinary question, which immediately introduces a religious dimension: *Is the mother lying to the child?*

Berger thinks that in uttering her "everything is all right" the mother is making a metaphysical statement, that is, a statement about the ultimate nature of reality. Obviously she has not done so in a deliberate, calculated way. The utterance just flows forth unreflectively. Yet it is still meaningful

for us to ask: *Is she lying?* According to Berger, "the answer, in the most
profound sense can be "no" only if there is some truth in the religious
interpretation of human existence." (55)

Religion and Trust

Religion is connected *in some way* to the ineradicable trust that undergirds so much of our everyday lives. From its primitive beginnings,
through the emergence of the great traditions, religion is essentially about
trust. But it is a tricky business to show *exactly* how religions and religious
activities are related to it. Religions are transformative bodies of symbols,
myths, stories, rituals, practices and ideas, often pointing to an other than
ordinary dimension of reality and encouraging us to trust in it. They flow
out of our native capacity to trust. But we *already* trust to one degree or
another, whether we are religious or not. So where does religion come in?
And why? If trust takes place even in the absence of religion, then what
does religion add? We do not get very far simply by defining religion as
trust. After all, there are many other, apparently non-religious, manifestations of basic confidence. What then is distinctive about religion?
    Simply this: religions provide ultimate *re*-assurance. They relate to
our natural confidence by pointing symbolically to an *ultimate basis in
reality* for our trusting *again*. I use the term "reassurance," because I mean
not just assurance, but precisely *re*-assurance, implying "being assured
again." Schubert Ogden whose ideas we are employing here observes:

> . . . the function of religious assertions is to provide "reas-
> surance." As we know from our everyday experience, to reassure
> someone is to restore to him an assurance or confidence which,
> for some reason or other, he seems to have lost. And this can be
> done only in the one way suggested by the word "*re*-assure"
> itself, namely, by assuring *again*, by re-presenting assurance.
> (Ogden, 32ff.)

But why do we need to be assured "again"? Because somewhere along
life's way we have quite likely lost at least some of our native tendency to
trust. Negative experiences that we have had from very early in our lives
can tempt us to *dis*-trust. The weakness and anger of our parents, the
hostility of siblings, the feeling of pain, the experience of our physical and
mental limitations, temperamental peculiarities, frustrated desires, the
awareness of our own mortality, and the apparent indifference of nature

and other people—all of these can lead us to suppress the natural persuasion of interior trust.

Threats to our basic confidence constitute a great deal of our life experience. And sometimes these menaces can be so overwhelming that we are tempted to lose heart altogether. Hence we need to be assured *again*. This is where religion comes into the picture. Religion in this interpretation is *not* the initial cause of our trust, but its confirmation. Original confidence comes with our humanity, not with religion. Our existence itself already presents us with the propensity for trust. Religion, therefore, is best understood as *re*-assurance, that is, as a *re*-presentation of trust. Ogden summarizes:

> . . . the various "religions" or "faiths" of mankind . . . are one and all expressions or re-presentations of a yet deeper faith that precedes them. Logically prior to every particular religious assertion is an original confidence in the meaning and worth of life, through which not simply all our religious answers, but even our religious questions first become possible or have any sense.
>
> . . . Because all religions are by their very nature representative, they never originate our faith in life's meaning, but rather provide us with particular symbolic forms through which that faith may be more or less adequately re-affirmed at the level of self-conscious belief. (54)

Our capacity for trust is first activated by our sharing life with others. But the attitudes of these others have *already* been shaped by a set of cultural symbols and stories, and many of these are religious in origin. Such stories are already a part of all cultures and linguistic systems. And by being born into such narrative contexts we learn to trust. So it is not as though our basic trust is ever completely isolated from the influence religions have already had on the shaping of human culture and language. But it is still useful to make the distinction between our "natural" capacity to trust as it is shaped by generic cultural systems of meaning, and explicitly religious symbols and stories whose purpose is to provide *ultimate* reassurance.

Stories of Origins and Order

One way religions provide such reassurance is by narrating how things began. You are probably familiar with the opening words of the Bible: "*In the beginning* God created the heavens and the earth." This is the part we know best, but look carefully at the next sentence: "The earth was

without form and void, and darkness was upon the face of the deep."
There is something terrifying about these images of desolateness. They
powerfully suggest the threat of nothingness. The threat of chaos lurks in
the background of the whole creation story, as well as throughout the
Hebrew and Christian scriptures. Indeed the threat of the "void" is an
aspect of a great deal of religious imagery. We noted in Hinduism and
Buddhism that the sense of the perishability of all things is a powerful
stimulus to construct a religious interpretation of the world. And in the
Christian scriptures the threat of chaos is imagined in a wide variety of
ways. For example, there is the story of Jesus and his disciples caught in a
storm out on "the deep." The disciples are in a state of panic at the turmoil
around them, fearing that they are about to perish. But Jesus is pictured as
asleep and undisturbed. When he is awakened he rebukes the storm, and
according to the Gospel accounts, calm is restored. Annihilation is kept at
bay. Such stories of Jesus' mastery of the threat of chaos are told again and
again by Christians in order that they too might experience in their faith
the reassurance felt by the disciples in the presence of their master.

The threat of disorder is a constant theme in the stories of religions,
going back to the earliest records of myth-making. But just as pervasive
is the conviction that darkness, nothingness and discord will not be
victorious: "And the Spirit of God was moving over the face of the
waters," the biblical story of creation continues. "And God said, 'Let
there be light . . .' " And after his death Jesus is pictured as returning to
his loved ones and breathing on them the word "shalom" (peace), signifying a new beginning, a new creation. Order always wins out over chaos,
in the long run at least. This is perhaps the central instruction of all
religion. In the final analysis, says religion, "all manner of things shall be
well." Religion is *ultimate* reassurance.

It is hard to overestimate the reassurance that religious stories about
the conquering of chaos have always instilled in the hearts of the devout.
The capacity of such stories to dispel the terror of chaos is one of the most
important features of religions. Stories of God or the gods provide a "way"
through the clouds of darkness that hover over human lives and threaten
the capacity to trust. And this is especially true of the stories that tell about
how things began. There is something enormously consoling and solidify-
ing about knowing origins. That is probably why creation stories, and
other accounts of how things came into being, abound in sacramental
religion.

A similar passion for beginnings still thrives in the modern scientific
obsession with the origins of the universe. Recently, for example, there has
been a flurry of books by physicists and astronomers with such titles as
"The Origin of the Universe," "The First Three Minutes," "Cosmic

Dawn," or "The Moment of Creation." Such scientific curiosity exhibits the unshakable habit we humans have, even if we are not ourselves explicitly religious, of seeking to know how things began.

Why? Why do we want so passionately to know our own "roots" or those of the universe itself? Why do we seek to know where our ancestors came from, how our country was founded, how the universe originated, how evil and suffering came into the world? In raising these questions we are simultaneously inquiring why our species has been so habitually religious. For religion, particularly in its sacramental aspects, has been inseparable from the quest for origins and stories about the beginnings. The biblical book of *Genesis* (a term which means "origin") is the most familiar example we have of this religious concern, but the quest for origins and the attempt to picture them symbolically and mythically has been a persistent aspect of most religions.

Any account of how the world began is called a *cosmogony* (from the Greek *cosmos*, meaning "order," and *genesis*, "coming into being"). The passion to know how things were "in the beginning" has given rise to numerous cosmogonies from all parts of the world, going back at least to the late Stone Age. Biblical religion is not alone in attempting to picture how things were in "primordial time," or how the world came into existence and how things got to be in the often sorry shape they are in now. In fact, the biblical story of creation, of Adam and Eve, of how evil entered the world, has obviously borrowed items from other ancient accounts of origins.

One of the most famous of such stories of origins, the *Enuma Elish*, was composed in Mesopotamia early in the second millennium B.C.E., and a version of it seems to have been available to the authors of the much later biblical account of creation. The Babylonian cosmogony can serve here as an example of how the many myths of origins from all over the world represent ultimate reassurance.

According to this creation story, there are two world-parents, Apsu and his wife Tiamat, who are present "before" the beginning of the world. Tiamat gives birth to other gods whose noisiness irritates Apsu, and so the latter makes plans to kill the annoying children. But Ea, one of the younger gods, learns of Apsu's designs and slays Apsu instead. This murder angers Tiamat, and so she conspires to avenge her husband's death. Then the most important character in the myth, Marduk, rises up to meet the challenge of Tiamat's hostility. Marduk is declared king of the gods and goes off to do battle with the she-monster, Tiamat. He slays her in a vivid and bloody scene, and then proceeds to make the heavens and the earth out of her body. It is in this terrible struggle between the forces of chaos and order that the world began.

The ancient myth then tells of how the people of Mesopotamia were created, and how Marduk was enshrined and celebrated for his victory over chaos. Annually, during the new year's celebration in ancient Babylon, Marduk's conquering of chaos was ritually re-enacted. The new year's ritual gave the participants a vibrant feeling that their society was contemporaneous with the creation of the world itself, thus providing them with a basis for confidence in living with the expectation that order ultimately wins out over chaos.

Thus the quest for origins is an expression of the more basic human need for reassurance. It is no secret that confusion constantly threatens our existence. Order of some sort is necessary for living. But at the margins of awareness lurk the many possible ways in which disorder can invade our lives at any time. The unpredictability of climatic conditions, the hostility of foreign peoples, sickness, famine, death and other uncontrollable happenings demand that we find a way to establish some degree of order within an otherwise chaotic world. Knowing the beginnings of things is one way of keeping out the terrifying indefiniteness of the universe. A sense of origins puts a clear barrier between our lives and the obscure past, and this perception of boundaries allows us to nestle more comfortably in the present. Religious myths of origins and order have reassured many of the earth's inhabitants that chaos is not the final word.

Reassurance "in spite of"

The first thing to note about religion, then, is its intention to *restore* our sagging confidence. Religions, though they may not initiate our trust, may well be the most important vehicles by which *re*-assurance has been provided to people throughout the ages. One of the most familiar examples of such religious reassurance may be found in the Twenty-third Psalm of the Hebrew Bible:

"The Lord is my shepherd, I shall not want;
he makes me lie down in green pastures.
He leads me beside still waters; he restores my soul.
He leads me in paths of righteousness for his name's sake.
Even though I walk through the valley of the shadow of death,
I fear no evil; for thou art with me;
thy rod and thy staff,
they comfort me." (Ps 23:1–4)

Notice not only the spontaneous trust expressed here, but the "even though," the aspect of "in spite of," that accompanies this religious utterance. The psalmist is quite aware of the dark side of experience. Religious people are by and large fully cognizant of the negativities besetting their lives. But they refuse to accept such experiences as the final word. Skeptics will question whether this refusal has any basis in reality, but as far as the religious person is concerned there is an *ultimate* ground in reality for our resisting the temptation to distrust. Beyond or deeper than our immediate environment, in which suffering and death seem to have the last word, there is, according to most religious traditions, a larger world, a transcendent environment, or an ultimate state of perfection, in terms of which the tragedies and limitations of our present existence are relativized and conquered. Religions typically point to this alleged transcendent world, this "other dimension," in a sacramental manner, that is, by way of symbolic, mythic and ritualistic expressions.

There are innumerable religious representations of trust. But the one with which we are most familiar is known as "theism." Theism (from the Greek *theos* = God) is the name scholars have given to a brand of religious reassurance in which the idea of God is the essential element. It is exemplified especially in Judaism, Christianity and Islam, but in a broad sense also in Asian and other religions. In brief, theism may be understood as the kind of religion that posits the existence of a transcendent (and often personal) "God" as the ultimate basis in reality for trusting in spite of life's negativities. One way to grasp what the word "God" means to the believer is to understand it as the deepest "ground" for trusting in reality and in the significance of life. The theist receives reassurance or bolstered confidence from the conviction that there is indeed something or someone at the heart of the universe that makes it trustworthy and renders the world and human existence meaningful. This something or someone is usually called "God" in our own culture and language. (Ogden, 44ff.)

As is typical of religion, this ground of confidence is pointed to by way of symbolic expression. By dwelling in the symbols and stories of God found, for example, in the sacred texts handed down in the traditions of Judaism, Christianity and Islam, the theist is given a "sense of God" as the basis for trusting in reality and in life. For those who do not share in any of these traditions, and the stories that carry them down through the centuries, the idea of God may be little more than a lifeless and meaningless abstraction. Normally, in order to appreciate and feel the trust communicated by the idea of "God" one has to have been steeped in a traditional set of symbols, rituals and stories that tell about the love and "deeds" of God.

"God," however, is only one of countless names that people all over the world have used to name what they take to be the depth and ground of their confidence in life. Hebrews named the basis of their hope "Yahweh." But Hindus have often referred to it as "Brahman," Taoists as the "Tao" (meaning "Way"), Sioux Indians as "Wakan Tanka," ancient Egyptians as "Re" or "Ma'at," Romans as "Jupiter" and the other gods, Buddhists as "Dharma" or even "Buddha" etc. What characterizes religions of all times and places is their tendency to provide ultimate re-assurance in spite of the negativities of life. And they do so sacramentally, by way of symbols that point to a hidden and transcendent foundation in reality for our trust.

"Ultimate" vs. "Proximate" Bases of Trust

Religion seeks an *ultimate* basis of confidence. This ultimate basis is to be distinguished from immediate or *proximate* sources of strength. Every one of us has proximate, near-at-hand sources of confidence, such as parents, friends, our country, job, car, or favorite sports team, etc. It is relatively easy to identify these immediate sources of courage, though we may be less conscious of some than of others. But religion is not satisfied with merely pointing to the obviously proximate sources of confidence. According to the religious visions of humanity, these close-by sources of strength are not enough to provide a sufficiently solid reason for trusting.

Why not? Religions answer: because the proximate sources of strength are all finite and transient themselves. They are themselves threatened with extinction. In the final analysis they will prove to be disappointingly perishable. And so religion usually directs its devotees toward an "ultimate" and "transcendent" basis of trust, one that is incorruptible, immune to disintegration.

Jewish faith may do so, for example, through its stories of God's unflagging activity on behalf of a specially chosen people. During the Passover feast the father of the family recounts the events surrounding the liberation of Israel from an apparently desperate situation of slavery and genocide in Egypt. By participating in this ritual meal the believing Jew is brought into deep intimacy with the idea of a divine power that has shaped Jewish history. And this God (*Yahweh*) is understood not only as the liberator of the Hebrew people during the Exodus from Egypt, but also as an eternal reason for contemporary religious trust. According to Judaism such a vision of ultimate care points to an imperishable reason for our living with confidence. Beyond all immediate sources of assurance there is an ultimate one that manifests itself, or "reveals" itself, through the sacramental mediation of our proximate bases of strength. This ultimate source of trust is what Judaism means by God.

In a similar way, when the Christian attends a Eucharistic celebration there is a "contact" with what Christians consider to be the ultimate ground of their trust. The belief that God entered fully into the human world in the person of Christ provides the Christian with a sense of reassurance that in spite of suffering and death there is every reason to hope and to live with joy. It is especially through its sacramental faith in God-incarnate that Christianity provides ultimate religious reassurance to its followers.

By making a pilgrimage to Mecca, a religious journey referred to as one of the "Five Pillars" of Islam, the Muslim participates bodily and geographically in the story of Allah's faithfulness and mercy to Muhammad and his followers. Pilgrimage is capable of bringing the Muslim into deep communion with "Allah," the Islamic name for what we are calling the ultimate "ground of trust." The exceptional action of pilgrimage to the main shrine of Islamic faith symbolizes both the journey to God and God's coming to meet the devotees as the basis of their confidence. Thus through the medium of this and other religious exercises, shared with millions of fellow believers, the devout Muslim is reassured that the world and human existence are grounded in an ultimate source of trust.

Religion, then, is a set of symbolic expressions whose function is to reassure us that in spite of our fragility and the perishability of the things and persons around us there is still reason to trust. But to understand religion correctly we must recognize its characteristic tendency to push beyond the "proximate" sources of our confidence in order to arrive at an "ultimate" and "transcendent" principle or experience. Religion notices how truth, justice, love, friendship, caring, human warmth and other things *proximately* give us the courage to trust, but it requires a transcendent ground beneath or beyond them. It usually seeks an "alternative reality" as the final *foundation* of truth, love, justice, friendship, and other values. According to the religious outlook this foundation is empirically unavailable. That is, it cannot be grasped by our senses, or by science and ordinary experience. We must spring toward it with the risk-taking disposition of trust. Otherwise it will not show up in the horizon of our awareness. To the religious mind the reality of such a transcendent ground cannot be discerned by way of any type of understanding in which trust is left out.

The skeptic will question whether such trust is reasonable. For the religious mind, however, the idea of the transcendent is required as the underpinning that makes our confidence in life reasonable. If there were no such *ultimate* basis for confidence underlying all our immediate sources of strength, then would it be honest for us to trust at all? Religious people and theologians are inclined to say no. For them, it would be unreasonable to go on trusting in a reality for which there is no *ultimate* basis of trust! One may or may not agree with this conviction, but it is important to recognize that, for the religious person at least, such a definitive basis of trust is absolutely *real*. Its supposed reality is indispensable to an adequate interpretation of human confidence.

Religions maintain that ultimate reality is beyond the controlling grasp of our consciousness. Our awareness of it is "revealed" or becomes transparent to us by way of proximate sources or sacraments of confidence. In Christianity, for example, the friends of Jesus found a great strength simply by living in his presence. However, they did not see him standing alone and unconnected with the world of the divine. They interpreted his own compassionate character as a manifestation of the mystery of God which he seemed to them to express. And, especially after his death, they looked upon him as the decisive "symbol" of the God whom they thought to be the ultimate basis of their trust. Typically sacramental religion "sees through" the immediate environment and finds the only solid basis of trust in an "ultimate environment" of transcendent order and care.

Conclusion

However, it is precisely this religious jump from proximate bases of trust, which are obvious to all of us, to an *ultimate* ground of confidence that is especially troubling to the sincere skeptic. Religious people make this leap by way of what we may call "symbolic consciousness." Symbolic consciousness "sees through" the ordinariness of things to some mysterious presence that lies behind them or in their depth. These ordinary things then become "revelatory" of this depth, and religious people feel that something extraordinary and momentous, a sacred mystery, is coming to expression in them. It is impossible to be religious without participating in this symbolic consciousness. And that is why any attempt to understand religion will have to pay considerable attention to critical questions about the nature and truth-value of the symbolic expressions used by religion. In Part IV we shall discuss some of these questions.

One of the major concerns of modernity, and especially of our present century, is whether there is any reason for trusting that our lives on this planet have any final significance. So many horrors have occurred in the present century, and now the ultimate terror of nuclear annihilation threatens us. The scientific picture of the universe gives us a picture of the cosmos so vast and seemingly forbidding that we begin to wonder about our personal value in the total scheme of things. The question of our significance, or whether there is any basis in reality for confidence in the worthwhileness of our lives, lies at the forefront of many a thoughtful person's concerns today.

A recent and widely read presentation of cosmology states that there is no scientific reason to trust the universe: ". . . this present universe has evolved from an unspeakably unfamiliar early condition, and faces a future extinction of endless cold or intolerable heat. The more the universe seems comprehensible, the more it also seems pointless." (Weinberg) Since the cosmos appears to many scientists to be ruled by chance and impersonal laws that have no regard for our personal aspirations, we cannot look to it for support in our own struggle for significance. Because the universe sustains the life of organisms only for a moment, and eventually frustrates our deepest desires, it appears to be stretching things to call it purposeful.

And so when we look at the complex world of religion from the perspective of our own situation we are curious about what it might be able to teach us about coping with contemporary threats to our own native confidence. What possible reassurance can it provide in terms of our own situation?

The persistent viewpoint of religion, as expressed by the medieval English mystic Julian of Norwich, is that in spite of all appearances to the contrary, ultimately "all manner of things shall be well." This indomitable trust remains a central characteristic of religion. Such faith represents either the most naive credulity imaginable or the most important posture that we could possibly live by. But in either case it seems to be more controversial in the present century than it may have been in other periods of history. Other ages and times might lead students of religion to single out alternative qualities such as gratitude, worship, ethical conduct or sense of dependency and offer these or any other qualities as the heart of religion. But our present situation in the twentieth century suggests that a more meaningful path toward understanding religion is to focus especially (though not exclusively) on its pervasive exhortation for us to trust in an ultimate mystery in spite of all the apparently sound reasons not to do so. But whether it is *reasonable* to do so is a question that we shall have to consider also.

10.

Mystery

We are trying to understand how religion fits into the "natural" context of human life and experience. Exactly where does it enter into our awareness and set itself up as a transformative influence distinct from but still related to the ordinariness of our life? In this chapter we shall note that religion takes root especially in our natural enchantment with the "unknown." Religion "shows up" in an especially clear way at those points where we experience the "limits" to our ordinary life and thought. It is at these limits that we begin to feel the presence of the unknown in an exceptional way. And it is at the limits of life and thought that we may locate with some precision how religion fits into the texture of human existence.

It is difficult to deny that we are attracted to the unknown. It is true, of course, that we are also terrified by it. We anxiously shrink away from it. We suppress our underlying awareness that the real world is mostly unknown and unfamiliar to us. We seek to make everything predictable. Magic is one way of doing this. Science may at times be another. But all of our attempts to make the world completely familiar eventually fail. And part of us rejoices in this failure. There is a portion of us that resists any efforts to subject all reality to our cognitional control. We remain curiously in need of and enchanted by yet unexplored regions of reality. For we realize that the deepest nourishment for our lives comes from the novelty of the unknown. Religion is born out of this enchantment with the unknown.

Religion is the most explicit way in which human beings have expressed their cherishing of the unknown. Religion, as we have been noting all along, is very much about "mystery." What distinguishes religion from ordinary life and consciousness is its explicit openness to an other-than-ordinary dimension of reality for which we can probably find no better word than "mystery." In this text the term "religion" is used to designate only those modes of living, thinking, speaking and acting that display a consciousness of and a trust in mystery.

Generally speaking, religious people have had an "intuition" that there is an "awesome and fascinating mystery" of total otherness surrounding our ordinary lives, giving substance and meaning to human existence. In his book, *The Idea of the Holy*, the famous religious scholar Rudolf Otto writes that religious people always and everywhere have felt a "numinous" (holy) presence of inexhaustible mystery lurking behind, beyond or in the depths of ordinary things, persons and events. He defines this intuited dimension of otherness as a *mysterium tremendum et fascinans*. The term *mysterium* points to the religious sense of an inexhaustible realm of "holiness," for which there are no adequate words in our languages. The word *tremendum* indicates that the experience of mystery often evokes a feeling of awe and even anxiety in those who have encountered the mystery of the "sacred." And the final term, *fascinans*, expresses the satisfaction, fascination and sublime joy to which religious participants in the sacred mystery also testify. Religion, then, may be understood here as a special discernment of and response to *mysterium*.

But what exactly is mystery? Where does the sense of mystery come from? Is there indeed a dimension of mystery to reality, or is the notion of mystery simply a cover-up for our ignorance? Is it merely a notion we use to characterize the yet unknown parts of the secular world and human experience? And as we learn more about the world and ourselves is the realm of mystery going to shrink and eventually disappear?

Or is mystery a reality that can never be fully known? Does it perhaps have a quality of being so "other" and distinct from what we are capable of knowing that it remains quite inaccessible to our ordinary awareness?

Religions usually understand mystery as having the quality of "total otherness." Mystery, in other words, is "holy" or "sacred." The term "sacred" comes from the Latin word *sacer*, meaning "cut off from." The "sacred" or the "holy" mystery of reality appears to religious people to possess the quality of irreducible otherness. And in the post-axial phases of religious development, this sacred mystery takes on an exceptionally sharp distinctiveness from the secular or profane world.

Religion is a mode of awareness sensitive in a special way to a dimension of mysterious otherness. And since the whole business of religion revolves so centrally around the discernment of mystery, we need to devote some time to a discussion of it.

Isaiah and Black Elk

The sense of a sacred mystery may be found in the most diverse religious settings. We can observe it in testimonies as far removed from each other, for example, as those of an ancient Hebrew prophet on the one hand and a native American tribal chief on the other.

When the Hebrew prophet Isaiah recalled his vision of the "Holy One" in the temple on the occasion of accepting his vocation as a prophet, he told of how this experience proved to be too much for him, leading him to a deep sense of unworthiness before the divine mystery. Composed in the eighth century B.C.E., Isaiah's account of his encounter with the mystery of God illustrates well the three components of Otto's definition:

> In the year that King Uzziah died I saw the Lord sitting upon a throne, high and lifted up; and his train filled the temple. Above him stood two Seraphim; each had six wings: with two he covered his face and with two he covered his feet, and with two he flew. And one called to another and said: "Holy, holy, holy is the Lord of hosts; the whole earth is full of his glory." And the foundations of the thresholds shook at the voice of him who called, and the house was filled with smoke.

Thus, in highly imaginative language, Isaiah describes the *mysterium* that he has encountered in an exceptional moment of religious ecstasy. Then he goes on to express the sense of the *tremendum,* the disorienting aspect of mystery, and a feeling of deep unworthiness in the face of the "holiness" of God:

> And I said: "Woe is me! For I am lost; for I am a man of unclean lips; for my eyes have seen the King, the Lord of hosts!"

But the other side of the *tremendum* is the *fascinans,* the fulfilling and peace-bestowing aspect of the mystery of the holy:

> Then flew one of the seraphim to me, having in his hand a burning coal which he had taken with tongs from the altar. And he touched my mouth, and said: "Behold, this has touched your lips; your guilt is taken away, and your sin forgiven." And I heard the voice of the Lord saying, "Whom shall I send, and who will go for us?" Then I said, "Here am I! Send me."
> (*Isaiah* 6:1–9)

Strengthened and "reassured" by his experience of mystery, Isaiah then takes up the burdensome but fulfilling vocation of a prophet, devoting his life to the unenviable task of being a spokesperson for his God.

Another example of a vision not unlike Isaiah's, but from a completely different time and culture, is narrated by the famous Sioux Indian, Black Elk. Recounting the results of the vision-quest he undertook as a very young lad, he clothes his description of sacred mystery in the specific terms of his native Lakota experience:

> It was when I was five years old that my Grandfather made me a bow and some arrows. The grass was young and I was [on] horseback. A thunder storm was coming from where the sun goes down, and just as I was riding into the woods along a creek, there was a kingbird sitting on a limb. This was not a dream, it happened. And I was going to shoot at the kingbird with the bow my Grandfather made, when the bird spoke and said: "The clouds all over are one-sided." Perhaps it meant that all the clouds were looking at me. And then it said: "Listen! A voice is calling you!" Then I looked up at the clouds, and two men were coming there, headfirst like arrows slanting down; and as they came, they sang a sacred song and the thunder was like drumming. I will sing it for you. The song and the drumming were like this:
> "Behold, a sacred voice is calling you;
> All over the sky a sacred voice is calling." (Neihardt, 15f.)

After the age of nine, the visions came to Black Elk again, more and more vividly. Often the mystery of the sacred was embodied in the form of horses or of his "Grandfathers." The visions summoned him to something akin to a "prophetic" vocation, one of caring for his people and their welfare, especially since they were threatened by the "white man." And, as in the case of Isaiah, the visions produced both anxiety and courage. They were instances of a *mysterium tremendum et fascinans*. Speaking of the Grandfathers encountered in his visions, Black Elk recalls one in particular:

> The oldest spoke again: "Your Grandfathers all over the world are having a council, and they have called you here to teach you." His voice was very kind, but I shook all over with fear now, for I knew that these were not old men, but the Powers of the World. (21)

But the experience of "fear" (the *tremendum*) was conquered by an enormous influx of power and courage communicated by the vision.

> The second Grandfather, he of the North, spoke again: "Take courage, younger brother," he said; "on earth a nation you shall make live, for yours shall be the power of the white giant's wing, the cleansing wing." (21f.)

The *mysterium* is also *fascinans*, fulfilling, ennobling and empowering. Black Elk's account is a good illustration of the effects on religious participants of an experience of sacred mystery.

This feeling of being surrounded by and grounded in a world of mystery is typical of the experience of most peoples of the ancient world and of many societies in various parts of the world even to this day. Educated modern thinkers will sometimes wonder whether Isaiah's or Black Elk's visions are anything more than hallucinations, but in the religious environments in which the visions occurred they are not all that exceptional and certainly not considered pathological. Rather they are taken for granted as revelatory of the deepest levels of reality, hidden to mundane consciousness. It was expected of many Indian lads, for example, that they would undertake a "vision quest" and cultivate a disposition open to revelations of sacred mystery. Black Elk laments the fact that our secular experience, including his own later life as a circus performer, has sealed us off from the religious world of his youth.

The Eclipse of Mystery?

It is often said that many of us living today have lost the sense of mystery. It is even said that we live in an age of the "eclipse of mystery," that we can no longer take for granted that people have experienced "the sacred" in the manner of an Isaiah or Black Elk. Some scholars suspect that this opaqueness to mystery is more characteristic of those of us in the universities of the Western world than of people less involved in a theoretical or scientific orientation to the world. But for many, both within and outside of the academic world today, the sense of a distinct realm of mystery does indeed seem to be out of vogue.

Thus we have to ask why mystery has apparently vanished from the consciousness of many of us, and whether it is at all possible, or for that matter worthwhile, trying to recover it again. It is important for us to make this inquiry, if for no other reason than that it may be difficult to understand much about religion at all unless we ourselves have had at least some inkling of mystery in our own experience. Is it possible for us truly to understand religion unless we have felt at least something of what Isaiah and Black Elk are talking about?

The alleged demise of mystery is partly a result of the scientific aim to "eliminate mystery," to use the words of the famous Harvard psychologist B. F. Skinner. (1972, 54) A number of modern scientific writers echo Skinner's sentiments that science will eventually do away with what we call mystery, and that therefore mystery and the religious sense based on it have an extremely precarious existence. For these scientific thinkers mystery is simply a convenient word pointing to yet unexplored aspects of the physical world. In other words, mystery means for them a temporary gap in our present understanding, a hollow space that will be filled in by scientific knowledge if we just wait long enough. This is not by any means what Otto or the religions mean by mystery, but it is such a common way of understanding the term that it is worthwhile dwelling on it for a moment.

"Mystery" today often means nothing more than a set of problems that will eventually be solved by scientific exploration. For example, physicist Heinz Pagels in his recent book on the origins of the universe writes:

People once worshipped the sun, awed by its power and beauty. Now that astrophysicists understand the physics of the sun and the stars and the source of their power, they are no longer the mysteries they once were. In our culture we no longer worship the sun and see it as a divine presence as our ancestors did. But many people still involve their deepest feelings with the universe as a whole and regard its origin as mysterious. The size, splendor and glory of the universe still provoke the sense of transcendent eternal being. (Pagels, 367)

However, Pagels thinks that physicists will someday understand the basic laws of the quantum creation of the universe. When that happens, he continues, "the existence of the universe will hold no more mystery for those who choose to understand it than the existence of the sun." In other words, "as knowledge of our universe matures, that ancient awestruck feeling of wonder at its size and duration seems inappropriate, a sensibility left over from an earlier age." (xiv)

Another scientist, Richard Dawkins, a young British biologist of considerable renown, begins his recent treatise on evolution with these words:

"This book is written in the conviction that our own existence once presented the greatest of all mysteries, but that it is a mystery no longer because it is solved. Darwin and Wallace

solved it, though we shall continue to add footnotes to their
solution for a while yet." (Dawkins, 1986, ix)

Dawkins is amazed that after Darwin's *The Origin of Species* any intelligent
person can still look upon the marvelous design of organisms or the existence of humans as a mystery, when "everyone knows" that natural selection working on random changes over a sufficiently long period of time
gives an "elegant and beautiful solution" to such problems.

Notice that both Pagels and Dawkins are using the term "mystery" as
the equivalent of "problem to be solved," or "present gap in our knowledge." By such usage the unknown is destined to dissolve into the void in
direct proportion to the advance of our scientific knowledge. To many
scientific thinkers "mystery" is nothing more than a name for our temporary ignorance. And since religion apparently feeds parasitically on this
gossamer of the unknown, there is little wonder that the likes of Skinner,
Pagels and Dawkins see little substance in religion. The countless epochs
of human religious encounter with an alleged mystery is all a huge mistake.
Science, they say, has now eliminated, or is in the process of eliminating,
any special area roped off just for religious consciousness. Today we should
learn to accept things "as they are" in their utter ordinariness and complete
explainability.

A more congenial response by a scientist to the idea of a distinct realm
of mystery is that of Albert Einstein. Though Einstein was not a theist,
and even thought the notion of a personal God was the creation of primitive superstition, he nonetheless took seriously the dimension of mystery.
He was never so sanguine as to suppose that the advance of science would
"eliminate mystery" altogether. For Einstein mystery was a more substan-
tive and irreducible aspect of things than it is for many other scientists and
philosophers. In his words, religion is a "rapturous amazement at the
harmony of natural law, which reveals an intelligence of such superiority
that, compared with it, all the systematic thinking and acting of human
beings is an utterly insignificant reflection." And, he continues,

> "The most beautiful experience we can have is the mysteri-
> ous. . . . Whoever does not know it and can no longer wonder, no
> longer marvel, is as good as dead, and his eyes are dimmed . . . it
> is this knowledge and this emotion that constitute true religiosity;
> in this sense and in this alone, I am a deeply religious man."
> (Einstein, 11)

For Einstein, unlike Pagels and Dawkins, mystery is a permanent
dimension of reality, and not a merely temporary cover-up for our scien-

tific ignorance. And in his view the sense of mystery may actually grow more explicit as scientific knowledge advances. Thus he comes somewhat closer to capturing the perennial religious intuition that mystery is a reality underlying or transcending all phenomena. It goes without saying that many scientists, possibly the majority of them, share at least some of Einstein's mystical sensitivity. They experience science as an opening to, rather than a narrowing of, the domain of mystery.

There is little hope for our understanding much about religion if we cannot resonate, like Einstein, with some notion of mystery. But there remains a need to clarify more carefully the difference between *religious* mystery and other aspects of the "unknown." For not all aspects of the unknown qualify as religious. Science, for example, is aware of a type of unknown that will eventually be known. The knowable unknown is not what religion means by mystery. For religion mystery is an area of incomprehensibility that cannot, even in principle, be mastered by scientific expertise. And because this incomprehensible aspect of mystery is so basic to religious awareness the world over, we must ask whether it shows up in any way in our own experience today, in spite of what has been said about its possible "eclipse."

Problem and Mystery

The term "mystery," we have seen, is often understood today simply as a gap in our knowledge that will eventually be closed up by the process of scientific advancement. According to this usage, as long as our intellectual mastery of the world progresses we will find answers to the "mysteries." The realm of the unknown will be gradually diminished, and "knowledge" will take its place. When "mystery" is understood in this fashion, we can scarcely wonder that the word no longer functions to evoke a religious sense of the *tremendum et fascinans*. For on this reading "mystery" is merely a vacuum begging to be filled with our intellectual achievements, and not an ineffable depth summoning us to surrender ourselves religiously to it.

However, according to many theologians and philosophers today such gaps in our knowledge should be called *problems*, not mysteries. The term "problem" points to an area of ignorance that is able eventually to be filled in by the application of human ingenuity. Mystery, on the other hand, is incapable of "solution." (Marcel)

A problem is open to eventual scientific, logical or technological disposal. It is somehow under our human control and can be mastered and removed by our intellectual or technological abilities. But "mystery" denotes a region of reality that, instead of growing smaller as we grow wiser and more powerful, appears to grow deeper and more incomprehensible. Einstein mentions, for example, that the greatest of all mysteries, and one for which there can never be a scientific "solution," is that the universe is even intelligible at all. The realm of mystery, as many other mystically oriented scientists testify, seems to expand as we solve more of our scientific and other problems. It is like a "horizon" that keeps receding into the distance the more our knowledge advances. While problems can be solved and thus gotten out of the way, mystery becomes more prominent the deeper our questions dig and the more secure our answers to problems become.

But where, more precisely, does mystery show up? At what points in our experience and questioning do we brush up against it? Where, in other words, can we appropriately locate the place of religious consciousness in the total context of our lives? One way of approaching these questions is to become aware of the notions of "limit-experience" and "limit-questioning." (Tracy, 91–118; Toulmin, 202–21)

Limit-Experience

Usually we are preoccupied with the ordinary "problems" of life, with everyday concerns such as how to pay for food, shelter, recreation, college tuition, how to gain friends and have a fulfilling social life, how to find the kind of work that fits our temperament, etc. In other words "functional" or "pragmatic" questions consume our ordinary lives. But there are certain exceptional moments when something breaks into the routine of our lives and causes us to look at our everyday world in a new and startling light. More often than not these are moments of "shipwreck" or "earthquake." One philosopher may call them "boundary experiences," another may name them "marginal experiences." Still others call them "limit-experiences." The point is that they lie at the edge of normal life and seemingly thrust us toward a terrifyingly unfamiliar (*tremendum*) but also perhaps promising (*fascinans*) dimension. They may initially evoke in us a feeling of anxiety causing us to cling all the more desperately to familiar things. But at the same time we may experience something deeply alluring about the unknown horizon they open up. In these moments we apprehend mystery in an especially sharp way. The death of one's spouse or child, the experience of deep embarrassment, the collapse of one's career plans, the infidelity of a close friend—one could easily multiply examples—can challenge us to raise provocative questions about the meaning or value of our existence as we have understood it up to now. They can bring us to a point of crisis in our lives, and at these moments we are faced with a decision as to whether we may still trust in the worthwhileness of life or give in to despair. Such events bring home to us the confining nature of ordinary existence. At such fragile times we may become more permeable to the reality of another dimension, beyond or infinitely deeper than the everyday. The experience of our vulnerability may expose us in a dramatic way to a depth beneath the surface of our lives that we may never previously have known. The term "mystery" seems appropriate as the name for this newly intuited territory.

To the skeptic, of course, this intuition of mystery will seem to be mere escapism and wishful thinking. But to countless others limit-experiences are openings to what religions, especially in their more mystical moments, interpret as ultimate *reality*. This intuited reality seems to provide religious people with a solid basis for continuing trust, in spite of the most devastating circumstances in their lives. Religion is meaningful to them as a way of articulating their sense of being connected with a mysterious "something" or "someone" sustaining them in their suffering.

Limit-experiences often consist of "shipwrecks" that force us to ask the so-called "ultimate" questions, and these in turn provoke us to rethink and perhaps deepen the context of our lives. Yet it would be a mistake to say that awakening to a sense of mystery is the result only of such extreme experiences. For the unsettling experience of discontent with the limits of the ordinary, and a novel fascination with the unknown, may creep up on us in those very moments when things are seemingly in perfect order. At the pinnacle of successful achievement, when nearly everything we have longed for has been realized, we often begin to sense the suffocating limits of our ordinary lives. We may begin to ask: what next? What do all my actions and accomplishments mean in the final analysis? What is the purpose of my endeavors? Where is my life ultimately leading? These questions are indications of our underlying awareness of the limits of the ordinary. They arise at the boundary of our efforts to make something of our lives, and they point no less than tragedy, suffering and death to the domain of mystery.

And, lest we appear to be too sober about all of this, we should emphasize that a grateful intimation of mystery often arises also in the context of simple human happiness. Moments of deep joy can transport us beyond the restraints of everyday existence. Some people testify that ecstatic experiences introduce them to the mystery of life much more decisively than the negative variety of limit-experience. The feeling of being deeply loved by another person or of being drawn into the experience of great beauty has made countless people suspect that their lives are enshrouded by an ultimate and gracious mystery. At such moments the world of everyday experience fades into a mere shadow, as unreal as the figures in Plato's cave; and a fresh, inexhaustible realm of mystery comes into the sweep of awareness, even if only for a moment. Often after having had such experiences it is quite difficult to "return" to ordinary life with its mundane duties in the same way as before. One has found a deeper level of "reality" and understandably wants to abide there, viewing life from a totally new perspective. Religion, especially of the mystical type, often cultivates this type of experience.

Limit-Questions

The realm of mystery may also come into view at the "limit" of our intellectual inquiries and disciplines. Mystery shows itself most explicitly at the point where we momentarily step out of our various academic pursuits and begin to ask what might be called "limit-questions." These limit-questions, lurking at the "boundary" of our academic disciplines, ask why we are involved in these pursuits in the first place. In raising such questions we are once again on the brink of an aspect of the unknown that cannot be removed by our intellectual efforts. (Tracy, 94–100)

A scientist, for example, is ordinarily preoccupied with *problems* for which some definitive answer is expected. He or she may spend months or years seeking a unified field theory, a room temperature super-conductivity, or an explanation for the deterioration of the ozone layer. The expectation is that someday such scientific problems can be solved and removed, or that at least a solution may be approximated. It is the nature of problems to be eventually disposed of so that the scientist can get on with new ones. But someday the problem-solving scientist might find himself or herself suddenly asking: why am I doing science at all? Why am I always looking for answers to my questions? Is the universe completely intelligible? Is it worthwhile spending my days in pursuit of the truth? These are examples of limit-questions, and it is around them that mystery hovers.

Such questions do not fall within, but rather only *at* the boundary of ordinary scientific inquiry. Limit-questions are not "solvable" in the same sense as the scientific problems on which one works in the laboratory. Instead, the deeper one becomes involved with limit-questions, the further any clear answer to them recedes. Perhaps this occurs because in limit-questioning one begins to have an inkling of the inexhaustible mystery of the world and of the incapacity of science to "solve" this mystery.

To give another example: the field of ethics attempts to provide answers to our moral problems. Ethicians engage in vigorous problem-solving exercises trying to decide whether this or that action is the violation of principles of justice, or whether a certain action involves infidelity to a contract or promise. Ethicians debate whether abortion, capital punishment and war are legitimate taking of life, or whether certain public policies violate human rights, etc. But, at the limits of ethical discussion, stepping out of the discipline of ethics for a moment, the moral philosopher may suddenly ask: why bother about ethics at all? Why be responsible? Why pursue the good life? Or at a certain point the following questions may arise: "Why should we be faithful at all? Why keep promises? Why be concerned for human life or human rights at all?" At this juncture the ethician has shifted from ethical problems into the irremovable and constantly pressing limit-questions that lead us into the realm of the mysterious.

The "Location" of Mystery and Religion

One way of understanding religion, therefore, is to see it as a kind of symbolic understanding that addresses these limit-questions. Religion fits into the context of our questioning consciousness not as another type of problem-solving, but rather as a source of reasons why we should get involved in problem-solving at all. At the limits of all the various fields of human inquiry we come to an impasse that we cannot get beyond with the tools of the disciplines themselves. No matter how much intellectual effort we expend there are still imponderable issues left over. Our problem-solving techniques bring us up to, but cannot get us over, the encompassing horizon of mystery that gapes open beyond our limit-questions. This is where religion may come into the context of our intellectual endeavors.

The place of mystery, and hence the appropriate place to locate religious symbols, acts and ideas, is at the limits of our problem-oriented questioning. If we have arrived at such limits we may find ourselves asking questions that we realize no human ingenuity will ever solve or "remove." Why should I seek truth? Why is the world intelligible? What is the purpose of learning? Why continue to work on problems? Is the intellectual life worthwhile in the final analysis?

Some religious thinkers even hold that the very fact of our asking limit-questions implies that mystery has already grasped hold of our consciousness. The horizon of mystery addresses us from the other side of our limit-questions and invites us to move beyond the scientifically yet-unknown toward the acknowledgement of an unknowable unknown. And we show our penchant for this dimension of mystery whenever we find ourselves asking limit-questions. At the "limit" of our ordinary experience and our problem-solving questions we are alerted to the nearness of mystery. We sense that it has been intimately present all along, but that it may not have entered into our explicit awareness. In limit-experience and limit-questioning we are invited to make the dimension of mystery the most important and enlivening aspect of our lives.

However, whenever we are brought to the limits of ordinary consciousness and experience we are tempted to take flight back to the "safer" refuge of the ordinary, to turn away from the *tremendum et fascinans*. We do so typically by trying to transform mystery into problem. The existence of a mysterious dimension that grasps us is repudiated by our efforts to subject all things to our own intellectual or technological mastery. "Mystery" then becomes only another word for "problems to be solved." The result may be not only an artificial delimiting of the world around us, but also an unfortunate diminishment of ourselves and a denial of our fundamental dignity as beings endowed with a capacity for growth into mystery.

This suppression of mystery by our inclination to mastery may also occur at times even within the world of religion. The degeneration of ritual into magic, the perversion of our quest for understanding into an obsession with certitude, the transformation of doctrine into rigid dogma, or the reduction of ethical aspiration to narrow moralism—these are all instances of the wilting of mystery into problem, into a domain where predictability and control are the chief authorities. Mystery, however, seeks the response of trust and surrender.

Conclusion

To the notion of *trust* then we must add the *sense of mystery* as an essential part of our understanding of religion. And just as there are temptations that challenge our capacity to trust, there are also experiences that seem to diminish our intuition of mystery. In fact, in modern times there has occurred a phenomenon, broadly known as secularization, that has seemingly exposed the realm of mystery and the sacred as insubstantial, or as lacking reality altogether. In Part IV therefore we shall explore further the skepticism that questions both the reality of *mysterium* and the religious affirmations that there is in reality a transcendent basis of trust.

One final word. Religions are not content with a vague impression of the *mysterium tremendum et fascinans*. They also insist on giving a name, or names, to the intuited dimension of mystery. Religions discern a *face* in mystery, often an intensely "personal" one. In theistic religions it is called "God," but other religious traditions have a variety of names and faces for this dimension of mystery. It is apparently not sufficient for religions that we simply have a generic sense of the horizon of mystery. We must bring it near to ourselves by way of a specific image. And different religions, as we have seen, accomplish this imaginative representation in amazingly rich and complex ways. The mystical way is the one most explicitly aware of the dimension of mystery. But sacramental religion brings this mystery very concretely into the ambit of actual human life and awareness.

11.

Adventure

It is hard to ignore the ring of truth in the Buddha's First Noble Truth. We are seldom able to reach a point in our lives where we can say that everything is just right or that life is absolutely perfect. Can we honestly deny that, along with its moments of joy and satisfaction, life is often frustrating? We are constantly brought up against insurmountable "limits" that interfere with our dearest longings in life. The facts of suffering and perishing are all we need to remind ourselves of the "unsatisfactoriness" of life.

Religions have been so attractive to people because of their promise of a state or realm of "perfection" in which we can finally surmount the frustrations that sometimes dominate our lives. The sacrificial rites of primal religion promise devotees a way out of sheer helplessness before fate and death. Hinduism promises *moksha.* Buddhism holds out the prospect of *nirvana,* and prophetic religion promises ultimate redemption. No other human ways of thinking and acting are so focally concerned with the attainment of perfection as is religion.

We are seeking to gain some understanding of what religion is by observing how it is connected to several inclinations that we all experience in our everyday lives, whether we are religious or not. The first of these is the need for reassurance. The second is our enchantment with the unknown. And a third is our longing for "fulfillment." A fourth, which we shall explore in the next chapter, is our aspiration toward morality. Such impulses are not themselves religious, and our having them does not make us religious. But religion is intimately related to them. It blossoms out of our tendency to trust, our need for the unknown, our desire for perfection, and our attraction to goodness. Religions articulate visions of reality that point to an ultimate reason *why* we should trust, *why* we are attracted to the unknown, *why* we often experience disappointment, and *why* we should aspire to morality.

In this chapter we shall bring into focus the relationship between religion and our experience of frustration. It is especially in Buddhism that this experience comes to religious expression. "All life is suffering" according to the First Noble Truth. And the way of silence, the *via negativa*, present in all the major post-axial religions also speaks to the universal human awareness of the "unsatisfactoriness" of life. Generally speaking, religions are convinced that we experience the imperfections of life in so vivid a manner because, in the deepest regions of our being, we are in quest of an ultimate "perfection." Religions respond, as it were, to a boundless "blank space" inside of each person. And they tell us that if we attempt to fill in this space with anything less than infinity we shall remain restless. Augustine of Hippo prayerfully expressed the conviction of many a religious person: "You have made us for yourself, O Lord; and our hearts are restless until they rest in you."

It is not difficult to recognize in ourselves a vague anticipation of perfection. Every time we become bored or discontent it is because things do not measure up to some expectation we have of what is ideal or perfect. If we had no inkling of "perfection" then things would never seem imperfect. If we had no intuition of what would be satisfying we would never feel dissatisfied. Whenever we experience "absurdity" we recognize it as such only because we are implicitly comparing that experience with "something" not absurd. Religion displays in a symbolic way what this vaguely apprehended "non-absurdity" is. In an always inadequate fashion it tries to bring the dimly intuited "perfection" out into the light of day. As the way of silence insists, any sacramental representations of perfection will themselves always be imperfect. But they still arouse the human hope of attaining an ultimate perfection. According to most religions, only the hope of ultimate fulfillment can allow us to accept the pain and disappointment of life.

Adventure

The religious intimation of ultimate perfection invites us to loosen our grip on the familiar. Sacramental religion discerns the possibility of a wider enjoyment symbolically transparent within and beyond the familiar world of enjoyable goods. Mysticism leans even more emphatically toward the unknown perfection of a transcendent One in the depths of our ordinary experience. The religious way of action, typified especially by prophetic religion, lures us toward an unpredictable, though promising, future perfection. And religious silence is so impressed by the human need for perfection that it abandons talk of the perfect altogether for fear of rendering it imperfect. The *via negativa* strips us of all familiar images and thoughts in order to open us to a pure experience of perfection.

By awakening people to a realm of ultimate perfection, however, religion requires a "renunciation" of the familiar world. This does not mean escapism, although that is one of the most serious temptations of religion. Instead, the religious spirit of detachment means we must constantly seek a *wider* world. In the mystical quest for the unknown, religion is a search for inexhaustible depth. But in the apophatic quest for perfection religion is the search for an all-encompassing *breadth*. Religion looks for a *wideness* of vision in which life's disappointments can be reinterpreted and given a new and surprising meaning that we would never discern apart from such an expanded perspective.

Any such widening movement of consciousness can be called *adventure*. And because of its yearning for the boundless breadth of absolute perfection religion may be called an adventure. The heart of religion is trust. Its orientation is toward mystery. But its distinctive style is adventure. Although, as we shall see, much that passes as religion seems undeniably far from adventurous, religion, as a quest for seemingly unattainable perfection, is at heart perhaps the greatest adventure of the human spirit. (Whitehead, 1967a, 191–92)

Adventure may be understood more specifically as *the search for ever more intense forms of ordered novelty*. (Whitehead, 1967b, 252–96) It is the restlessness that moves a process beyond narrow and monotonous order toward wider and more nuanced forms of harmony. Adventure is the expression of a discontent with the banality and narrowness of the familiar world. It goes in search of new forms of harmony.

In other words, the goal of adventure is *beauty*. Beauty, according to Whitehead, is a "harmony of contrasts." What makes things beautiful is that they combine harmony, order and unity on the one side with contrast, complexity and novelty on the other. For example, a great musical symphony combines a rich array of movements into an overall harmony. Without complexity there would be only monotony. Without nuance there would be mere triviality. On the other hand, without an overarching and harmonious arrangement of the component parts there would be utter chaos. To have genuine beauty there must be both order and novelty, harmony and contrast. If the composer of a piece of music were too concerned about harmony the outcome would be tedious. But if the composer were excessively preoccupied with complexity at the expense of unity, the musical composition would degenerate into the unpleasantness of discord. Both monotony and chaos in themselves lack beauty.

Beauty is the harmony of contrasts, and adventure is the quest for more and more intense beauty. Adventure is the struggle to move beyond monotony and chaos toward a wider and richer harmony of contrasts. It is a movement toward the breadth of perfection. But such a quest always implies *risk*. There is always a possibility that the novelty and freshness sought by an adventurous process, as it becomes broader and more complex, will bring about disorder and chaos, at least for a time. A risk of chaos is the price paid for adventure as it moves toward the attainment of wider beauty. Adventure involves danger, even though it promises deeper "enjoyment" also.

Viewed in broad terms, and over a period of thousands of years, religion presents itself to us as an adventure. If we look at it in a sweeping way, it appears as a whole, if not always in its various parts, to embody the quest for more intense versions of ordered novelty. Behind any adventurous movement there is the quest for breadth. And religion is perhaps the most dramatic and far-reaching way in which the quest for the breadth of perfect beauty has been undertaken by human beings. For religion seeks the widest possible synthesis of order and novelty. Such a synthesis may be called "perfection."

Peace

In Whitehead's terminology, the feeling that comes from experiencing perfection is called *peace*. The feeling of peace generally occurs at the end of a long and difficult journey through complexity that culminates in the perception of a wider and more pleasing harmony of contrasts. A flickering sense of "peace" is provided in the feeling one gets at the end of reading a difficult novel or attending a tragic drama. Having gone along with the characters through the twists and turns of their lives, one is given a new sense of the breadth of human experience. While going through the novel or drama we may have wished at times for a simpler plot or a crisper resolution. Less complicated story-lines would have been more immediately gratifying. But too simplistic a narrative would not have produced the satisfaction bestowed by a greater work of art. For the feeling one gets at the conclusion of a well crafted novel or drama is neither frivolous gratification nor despair, but—peace. It is a sense of "fullness." It is a perception that widens our appreciation of life. Peace, in other words, is the impression of having been taken into a continually expanding beauty. An unsurpassable experience of such "peace" is the disposition promised by religious traditions as well.

When one has gone through a difficult life involving joys and tragedies, agonies and ecstasies, ups and downs of many sorts, it may seem at any particular point that one's existence has had little significance. Disappointment, monotony or disorder seems to rule at various times. It would have been better if some things had gone along more smoothly. Or it might have been better if certain other things had not happened. But in retrospect such twists and turns can contribute to the richness of life. We often meet elderly people who in the twilight of their years express the sentiment that they would not trade such a life for anything. They now value their lives, including the rough spots, the precipices along with the heights. From a seasoned perspective they cherish their rough but adventurous journeys more thoroughly than a life undergone without all the contrasts of joy and sorrow. They are happy that they have weathered the storms because their horizons have been widened, their vision of the world enlarged, and their courage deepened in the process. They are at "peace," and often they will say so explicitly.

Religion, especially as the result of its apophatic aspects, promotes something like this state of peace. It does not try to avoid the tragedies of life, but leads instead toward a point in which the experience of tragedy is transformed into a larger picture that evokes the sense of peace. If religion's style is adventure, then one of the most representative religious feelings is that of peace.

Anaesthesia

In contrast to the feeling of peace there is "its bastard substitute," *anaesthesia*, the settling for monotony and triviality when it is appropriate to move on toward more intensely complex order. (Whitehead, 1967b, 284–96) The goal of adventure is the peace that comes with "perfection," but anaesthesia is content with the premature closure of banality. Does not religion also fall here, settling as it often does for monotony, and exhorting us to steer clear of adventure? To a great extent, yes. For religion is concerned not only with the novelty of the unknown. It is also preoccupied with order. And at times the obsession with order dominates and rules out the equally important need for novelty of contrast.

The need for order is one of the most urgent longings shaping human life and consciousness. It has always been so. Given the threat of chaos in our lives and those of our ancestors, it is not surprising that from the beginning our species has devised ways of guaranteeing the order of nature and human social life. And religion has generally provided this guarantee by painting symbolic pictures of a cosmic or sacred order beneath whose protection people can gain the confidence to build a human and social order.

A good illustration of the close connection between the religious sense of cosmic order and the shape of social and political life may be found in Egypt of the pharaohs. Ancient Egyptian religion centered around the sun, the river and the pharaoh. The miracle of the sun's "rebirth" every day, and the annual depositing of fertile soil along the Nile, were so significant for survival that they became the basis of religious life as well. They were matters of "ultimate concern." Sustained by these two natural recurrences, the Egyptians learned to trust that order is victorious over calamity, and they expressed this trust in their myths and rituals. This conviction had to be articulated in the face of the obvious fact of the threat of chaos. For the river was itself often unpredictable and destructive, while the sun's heat could be nearly unbearable at times, causing the precious reserves of water to evaporate. So the river and the sun had to be situated within a sacred cosmic context to guarantee their orderly conduct.

The figure of the pharaoh became the main link between the precarious "natural" world and the trustworthy sacred environment. The pharaoh was himself considered to be a descendant of the gods, the offspring of the sun-god Ra. It was his task daily to celebrate the ritual of awakening the sun-god in the temple. And it was through the pharaoh that the divine cosmic order, called *Ma'at*, was mediated to the people. The visible figure of the pharaoh served to hold chaos at bay, at least in the minds of the Egyptian people. The pharaoh defended Egypt from its enemies. As the high priest of the nation he conducted the rituals celebrating the creation of the world, and he carried the shepherd's staff indicating his and the gods' love of the people. He was quite literally worshipped, considered immortal and given special burial privileges.

Thus the pharaoh's own person sacramentally represented the victory of order over chaos. Just as the religion of hunters and gatherers seeks to transcend the limitations on life by investing so much in the shaman, so the Egyptian people symbolically felt their way through the threatening limitations of drought, heat and death by enshrining a single individual, the pharaoh, in a specially charged position of sacral significance. Since so much of the religious burden was placed on his shoulders it is no wonder that special care would be taken to ensure his immortality. If he were a mere mortal how could he function as such a light to his people? The great pyramids of Egypt, where the pharaohs were entombed, are expressions of the enormous human passion poured into the quest for a way beyond the transience of life toward an ultimately secure order of being.

Whenever the ruler of a nation is perceived to be the incarnation of an ultimate order, this divine aura will give the potentate an extraordinary authority. People will be less inclined to question his (or her) rule if they perceive it as the expression of an eternal principle of order. Pharaoic Egypt is an instance of the *legitimating power of religion*. It exemplifies religion's potential for sanctioning almost any given social or political order, sometimes to the point of excluding all novelty and therefore adventure. Religions give "legitimacy" to social or political order by situating the latter within the framework of a "cosmic" or sacred order. (Berger, 1969) And in doing so they give a semblance of immutability to the imperfect human order. Instead of adventure they uphold sameness. Instead of peace they offer "anaesthesia."

Its special power to provide social and political legitimation for mundane political orders is one of the most important, if controversial, features of religion. We could provide numerous illustrations of it. Nearer to our own times, for example, lie the Holy Roman Empire and the notion of the divine right of kings. Or we might note how the papacy has been able to wield so much political clout at times in its often ragged history, or the way in which the Ayatollah Khomeini was given such high status in Iran because he was understood by so many of his followers to have a special connection with an unchangeable divine order. Whenever the immediate, "secular" order is encompassed by an ultimate, transcendent and sacred order, some of the "eternity" and immutability of the "above" will inevitably seep into the observable order here "below." The religious intuition of an infinite perfection may then be identified with a very imperfect human arrangement. Religions will therefore often justify oppressive forms of human order. Sacred monotony will stand in the way of ultimate perfection. Anaesthesia will be substituted for peace.

Order and Adventure

Through its religious symbols, myths and rituals a people such as the ancient Egyptians finds a way of countering the threat of chaos (in the form of famine, drought or death). And once a plausible way is accepted as appropriate for keeping the threat of chaos under control, then the successful religious cosmology generally gains an enormous staying power in the lives and consciousness of a people or community. Egyptian religion persisted relatively unchanged for more than two thousand years. Even though all religions undergo change, and most of them eventually become fused with others, they are still one of the most change-resistant ingredients of human life and culture. They often seem, therefore, to be utterly opposed to any spirit of adventure.

Why do religions tend to be so conservative? Bowker (1988) explains that whenever a religious group has hit upon what it considers to be a plausible way through the most stubborn obstacles to the continuity of life, it experiences a strong responsibility to pass on its specific "techniques" to others and to subsequent generations so that they might benefit from them also. Any challenges to what has been successful in the past will then be taken as a new invasion of chaos. The need to salvage the order that has "worked" effectively to control chaos will often motivate a religious community to suppress new ideas, and at times it may even lead to the condemnation and execution of aliens or heretical innovators. Persecutions, executions and genocides, along with the suppression of minorities and women, have all been carried out in the name of preserving a religiously upheld order against the importation of novel and alien ways of dealing with limitations.

A compulsion to maintain the *status quo* is an undeniable part of religion. If religion is essentially an adventurous phenomenon in quest of breadth and perfection, in practice it is often, if not usually, linked with the human tendency to maintain stability in very narrow and restrictive ways. Religions often seem to be anything but adventurous. Indeed they are often the very opposite. In what sense then can we say that religion is an adventure?

Religion is the story of a *long* human search for perfection. And like any elaborate story, including that of our universe, it goes through lengthy periods where not much happens. It too awaits special moments where events ripen and come to a head. And at such exceptional times rapid change and exciting revolutions may occur in religion. But then things settle down once again, and a religion may stabilize and remain relatively fixed for centuries. The term adventure may not be applicable, therefore, to every single phase in the story of religion. But no adventure story can sustain the same level of excitement throughout every page or chapter, and this is especially true of religion.

To account for the conservative episodes of the religious story we need only remember how troubling life can be, and how grateful we are whenever order begins to vanquish the chaos that threatens to make life intolerable. Sometimes when things are in special disarray we are willing to settle for almost any form of order, even if it is narrow and restrictive, just to have some clear "space" in which to exist and move about. People are often even willing to make compromises with tyranny if it means the end of confusion, or if it brings an end to revolution and economic decline. This may also explain the appeal that religious cults have in our own day. (See Appendix A) The passion for order, it bears repeating, is one of our most powerful human longings.

And yet, it can also be one of the ugliest. For it can lead to an exclusivity, absolutism and arrogance that weed out the freshness we also need for the sake of a wider beauty. In settling for a monotony that suffocates human creativity, an obsession with harmony suppresses the urge to adventure and the longing for perfection. Correspondingly, there is an ugly side to religion whenever it is reduced to the absolutization of order. We can hardly ignore this religious obsession with order as we look at various ways humanity has dealt with chaos. For while religion exhibits a general trend of adventurousness, there are many episodes in its historical manifestations that frustrate this trend. The same passion for order that drives religion to conquer the threat of chaos can end up as an obsessive patrolling the boundaries of the world so as to keep out any new life. Calling religion an adventure needs to be carefully qualified.

The Longing for Novelty

Nevertheless, the need for order is by no means an adequate explanation of why people act and think in religious ways. For religion also originates in the need for novelty. It is the openness to novelty that makes a process adventurous. Order alone is not enough for the human spirit. What we long for is a *complex* order, *nuanced* unity, *contrast* within harmony, an increasingly *wider* combination of novelty and order. In short, we long for *perfection*. Religion is a quest for this perfection and the peace that goes with it.

For this reason it is questionable to maintain, as many do, that religion is concerned *only* with upholding a given order. Often social sciences give us the impression that this has been the sole function of religions. But even though social and political orders have exploited religion for purposes of sanctioning specific institutions, legitimation is not the only business of religion. Obsession with order may actually be a sign of the death of religion and the beginning of its decline into magic. As its central figures (such as Abraham, Gautama, Moses, Muhammad, Jesus, Luther, St. Francis of Assisi and numerous others) have understood it, religion's authentic style is adventure. It is a quest for more and more intense forms of ordered novelty, a striving for a wider and more inclusive harmony of contrasts. Recall, for example, how many religious figures were rejected as heretical innovators and troublemakers because they disturbed the reigning ideals of order. That religious people often grow weary of novelty and adventure is, of course, a fact of history. And their willingness to acquiesce in monotony needs to be recognized and explained. But an adventurous thread runs, at least precariously, through religion's most important figures and manifestations.

Adventure and Evil

This adventurous quality is already observable in the earliest religious myths about how evil came into the world. The general structure of these myths of evil is repeated over and over in all parts of the religious world. They begin by painting the scene of an "essential" or paradisal situation that prevailed in some "primordial time" before calendrical or historical time began. In this "time beyond time" (exemplified in the story of the Garden of Eden) all things are in order. Complete harmony reigns; there is no suffering; people get along with one another; a paradisal innocence prevails.

And then something catastrophic occurs. It is often triggered by an event that may seem trivial (such as eating an apple, transgressing an artificially fixed barrier, opening a forbidden box, etc.). But this trivial deviance unleashes a suffering that is often cosmic in scope. Upon hearing such myths today our first reaction is likely to be puzzlement at the lack of proportionality between act and result. We wonder how a minor delinquency could open a breach so wide that all the evils of the world would stream forth from it. It is almost as though the potential for evil and suffering was already lurking in the background, waiting for any small aperture in order to explode out into the open. And in fact it seems that the myth-makers themselves often had such an impression also.

A myth from the Dinka tribe in Africa about the origin of evil may serve to illustrate this intuition of impending disaster. According to this myth (as narrated by the scholar of religion, Godfrey Lienhardt) God and humans, sky and earth, originally constituted one harmonious world. God and the sky were connected to humans and the earth by a rope, and people could climb at will into the divine world. There was no death, hunger or suffering in this paradisal situation. The first human beings, a man and a woman, Garang and Abuk, lived a serene, uncomplicated life. They only had to be careful to heed divine instructions not to plant more than a certain amount of grain. But one day the woman "because she was greedy" decided to plant more than the allotted portion. For this purpose she took a long handled hoe to dig up the ground. But the handle of the hoe struck the divinity and he withdrew from the earth. The rope connecting earth and sky was severed, and ever since then the world has been full of misery. (Lienhardt, 33–34)

Notice the elements in this myth: an essential order, a triggering circumstance, and the invasion of evil. It has many features in common with the story of Adam and Eve. There are countless such myths of evil, and all of them move between the poles of an "essential order" on the one hand and an "actual order" of imperfection and frustration on the other.

But they also share a hope for final perfection, for redemption from evil. (Eliade, 1968)

Such myths already exhibit a zest for adventure. They tell of some ineradicable tendency in reality that seeks to break down an initial state of narrow harmony (represented by a primordial "paradise") and undergo an experience of chaos, in order perhaps to widen the boundaries of the universe. While we inevitably have a certain nostalgia for the lost harmony the myths tell about, there is also an appreciation of the adventurous journeying in exile from paradise. This exile is evil and painful, but in the long run it gives breadth to human existence. That is, it augurs a wider peace and perfection that rejects anaesthesia and accepts tragedy as one of its contrasting components. Would we be fully satisfied abiding in a realm of simplistic paradisal harmony? We would experience the security of anaesthesia, not the perfection of peace. Could we endure living indefinitely in a fixed world devoid of the risk of adventure? The myths about the origins and end of evil seem to suggest not. They express our intuition that the "adventure of evil" is almost an inevitable part of the quest for a wider vision. They are aware that tragedy, in spite of its horror, can in the long run give breadth to the beauty of reality. And this in part constitutes their response to the problem of suffering.

Perhaps this is why the Catholic Easter Vigil rite refers to the sin of Adam as a *felix culpa*, a "happy fault" that made possible the wider, more intensely beautiful story of salvation by Christ, the New Adam. Without the breach of paradisal harmony at the time of the beginnings, there would have been no adventurous history of redemption, no Savior of such magnitude. Without the crises and complications that tragedy brings, our concepts of God would be trivial, and our sense of mystery would fade into monotony. The myths of evil, of course, do not justify or celebrate evil. But they do imply that the tragic moments of human life can be transformed into contrasts that enhance the total adventurousness and beauty of the world. It is one of the functions of religion to attune our lives and awareness to this wider beauty.

The Religious Adventure

Therefore, as we look at its various manifestations over the centuries we cannot help being struck also by the strain of adventurous restlessness that characterizes the religious outlook. Its spirit of discontent with the mundane, its relentless urge to forge a way through appearances and superficialities, and its excitement about the unknown—these features make religion perhaps the most adventurous of all the movements of the human spirit. In its revolt against monotony religion is adventure. In its refusal to settle for the familiar and immediate, religion is adventure. In its quest for peace and perfection religion is adventure.

Adventure always implies risk, and there is a definite risk to being religious. Religions at times even demand that we have the courage to stake everything on its intuitions. They teach that in order to find fulfillment we must cease clinging to the illusory security of near-at-hand objects. They invite us to ply our ships on the open sea of mystery as alone proportionate to our deepest strivings. Although the admonition to break free from the familiar dawns only slowly in the course of the individual's religious development, the major traditions deem this transcending of the limits of ordinary perception to be the very core of authentic religious life.

In "primitive" animism and shamanism there may already be the beginnings of the religious search for a perfection beyond the confinements of death and ordinary life. In the several "ways" that later religions have devised to combat our tendency to acquiesce in immediacy there is still more evidence of religion's adventurous character. The "mystical" way exemplified by Hinduism invites us to look beneath the surface of our experience, to join the long search for a perfect unity and inexhaustible depth beyond the deceptive multiplicity of appearances. The "way of silence and renunciation" represented especially by Buddhism challenges us, perhaps more than any other way, to cease our clinging to things as though they were permanent. For such clinging narrows our lives and inhibits the human adventure toward the breadth of true perfection. Only in letting go of our securities, in detachment from what we mistakenly think to be enduring things, do we find fulfillment.

Buddhism knows all about our longing for the security of something solid to hold onto. After all, the Buddha himself spent thirty years of his life "clinging" to luxury and his family's established name and place in society. But Buddhism advises us that such security is insufficient and that genuine peace comes only from letting go of the illusion of permanence. In such advice there is a protest against the monotony that would result from a premature unity and finality imposed on our lives. The phenomenon of Buddhism will forever stand out, in terms of adventure, as the negation of premature harmony. It revolts against the ideas of substance, soul and even God not because it has no interest in ultimate perfection, but because it is sensitive to the monotony and triviality resulting from our typical religious attempts to represent this perfection in meager and inappropriate ways.

Its restraint about God-talk does not mean that Buddhism is disinterested in perfection. The Buddha's thirst for enlightenment, salvation or *nirvana* shows that he is not unlike the rest of us. But it is noteworthy that he greets with silence all our attempts at speaking positively about the ultimate. Those who look at religion in the long run may see great wisdom in the Buddhist silence. The Buddha is the ally of those who seek perfection. Within the larger human quest for perfection there is a need for moments of silence lest we settle too early for a sketch in place of the whole picture. Buddhism and the *via negativa* provide this respite as they seek to guarantee the breadth of our religious visions.

The *bodhisattva* actualizes religious adventure in the refusal of solitary enjoyment. This exemplar of compassion refuses the premature experience of *nirvana*. The *bodhisattva* rejects self-serving anaesthesia and seeks a peace that can only accompany the "wider vision" embracing all humans (and all living beings for that matter). Whitehead speaks of the tendency of humans and of their religions at times to acquiesce in monotony, to "substitute a sketch for the whole picture." Our natural need for order and stability can obscure our deeper need for "perfection." Buddhist teachings are especially sensitive to the stagnation stemming from our clinging to low-grade forms of order. And in Mahayana Buddhism the ideal of the *bodhisattva* epitomizes the revolt against monotony. This ideal of universal compassion seeks to widen our world considerably beyond the narrowness of self-interested goal-seeking. In reaching out to enfold the entirety of life, the *bodhisattva* stands at the cutting edge of the religious quest for perfection.

In this connection we may conjecture that the impetus toward selflessness that we find in all the great traditions resonates well with the ideal of adventure. In their nearly unanimous espousal of the ideal of love, religions express their discontent with any vision of reality that centers on the individual's own egotistic desires. Their common advocacy of the "renunciation" of selfishness is not intended to make us uneasy (as it often does, at least initially) but to expand our vision of reality so that a deeper enjoyment of beauty and peace might eventually become possible. Whenever it is linked with self-giving love religion shows itself to be an adventure.

The "way of hope" or the "prophetic" style of religion held out by Judaism, Christianity and Islam also illustrates the spirit of adventure. The prophets demand that we widen our vision of social reality to include the poor and oppressed who are normally left out of our narrow political and economic designs. The prophets do not allow us to settle for any "separate peace" that ignores the totality of human conflict and suffering. And they encourage us, as Abraham's God did, to venture forth into the unknown mystery of an unpredictable future. They require that we abandon the stultifying safety of the past and present for the sake of the limitless future of God.

Conclusion

In the story of religion there is so strong a theme of uneasiness with monotony and sheer ordinariness that it is impossible to avoid the suggestion that we are dealing here with adventure in the boldest sense. But what starts out as adventure, as we know from our own experience, can eventually degenerate into a loss of enthusiasm. The effort to sustain any valorous expedition can sag. And the same is true of our species' religious journey. Religions can grow weary of their voyage into mystery and take refuge in the safety and banality of the familiar. Religions can often lose touch with the primordial human zest for perfection. They may become transformed into a style of life and thought that does little more than sanction the social or political status quo. Religion can lose its soul, and Whitehead thought that this is what has been happening to it in the modern age. "Religion," he said, "is tending to degenerate into a decent formula wherewith to embellish a comfortable life." (1967a, 188)

Nevertheless, this same philosopher thought he could still see through to religion's authentic core. In its strongest manifestations religion provides a "commanding vision" that arouses its devotees to move beyond complacency. Religious worship is ". . . not a rule of safety—it is an adventure of the spirit, a flight after the unattainable. The death of religion comes with the repression of the high hope of adventure." (1967a, 192)

12.

Morality

Religion seeks perfection not only in the sense of beauty, but also in the sense of "goodness." Over the centuries of its development religion has become more and more explicitly associated with the most intense expression of goodness known to humans, namely, unselfish love. In its major manifestations religion has increasingly intuited an unspeakable compassion at the heart of mystery. It has insisted upon the essentially loving character of ultimate reality. And it invites its followers to body forth that goodness in their own lives. Indeed, it holds that we can become deeply aware of the compassionate nature of ultimate reality only as our own lives are themselves transformed into examples of compassion. This motif occurs not only in the prophetic religions, but also in the religions of China and India. And the notion that sacred reality is caring and compassionate is also found abundantly in the oral traditions of primal religion.

Because of the frustrations and tragedies of existence we have a natural longing for reassurance. And the sacramental aspects of religion provide numerous hints that reality is ultimately trustworthy in spite of all the threats that beset us. We also have a natural tendency to unify, to seek a *oneness* or coherence within the multiplicity of experience. Mystical religion blossoms out of this unifying tendency, and assures us of the reality of an ultimate transcendent unity that holds all things together in spite of any impression we might have that the world is made up only of unconnected moments and meaningless fragments. Likewise, human consciousness has a spontaneous inclination to seek wider and more intense beauty. In the previous chapter we noted how religion grows out of this spontaneous longing for fulfillment. In its adventure toward "perfection" religion seeks an ultimate "breadth" of vision that gives fresh perspective and meaning to individual experiences. In a special way the religious "way of silence" expresses this need for breadth and a distaste for narrowness of vision.

Yet another of our natural human aspirations is the attraction we feel toward *goodness*. Goodness is embodied especially in human love. We are naturally attracted to people who love and care for us. In some way, it seems, religion also grows out of the human capacity for and attraction to love. The "way of action" is an especially noteworthy illustration of the connection between religion and the impulse to care for and be cared for by others.

Once again, however, we must be careful not to identify religion with love or with the natural attraction to goodness. These are inclinations of people as such, and they can flourish quite independently of religion. Many non-religious people are naturally much more generous and caring than religious people. The love of goodness is quite instinctive in their lives. Many of them see no value in religion as a way to make them more loving, and they do not need it to satisfy their own longing to be cared for. And some skeptics even maintain that religion, by focusing on a totally other dimension, distracts us from the love we owe to our fellow human beings in our immediate world.

Nevertheless, if we are looking for a place where religion links up with our normal human aspirations, we can hardly find a clearer point of contact than the human capacity for love. By "love" is meant here nothing more complicated than the response to goodness. If "enjoyment" is the typical response to beauty, then "love" is the natural response to the "good." Religion, at least in most of its major manifestations, posits an *ultimate* goodness that embraces and endorses the natural human potential for love.

Religion and Morality

The human inclination toward the good comes to expression in a "natural" way in what is known as "morality." In its best sense morality implies a concern for others. It designates the attitude and actions that seek to make life satisfactory and enjoyable for others as well as ourselves. It also connotes the capacity to sacrifice one's self-interest for the sake of the wider community. Such a moral capacity is given with human nature, though it needs to be awakened by our life in common with others who express love for us. It is doubtful whether we would have any serious moral inclinations without having had the experience of being valued by others. But one need not be religious in order to be deeply moral.

Obviously there are selfish and "unethical" urges in us as well. But even the most immoral among us still have a glimmer of moral aspiration, however fragile it may be at times. Even mobsters have codes of conduct and are capable of experiencing compassion and even guilt. To be human is to be able to distinguish between what we are and what we could be, between our actual state and some ideal state of being. The capacity to imagine goodness or "value" makes us capable of acting morally, and of experiencing guilt when we have violated our sense of the good. Different cultures may have different ways of representing and grading what is good or valuable. But the capacity for moral aspiration is essential to being human. What then is the connection between religion and this instinct for morality?

At times it almost seems that religion and morality are indistinguishable. For religions face not only toward mystery but also toward the world in which people live their everyday lives. They are concerned not only with awakening us to a sense of the sacred, but also with shaping our conduct in the world. It is hard to find a religion that is not interested, to some extent at least, in ethical affairs. Even the most world-denying faiths are aware that religion has implications for social and political life. At times religions even seem virtually identical with codes of ethical and social conduct. However, the close association of religion with morality does not mean that the two are synonymous. And since people can be quite moral without being religious, the mistaking of one for the other is likely to make religion eventually seem irrelevant.

The "way of action," however, does make conduct an intrinsic aspect of religion. Earlier we noted that one of the four main religious ways of responding to the sense of mystery is action. Transformative action in the world is not just something religious people do in addition to being religious. It is in fact itself religion. The prophets, for example, considered working for justice to be itself a form of worship superior to the offering of sacrifice or the performance of other ritual observances. But even for the prophets and other religious activists the specifically religious quality of activity in the world cannot be sustained without a living connection to the sacramental, mystical and apophatic aspects of religious tradition. If the "way of action" loses its primal connection with the other three strands of the religious cord, and begins to unravel on its own, it then becomes no more than secularistic ethics. Being religious means more than simply acting morally.

Religion and morality may almost always walk hand in hand, but this does not mean that they are equivalent. It is quite possible for a person to have a strongly developed sense of mystery or the sacred and at the same time to be a thorough scoundrel morally speaking. (Jacob, 162) But because morality and religion are so intimately related, they are often identi-

fied with each other. The Bible and the Qur'an are filled with passages
where God is portrayed as one who gives specific moral directives, and so
Jews, Muslims and Christians have spoken of God's "moral will." And
they have referred to disobedience to the commandments as "sin." However, the notion of "sin" is itself an indication of the fact that being
religious adds some "mysterious" quality to the fact of being simply immoral. Sin implies the violation of an ultimate, transcendent *goodness*. In a
religious context when one person injures another more is at stake than
just the harm done to the other person. A "sacred order" has been violated. In the prophetic traditions when someone is called a "sinner," this is
not the same as being called an "immoral person." And being "righteous"
in the biblical sense is not quite the same as simply being an upright
individual. Both sin and righteousness are considered to be specific modes
of relationship to ultimate mystery, and not just qualities of human conduct. Language about sin and righteousness signifies that religion is not
reducible to morality. (Gustafson, 125–54)

Religion and the Stages of Moral Development

In order to clarify the relationship between religion and morality we
must first take note of the fact that there are degrees of moral development, and that "morality" can mean different things at different stages.
Recently there has been much discussion of the various levels of maturity
involved in the development of moral awareness from childhood to adult-
hood. People only gradually and sometimes with great difficulty arrive at
the point of mature moral existence. The new theories about graduated
moral growth are of considerable importance for our question concerning
religion's relationship to morality. (Kohlberg, Fowler)

It is convenient to delineate three general phases of typical moral
development. They may be called "pre-conventional morality," "conventional morality" and "post-conventional morality." (Thompson) Needless
to say, these three types are imprecise designations, only vaguely indicative
of the actual moral growth of any particular individual. But in a general
way they are useful and valid indicators of the possibility of becoming
more refined in the difficult art of moral discernment.

(a) In its most primitive or "pre-conventional" form human conduct is
governed by a system of rewards and punishments. This kind of morality
is not shaped by a sense of what is universally good and worthwhile in
itself, but by fear of punishment if we violate certain "taboos," and hope of
some reward if we obey the restrictions laid upon us. At this undeveloped
stage we may seem to be acting very ethically, while inside we have little

appreciation of the real value of our actions. We simply want to avoid pain and receive gratification.

This is the kind of morality present in very young children as well as in psychologically stunted adolescents and adults. Sometimes moral development remains arrested at this stage, and perhaps none of us ever completely outgrows this "taboo" sort of morality. Aspects of it continue to lie buried in the moral consciousness of even the most ethically enlightened people.

There is also a certain kind of childish religiosity that goes hand in hand with this primitive level of moral development. Those stuck at this immature level are inclined to interpret "God" primarily as a source of moral directives. For them the sacred is wrapped up with rules, rewards and punishments. Often, when they are ready to grow out of this phase of morality, they are also tempted to reject "religion," since they have identified it so one-sidedly with moral taboos which they may later find tiresome and restrictive. It is no exaggeration to say that much modern atheism has dismissed the idea of the sacred because of religion's close connection, in the minds of many believers as well as skeptics, with this taboo morality. Thus if religion is not carefully distinguished from "pre-conventional morality" it will eventually also become repugnant to those whose moral life has grown mature enough not to need the enticement of rewards or the threat of retribution.

(b) A second phase of moral development—call it "conventional" morality—is characterized by the need to belong to, and be accepted by, a social group, whether it be one's family, classmates, fraternity, sorority, place of work, country or even church. At this stage we may no longer need rewards and punishments to motivate us. To some extent at least we may have outgrown pre-conventional morality with its rewards and punishments. Instead we shape our conduct on the basis of what the group to which we wish to belong deems significant for its integrity and survival. Being a member of such a community of interest fulfills an inner need to mold our identity by sharing life with others. Here we are likely to follow an ethical "code" derived from what our esteemed social peers and other significant people consider to be appropriate. In other words, we allow right and wrong to be determined more by the group to which we belong than by appreciation of the inherent merits of a course of action. And often we follow the group ethic without at all questioning its judgments. We so badly want to be accepted that we are willing to go along with the reigning style of behavior, even when it becomes oppressive and narrowly self-interested. Our ethical conduct is then determined primarily by what is conventional rather than by sincere reflection on the correspondence of our actions with less precarious standards of value.

Some moral theorists observe that most of us remain mired in this "conventional" phase of moral development. We may not need elaborate systems of reward and punishment, but we do want acceptance by those in our social circle. And so we are willing to sacrifice a great deal of our individuality for the sake of this acceptance. We will be quite "moral" for the group's sake, even if it means smothering in ourselves the sparks of a more mature ethical sensitivity.

This second type of morality is resistant to criticism, whether from without or from within. It refuses to open itself to the challenge of alternative moral visions or of individuals in the group. Its main objective is to preserve the group identity. And for that reason it repudiates those who question this identity. Many Nazis, as they were leading their fellow humans to the gas chambers, probably thought they were doing right in "purifying" the human species of what they considered to be contaminating elements. Some may even have felt morally good about themselves because they were dutifully following orders, pleasing their superiors and fellow citizens, experiencing a strong sense of bonding and belonging. Most never seriously questioned Hitler's policies. In the conventional phase of moral development one might be a very decent and moral person, at least from the point of view of reigning standards of morality. But one can be moral in this conformist manner without ever internalizing values that would allow a true individuality to emerge distinct from the mentality of the crowd.

Conventional, like taboo, morality can get mixed up with religion in such a way as to become virtually indistinguishable from it. And because moral development often comes to a stop at this second level, the religion that accompanies it often remains no more than a divine sanction for the current ethos. Conventional morality is more than willing to invoke religious authority for the sake of legitimating its ethical style. And if "God" is understood as the one who has from all eternity authored the conventional moral code, then religious belief merges so intimately with the ethical life that it abandons any capacity for criticizing a society's morality. This wedding of religion and morality goes hand in hand with what we called "anaesthesia" in the preceding chapter. So much of the actual religious life of humanity is associated with conventional morality that it is not surprising so many of us have a hard time distinguishing religion from morality. Were it not for the fact that the most important persons in the history of religion are themselves so often anti-conventional, we might be tempted to see religion as little more than a "decent formula embellishing a comfortable life style." (Whitehead, 1967a, 188)

(c) Finally, though, there is a "higher" phase of moral development in which one does what is right for no other reason than that it seems intrinsically and unconditionally "good." This "post-conventional" morality flows out of the experience that one has been grasped by "universal values" that one must obey regardless of the consequences. Here our moral life is a response to (an "answering back" to) the summons of "eternal" values that place unconditional demands upon us. If we consider an action to be good we take it, no matter what happens to us. We have the sense of inviolable values existing "above" the plane of conventional moral consensus, and we feel these values calling us to an unswerving commitment to them.

Needless to say, it is difficult to sustain this level of moral existence. The fear of punishment and the longing for rewards remain stamped on us as powerful shapers of our conduct. The pressures to conform are enormous. And yet there are clear examples of people reaching this third level of moral development. Even though they usually come into conflict with those whose moral life is shaped by the first two levels, they maintain their conviction that some intrinsic goodness has made a claim on them. They cannot resist this goodness, even if, as occasionally happens, it leads to their death.

This stage of morality needs no extrinsic motivation of the sort that dominates in the first two phases. It is a truly "autonomous" morality. Here we act without consideration of rewards and punishment, and without undue concern about what those in our social circle might think of us. We feel that we have been addressed by inviolable values not of our own choosing. An easy example is that of Martin Luther King, Jr. The famous civil rights leader was grasped by the value of universal justice and could apparently take no other path in his life than one of obedience to it. He observed that the conventional racist "morality" was in violation of what he took to be a transcendent value. And so inevitably his program of inclusive human rights came into conflict with a conventional culture based on the unjust exclusion of ethnic minorities.

When our moral consciousness is shaped by what seem to us to be "eternal" values we may often find ourselves in conflict with conventional morality. But we are willing to sacrifice our need for social approval to what strikes us as universally and eternally good. However, we may then have to suffer the judgment by conventional standards that our moral stance is disruptive and immoral. Jesus, for example, was thought to be a criminal, a heretic and a blasphemer. He was found morally guilty and fully deserving of execution. The prophets, Joan of Arc, Mahatma Gandhi, Desmond Tutu and countless other courageous rebels have all been accused of upsetting the "moral" order, the "rightness" of things. A post-conventional morality often appears immoral from the point of view of conventional and pre-conventional morality. But a post-conventional morality flows autonomously out of a deep inward conviction of goodness.

And the sense of being embraced by this goodness can provide the courage to pursue an ethical ideal even when one is being assailed from all sides by those who have refused to go beyond levels one and two.

Recently a leader in South Africa angrily denounced the anti-apartheid movement for "disturbing our way of life." He considered the protests of black leaders to be quite immoral, for if their values of a more inclusive social justice were ever to become realized in that country it would inevitably bring about enormous upheavals. Many people would have to suffer a drastic restructuring of their lives. From the point of view of "conventional" morality this threat to a given social order seems to be immoral. And so it is denounced vigorously—in the name of "goodness" and "morality." And if one's conception of God and church are intertwined with conventional morality, as they often are, then the protests of a liberation movement will also be interpreted as contrary to "religion."

"Religious legitimation" gives a seemingly eternal sanction to the conventional order. And when injustice and evil are built into this order, religion simply places a sacred seal on the exclusivity and narrowness that a post-conventional morality would find contrary to ultimate values. Post-conventional morality is forced to be critical of "religion" whenever the idea of God or the sacred supports policies that violate what is taken to be an inviolable goodness.

But religion need not be associated only with conventional morality, even though the two are probably linked together more often than not. An example of a post-conventional religious and moral commitment may be observed in the life and death of an obscure Austrian peasant named Franz Jägerstätter. Jägerstätter resisted inscription into Hitler's army because the policies of the Nazis violated the values he associated with his rather simple Catholic faith. His friends and fellow Catholics, including members of the clergy, encouraged him to abandon his stubborn resistance. They did not consider it unethical for him simply to go along with what everyone else was doing at the time. Many acquaintances even encouraged him to do his "duty" by conforming to the popular standards of accepting what history was doing through Hitler. Jägerstätter, however, refused. He rebelled against the conventional moral wisdom. Consequently, he was apprehended and executed as a traitor. Recorded history has lost count of the many others who, like Jägerstätter, have pursued the more difficult moral path of commitment to an eternal goodness in the face of what is judged conventionally good.

This example demonstrates how what is considered moral at levels one or two might be considered immoral at level three. And what is considered moral at the post-conventional level may be taken as immoral by those firmly planted in the first two phases. Furthermore, it shows how the idea of "God" or "the sacred" plays a distinct role at each level. For pre-conventional morality God is essentially the source of taboos. For conventional morality God is the sanctifier of the status quo. But for post-conventional morality God is the ground upon which one stands in order, like Franz Jägerstätter, to criticize and transcend the conventional morality. Our whole discussion of morality and religion requires that we keep these distinctions in mind.

The famous psychologist C. G. Jung held the opinion that religion usually functions only to uphold a conventional morality. He referred to this use of religion as "creed." By this expression he meant that religion— and he was speaking especially of Christianity in the West—is little more than the sacral codification of a style of life based on a conformist morality. The temptation to conform is enormous today. In totalitarian societies, Jung observes, there is clear evidence of how willing people are to hand over their freedom for the sake of approval by the state. And in capitalist countries people at large allow their values to be shaped by consumer fads and other trends whose superficiality they seldom notice. In the case of the latter religion merely endorses such conformist trends. Religion as "creed" uncritically upholds conventional morality.

But, unlike Sigmund Freud and other critics of religion, Jung was aware of religion's capacity also to foster a post-conventional morality. If it is properly internalized and understood, religion can contribute to the process of personal and moral maturation. A personal relationship to transcendent reality, Jung argued, can give the individual a solid ground to stand on outside of the conformist pressures of modern society. A post-conventional religion can thereby support a post-conventional morality.

Jung also observed that the state, especially in communist countries, is often afraid of religion's potential for giving the individual an identity other than that approved of by the state itself. The state fears that if individuals have a basis of values outside of the official ideology, this might give them a ground for dissenting from any political and social system that conflicts with those personally ingrained values. Thus the state often tries to rob the individual of any source of criticism independent of the state itself. It may do so by overt religious persecution, as in communist societies. Or it may take pains to ensure that religion remains a purely private affair. If religion stays out of the public forum its ideals and reformist impulses can be domesticated and rendered innocuous. In eastern Europe, for example, communist governments seek to immunize the state against the criticism of religious people. And in Western capitalist systems religion is often made ineffective by being turned into a purely private affair with no political implications. Jung, however, insists that religion can nevertheless sometimes function as support for those individuals who resist the pressures of political conformism.

So religion, like morality, is riddled with ambiguity. It may be useful for us to distinguish three general phases of religious development parallel to those of moral development. (Barnes, 1986) First, there is a pre-conventional religion corresponding to the taboo type of morality. Here religion is very much a matter of fear and infantile desire. In the second place, there is a conventional sort of religion built around what is socially acceptable. This style of religion may assist the process of socialization, but it will usually resist the process of individuation. Thirdly, and perhaps much more rarely, there is also a post-conventional way of being religious. If one's life is determined by this kind of religion it can often lead one into conflict with those whose religion is pre-conventional or conventional.

It bears repeating that the most influential figures in the history of religion have belonged to this third variety, and their religious movements have been bitterly contested primarily by those whose religion is based on fear and obsession with a particular social order. Furthermore, religions that originate in the post-conventional insights of exceptional personalities eventually face the temptation to regress toward a conventional or pre-conventional style. In that case internal conflicts will develop within a tradition between those who want to keep alive the revolutionary spirit of its origins and those who want only to preserve the status quo.

Morality and God

In our post-conventional devotion to such values as love, peace or justice there is something very much like the religious person's surrender to God, Allah or Brahman. We feel grasped by a transcendent goodness, that is, by some framework of unconditional values existing independently of our own desires and preferences. In our encounter with these values we experience a *demand* upon us that cannot be explained in terms of taboos and conventions. For we are willing to commit ourselves to them regardless of such extrinsic considerations. It is as though a transcendent "goodness" were inviting us into its embrace and seeking a submission of our lives in service to it. It seems as if we were "answering back" to some mysterious summoning from beyond the plane of purely human existence. Such a response is almost indistinguishable from religion.

However, this response to universal values happens in the lives of non-religious as well as religious people. So it may not be fitting to identify religion, even at this third level, with morality. It would be insensitive of us to call those people religious who insist they are not. Sometimes, of course, the refusal by morally mature individuals to accept the label "religious" occurs because "religion" for them means only a pre-conventional or conventional way of existing. Understandably they divorce their post-conventional moral commitment from the immaturity of religion as they understand it. But beyond this, many morally mature individuals still have no use for religion, even in a post-conventional form. There is no need for them to think of God or the sacred in relationship to their morality.

In the final section of this book we shall return to some of the questions generated by this critical refusal. But we may observe even at this point that there are characteristics of a post-conventional "responsibility" that make it hard for us to overlook completely its "religious" demeanor even in the case of so-called "atheists." For the values that move such morally mature people seem to have an "a priori" status. They do not seem to originate in human caprice or convention. Rather they seem to be "already out there," inscribed in the nature of things.

Where does this apparent universality of post-conventional values come from? The skeptic, who denies the existence of an eternal source of values, would have to reply that they originate in a social consensus of sufficient strength and longevity to give our revered values the semblance of exceptional authority and "universality." As far as the skeptical point of view is concerned, even our highest values are only the products of social and linguistic conditionings.

Obviously, religious thinkers will not be satisfied by this answer. They would reply that if we were seriously convinced that "universal" values originate only in agreements among humans, then such values could no longer make an unconditional claim on us. This would be true no matter how many centuries the ethical consensus has endured. Mere agreement among humans is not enough to give values their absolute authority over our consciences. If we truly thought, for example, that the imperative to do justice or to care for our neighbors stemmed only from social or psychic mechanisms it would be too flimsy to exact the passionate surrender we often give to it. In order for values to function in a post-conventional manner we must respond to them as though they had their origin in something more solid than mere tradition or conventional agreement.

Religion, therefore, requires a timeless basis for the goodness that inspires us to morality. When our values truly move us to respond with consistency, without concern for rewards and punishment and without demanding the approval of others, they seem to be rooted in a transcendent realm of "goodness" that persists in a way that time and human opinion cannot obliterate. Goodness must originate in an eternal divine mystery "beyond" time, place and custom. Awareness of and submission to goodness seem to require a religious interpretation.

However, post-conventional morality is not simply identical with religion. In spite of its reverential obedience to universally valid norms of conduct it still lacks some of the qualities essential to religion. Religions, after all, require the acknowledgement of a dimension of inexhaustible mystery. Morality, on the other hand, is possible in the absence of any such mystical intuition. Furthermore, most religions also talk about the gods or God. Moral action does not in itself require thinking about God. Religion, as we have been interpreting it, requires at least some degree of all four of its elements: symbolism, mysticism, silence and action. For religion it is not enough simply to talk abstractly about universal values that guide our action. Religions need a sense of mystery on the one hand and concrete sacramental representations of it on the other. And they also require a sense of infinite distance from the ultimate, so that we are at times reduced to silence. These sacramental, mystical and apophatic aspects are not necessarily present in post-conventional morality, so it is misleading to identify religion even with the most highly developed ethical sense. When action is divorced from sacrament, mystery and reverential silence it becomes mere morality. When it is undertaken in consort with the other three, then it is religious.

Conclusion

Both morality and religion grow out of our awareness of goodness. Religion, however, seeks out a *ground* for the goodness that arouses the moral instinct. Talk about God and the use of specific symbolic representations is indispensable in this religious search. For religion, the quality of goodness in reality must be established by something mysteriously transcendent, but at the same time concretely real. Religion is distinct from the simple awareness of goodness. For it needs, in addition, a sacred order, or a deity (or sometimes deities) from whom the goodness emanates. Religion goes beyond morality and looks for an unshakeable, and often personal, sacred source of the goodness that awakens our moral sensitivities. It differs even from post-conventional morality in that it requires a divine basis of the values to which we commit ourselves.

PART IV

Critiques of Religion

13.

Secularism

Is there in fact an ultimate ground of trust? Is there an inexhaustible mystery seeking us out, as the mystics testify? Is there an ultimate fulfillment or state of perfection beyond the disappointment and frustration of our ordinary experience? Does our attraction to goodness entail the reality of God?

The extravagant claims of religion beg for a critical examination. And the questions we have just asked can push us further toward an understanding of what religion is. In this final section therefore we shall raise questions about the plausibility of religious interpretations of reality. Though we shall once again be looking at the four distinct ways of religion, in the final analysis we are dealing here with only one simple question: is there really anything to religion? We may begin with the question about religious reassurance. Granted that we humans need to base our lives on trust, is there any reason to posit, as religions usually do, an *ultimate* ground of reassurance beyond or deeper than our natural and secular environment?

Secularism

Secularism denies that we need to go beyond the natural and social world to find the sources of confidence that can allow us to accept our existence with confidence. Derived from the Latin word *saeculum* (which means "world"), secularism is the conviction that "this world," the immediate environment available to ordinary experience and scientific investigation, is all there is to reality. Secularism therefore rejects any idea of God or "ultimate reality." Reference to a transcendent ground of trust, such as is indicated by the word "God," is entirely superfluous. Furthermore, religion is an impoverishment of our life in this world.

Just what happened in the history of human consciousness that made this secularist dismissal of religion possible? What factors produced the cultural climate in which many people can now affirm so confidently that "this world" exhausts the limits of reality? After all, throughout most of the past thirty-five thousand years humans have taken for granted the reality of the sacred. And for the past three thousand years or so countless religious people have had a very pronounced sense of an ultimately unknowable divine mystery that makes nature and secular reality seem anything but final. Why then is secularism such an attractive option for many people today?

In part, secularism is a natural reaction to the emphasis placed by religious traditions, especially in their mystical and ascetical aspects, on the idea of a totally "other world." Most of the great religions since the axial period have proclaimed doctrines of detachment and withdrawal from the secular sphere. They have taught that our true destiny lies elsewhere. Secularism rebels against the ideal of withdrawal from this world. A radical other-worldliness seems to devalue nature and history. And so secularism understandably rejects what it considers an unnecessary flight from the goodness of the world.

In addition, for the past century or so a new sense of the earth and of its enormous possibilities has stimulated the secularist interpretation. Among many secularists there is now an unprecedented conviction that humans have a purely this-worldly future, and that we can work together, without the help of any supernatural influences, to transform the earth so as to make it a tolerable and fulfilling place in which to live. There are many reasons for this new attitude: the rise of humanism, science and technology, as well as economic, social and political developments. But standing out above all is the recognition that we live in a world that is moving, a world-in-process, with a future of its own. The impression given by science that the earth is evolving, and the modern conviction that politics and technology can help us shape our world into a suitable habitat have given people a fresh hope for the future of the earth itself. Now there looms before us a new horizon, not that of an other-worldly, but of a purely this-worldly future. Excitement about the development of our planet has gradually replaced the former urge to withdraw from the world. (Teilhard de Chardin, 272–82)

The medieval European world-view, by contrast, focused on the idea of the "other world." Our terrestrial abode was perceived in the popular religious mind and in much theology as not really leading anywhere itself. At most it was a stage upon which the human drama could be played out, not a place that could itself be transformed into utopia. It was the context for the soul's proving itself worthy to live eventually in heaven. In other words, it was a "soul school" in which people were expected to work out their salvation. It did not seem to have a significant destiny in its own right.

The influence of Plato and other-worldly spiritualities had for centuries convinced Christians and other theists that the material cosmos is quite dispensable in God's plans. People had been encouraged to turn their attention in a contemplative way toward the spiritual world beyond this material one. The soul's true abode is heaven, and this material world is merely a temporary way-station for the human pilgrimage. When the irrepressible question of the purpose of life arose in this "medieval" context it was easily answered in terms of images of the "other world." Our true destiny lies utterly beyond "this world." Literature on journeys to the next world abounded in the Middle Ages, and it held great command over the religious imaginations of people. The classic example, and one of the most influential bodies of religious writing ever composed, is the *Divine Comedy* of Dante Alighieri (1265–1321). In his graphic depiction of heaven, hell and purgatory Dante creatively synthesized the other-worldly preoccupations of an entire epoch, and the results of his work resonate throughout Western culture to this day.

However, with the development of modern science the Dantean vision of the soul's journey to the "other world" began to come under question, and the cosmology it implied no longer seemed believable to many learned people. The Copernican discovery that our earth is not the center of the universe shattered the cosmic scheme set forth by Dante and others before him. The earth was no longer a fixed point around which the rest of the universe revolved. Modern discoveries of astronomy showed our earth itself to be moving, and not a stationary platform for the performance of the human soul-making drama.

Furthermore, after Darwin, in this age of modern biology and physics, educated people have become even more attentive to the dynamic character of all physical reality. We now know that we live in a world-in-the-making, and this makes us wonder where *this* world might be going, if anywhere. "This world" suddenly has the possibility of itself undergoing a process of transformation that was formerly inconceivable. And we can no longer view our own species separately from the fifteen billion years of pre-human cosmic evolution. Humanity too is in the process of being fashioned by evolution. Our "souls" are no longer easily detachable from our bodies and from the earth out of which we are said to have evolved. The cosmological visions out of which all the great traditions were born have now been devastated by modern science.

Is it possible to plant a fresh religious fervor in the soil of the new cosmologies developing after Darwin and molecular biology, after Einstein and Max Planck, after Freud and neuroscience? Is there still room for a sacramental interpretation of the world? Secularists seriously doubt it, and they urge us to focus simply on this dynamic world with its own inherent potential for further evolution. They insist that religious symbolism is only an escapist human fabrication, not a way of "seeing through" to an ultimate ground of trust. There is no apparent need to go beyond the limits of this world for the promise and resources that can allow us to live confident and contented lives.

The Appeal of Secularism

Traditionally religions have commanded so much devotion partly because of their ability to provide reassurance in spite of the anxiety we experience in our lives. But now, the secularist argument goes, we have more and more purely secular means of confronting human anguish. We have pushed back, to some extent at least, the threat of suffering and even death. Who knows what further progress we will make in the future? It is our scientific and technological expertise, not religion, that has allowed this to happen, and there are no apparent limits to what our newly acquired skills can accomplish. Thus religion may no longer be needed to provide the reassurance we seek in the face of anxiety and suffering. Religion is "emotionally" superfluous.

Religion must have always been partly effective in confronting human suffering, or else it would not have survived to the extent that it has. It has given its devotees systems of symbols, stories and concepts that make at least some sense of human agony. Preliterate religious rituals, sacrifices and myths consoled people for their losses and pains. Hinduism has allowed many of its followers to interpret solitary suffering as part of an unreal world of *maya* that can be overcome when this illusory world is absorbed into the ultimate unity of all things. Buddhism's success has been a consequence of its directly addressing the problem of pain and disappointment. And prophetic religions have gladdened their followers by giving them hope in a divine promise, and by bestowing on human suffering a higher meaning. Such interpretations as these have comforted many in times of pain and in the face of death. It is safe to say that most of our human predecessors benefited in some way from religious "solutions" to their suffering.

To a great extent, however, modern medicine has been able to alleviate physical suffering, and it promises to do an even better job in the future. The threats of a sometimes hostile natural world can also be tamed by modern technology, so that we do not have to resort to ritual appeasement of the deities in order to survive. In short, many of the circumstances that gave religion a reason for existing in the past no longer seem to be serious limitations for us today.

Moreover, we now have numerous ways of dealing with mental suffering as well as physical. Various forms of psychotherapy and psychopharmacology have alleviated human distress. Pathological anxiety and depression, for example, are known to respond to certain chemical compounds. In fact, many psychiatrists now think that our mental problems are largely reducible to organic dysfunction or physico-chemical imbalances in the nervous system, or anomalies in the genetic make-up of certain individuals. And the environmental factors that contribute to mental illness can also be changed for the better. As medical technology continues to become more sophisticated human anguish, whether physiological, mental or environmental, will be treatable by purely medical or social techniques.

If this turns out to be true, we may well wonder whether religions will continue to be "relevant" in any way to the sufferings of human life. What might religions, with their sacramental reference to a transcendent basis of trust, still have to offer us, if anything? If our own secular and scientific techniques can deal so effectively with suffering, what justification would there possibly be for keeping alive any vestiges of the ancient religious interpretations of life and sorrow?

For secularists there can be no sound reason for halting the disappearance of religion. Religious "solutions" to physical and mental suffering divert us away from the purely human project of eliminating occasions for pain. Resorting to religious methods actually slows down the secular-scientific enterprise of bringing about a lasting answer to human misery. Trusting in "Something" or "Someone" beyond nature and history is a poor substitute for the actual relief provided now by science and medicine.

The Problem of Anxiety

Such a radical point of view, however, invites a critical question in return: is secularism able all by itself to give a fully adequate and coherent interpretation of human experience? Or is there still room for the sacramental religious approach that points us to an *ultimate* basis of trust? Secularism insists that religion's quest for a transcendent basis of reassurance is now unnecessary. How are we to evaluate such a stance?

The question raised by secularism comes down to this: can we humans solve the problem of anxiety all by ourselves, or is there still a legitimate place for religious "solutions"? Many observers wonder, for example, whether science has really demonstrated the potential for conquering our anxiety. They point to the persistence of a strain of uneasiness, and even its intensification today. The continued presence of anxiety among large numbers of people today seems to be not just in spite of, but at least partly *because of,* the emergence of a powerful arsenal of scientific, social and medical techniques designed to make our lives more secure. For as each scientific or technological breakthrough occurs, new risks of abuse arise along with it. Obvious examples are the developments in nuclear physics that have opened up the possibility of world-wide holocaust and, more recently, new knowledge of the chemistry of life, which if applied in careless ways by biogenetic engineering could become ecologically catastrophic. Fresh advances have brought new degrees of alarm.

In addition, many people in the modern world have felt a new and largely unprecedented type of anxiety in the wake of scientific "progress." It is a restlessness about the possible vanishing of a sense of mystery from the horizon of their lives. While secularists are often delighted with the prospect of human ingenuity's eventually disposing of the unknown, many individuals are horrified by the prospect of a world no longer open to inexhaustible mystery. They feel suffocated by the portrait of a world that could be totally comprehended by science. And in revolt against the poverty of such a world they look desperately for any sign of the irrational and uncanny. They seek instances of the "miraculous" wherever it seems fleetingly to appear. And in many other ways they display their distaste for a world so narrowly conceived that it could eventually be encompassed by something as limited as the human mind.

This quest for openings to the unknown can be observed, for example, in the Romantic movement of the nineteenth century and in the existentialist protests against rationalism in the present century. Many modern writers and thinkers have vigorously rebelled against the closed-in world of modern secularism. A deep strain of anxiety about the eclipse of mystery runs through much modern thought. Earlier in this century, for example, G. K. Chesterton argued that modern anxiety and even madness are not the result of untamed imagination. Rather they stem from secularism's absolutization of reason and science. Humanity cannot survive, he thought, without a permanent sense of wonder about the unknown.

Thus, in spite of the fact that physical and mental suffering can be offset considerably by purely secular or scientific ingenuity, we are still subject to the threat of anxiety. Is it possible that this enduring presence of anxiety leaves a meaningful place for religious reassurance? Or should we continue to look for purely secular ways of dealing with anxiety?

Before we move too hastily toward a discussion of possible responses, it might be well to define more precisely what we mean by anxiety. For there are different kinds of "anxieties." Some kinds do seem to be resolvable by science and human ingenuity. But others are apparently resistant to any advances we make in science or social engineering. Paul Tillich refers to the latter as "existential" anxieties. (1952, 32–85) They are the anxieties about not being in complete control of our destiny, about not being able to reverse the past, about having to die, about feeling guilty, about never fully realizing our dreams and possibilities as human beings, about always being somehow unfinished, incomplete. In short, existential anxiety is simply the awareness we all have of being finite, limited beings.

There are other kinds of "anxiety," of course, that we can do something about. We might call them "fears" in order to distinguish them from existential anxiety. Both terms, fear and anxiety, evoke the sense of fright and flight, but they are not identical. The difference is that fear always has a specific, identifiable object, whereas anxiety does not. (Tillich, 1952, 36–39) When we are in a state of fear we can always say exactly what we are afraid of. It may be a wild animal, a tornado, an authority figure, or failing an exam—something we can clearly put our finger on. In the state of anxiety, however, we do not know exactly what it is that causes our restlessness and uneasiness. We cannot focus on the object of anxiety as clearly as we can on the object of fear. Anxiety's object is unknown and unspecific, whereas fear's is easily identified.

This distinction is helpful in our discussion of whether religion is still an acceptable mode of reassurance. Today many religious thinkers are inclined to agree that religion is indeed superfluous if we reduce it to a set of responses to specific "fears." For if these fears can be conquered by purely secular means then religion seems to have become unnecessary. If religion were nothing but a response to fear, it would become outmoded to the degree that our present technological ingenuity is able to remove those objects that evoke fear in us.

When it comes to fear, we no longer resort to religious methods as much as our ancestors did. With the exception of scattered natural disasters like tornadoes, volcanoes, floods, droughts and earthquakes, do many of us have much fear of nature any more? And if we are afraid of it, how often do we resort to prayer alone rather than taking effective measures to eliminate the occasions for fear? Our secular way of combatting earthquakes is not to pray but to erect stronger buildings. And in the case of other kinds of fears that arise in the course of our lives, do we generally resort to religious "solutions"? If we are afraid of failing an exam, even if we pray for help, we know that unless we make the effort to prepare sufficiently, prayer will not help a bit. If we are afraid of other people, another country's armies, or even another college's basketball team, we work on our defensive strategies. If at the same time we practice a religion and say our prayers we hardly expect them to become a substitute for purely human preparations. What good then is religion if it makes so little practical difference to our success in combating our everyday apprehensions? And when religious people notice their non-religious acquaintances having greater success in battling fear than they themselves have had, does it not make religious visions of life seem quite extraneous? Why bother about religion at all?

Religion and Anxiety

Is it really fear, though, that arouses the religious instinct? Secularistic thinkers often assume that religion's primary reason for existing is to alleviate the fear of suffering some calamity or other. Sigmund Freud, for example, postulated that religion originates in fear. Religious thinkers today, however, would qualify this assertion. Religion's function, many of them would now insist, is not primarily that of responding to fear or alleviating specific suffering. It may do this too of course, for many people have testified to how their faith has brought them consolation and healing. However, usually religion brings comfort not by magically eliminating specific fears, but by "re-assuring" people in the face of their irremovable *existential* anxiety.

Such a reassurance appears essential to believers even apart from how successful they are in removing fear from their lives. For after all their fears and sufferings are removed (if that were possible at all) they still have their fundamental "existential" anxiety. They remain finite, mortal, unsatisfied beings. The value of religion, then, is to reassure people that in spite of fate, death, guilt, doubt and other insurmountable anxieties, their lives are still worthwhile. Religious devotion to an ultimate basis of trust provides for many what secularism cannot, the courage to deal with a life beset by existential anxiety. And learning to live with anxiety in turn gives the strength to cope with fears as well. The religious conviction that our immediate environment, in which fear occurs, is only a small part of the totality of reality, is inevitably a consolation to those beset by anxiety. So it is misleading to make religion just one among other solutions to the problem of fear.

In this theological interpretation religion has a more foundational role to play than simply delivering us from our everyday fears. Its primary role is that of providing the basis for a courage to accept our finitude. There are many means other than those of religion that can alleviate our fears, just as there are non-religious ways of solving intellectual, scientific and moral problems. So it is no more appropriate to reduce religion to a remedy for fear, than it is to make it a solution to intellectual, scientific or moral perplexities. Religion's primary role, according to much contemporary theology, is not to solve scientific problems or even provide definitive solutions to moral questions either. If it were defined in such restrictive terms it would soon become superfluous. For we are quite capable of doing science without the help of religious teachings. Likewise we can find responses to moral problems quite apart from whether we are religious or not. Religion is not needed to answer specific scientific and moral questions. Likewise, in the case of fear, the main focus of religion is not that of directly eliminating specific objects that arouse terror in us. Rather, religion confronts the more intransigent "limits" on life known as existential anxiety.

In religious stories, of course, there are many accounts of healing and other miraculous occurrences that might seem to indicate religion's potential for direct confrontation with specific ailments. But such "miracle stories" are not to be isolated from the larger context of religious reassurance. If they are taken out of that context they become nothing more than curiosities. Jesus, for example, is portrayed in the Gospels as working wonders, but not in order to show off. The evangelists narrated the so-called "miracle stories" in order to evoke trust or "faith" in the power of God. And they pictured Jesus as resisting the role of wonder worker if it would distract people's attention from an ultimate ground of trust.

The working of miracles does not seem to be the essential business of religion, especially since the axial age. In the great traditions an obsession with miracles is considered magical and childish. The Buddha did not eliminate sickness, famine and death, nor do his followers expect an easy end to suffering. Christians pray for healing but do not expect to escape the cross. Jews and Muslims do not reduce God to the role of problem-solver, but find a special dignity in being themselves the suffering instruments of God's involvement in and transformation of history.

Of course, we pray for specific goods, victories in sports, good grades on examinations. We are, after all, human, and it is quite natural to ask for things we want. This kind of supplication is an admission of our fundamental neediness, and praying for specific goods can be a sign of trust and humility. But if we have thought of religion *primarily* as a means to the satisfaction of our every wish, then we will eventually become disappointed with it. Or if we think of it as nothing more than protection against life's problems we will inevitably be disillusioned when it fails to come through for us.

It is possible then that we are expecting the wrong thing of religion if we look to it to remove all occasions of fear. For "fear" is parallel in the realm of emotions to "problem" in the area of the intellect, or "moral dilemma" in the area of the will. And so, if religion is out of focus when directed exclusively toward solving our intellectual problems or moral dilemmas, it may also be misinterpreted when seen as a direct response to fear. Religion is not reducible to one among other ways of removing fear. If it were, then as new ways of eliminating fear become more available, such as medical and other modern forms of technology, religion would indeed become more and more "useless," and eventually vanish completely. If people have magically related religion primarily to specific fears, they will inevitably abandon it when they discover they can stand on their own two feet.

Religion, Tillich says, points participants toward an ultimate source of courage to conquer anxiety. (1952, 86 ff.) Thus it is not reducible to an *ad hoc* technique for removing fear. For example, the Hindu mystical experience of *Brahman* absorbs and effectively vanquishes particular fears and sufferings, not by eliminating them but by contextualizing them in a new way. In their encounter with a gracious and saving mystery religious people notice that their specific fears and sufferings may not have disappeared. But they have lost their paralyzing power. Religion does, after all, respond to fear and suffering. But its characteristic way of doing so is to give people a wider vision of reality in terms of which formerly insurmountable agonies now appear paltry and insignificant. Anxiety has not been removed, but relativized. Many believing Christians have testified that they can accept inevitable sufferings if they interpret them in terms of the crucifixion of Jesus. The Christian hope for salvation that arises out of that calamity can give them confidence even in the midst of their own misfortune.

Religion, therefore, is trivialized if it is reduced to a simple technique for directly eliminating fear and suffering. As a magical remedy for fear, therefore, such "pre-conventional" religion is indeed emotionally dispensable. But the modern decline of religion as a magical solution to "problems" allows it to take up more explicitly its indispensable task of opening persons to what they need much more fundamentally than magic, namely, mystery and ultimate reassurance. Through religious symbols and stories people seem to be able to link their lives to a source of courage that allows them to live with their anxiety. And in the courageous acceptance of their finitude, fear and frustration are no longer perceived as the limits they would otherwise be.

In one of John's epistles in the Christian scriptures the writer says quite simply that where love abides there is no room for fear. "There is no fear in love, but perfect love casts out fear."(*1 Jn.* 4:18) An analogous experience is recorded in the *Bhagavadgita* where Krishna calms Arjuna's fears by placing the latter's existence in the context of the wider mystery of *Brahman*. And the Buddha teaches the end of fear as resulting from the quieting of greed. Fear is no longer a disabling experience if a more basic anxiety has been confronted. Religion's most appropriate objective is not to confront specific fears in a magical way, but to provide ways of reconciling us to the anxiety that always accompanies human existence as such.

The Attempt to Avoid Anxiety

Interestingly, though, we try (unsuccessfully) to remove the ineradicable threat of anxiety by transforming it into fear. (Tillich, 1952, 39) There is a certain logic in this attempted alchemy. For, as we have observed, any particular fear is capable of being terminated, whereas anxiety about being finite remains a constant, irremovable aspect of our existence. So if we could magically transform general anxiety about our finitude into a specific fear, then by removing that fear we could apparently step out of our finitude altogether.

Our efforts to condense all anxiety into a specific fear emanate from an unwillingness to be finite. A question that religious thinkers address to secularism today is whether the latter, in its program of removing fear, is also denying the undeniable fact of our finitude. Does secularism perhaps ignore the fact of existential anxiety by not distinguishing it carefully from fear? And is it possible to respond effectively to anxiety about finitude through purely secular means?

Religion, at least in its "post-conventional" forms, seeks not to surmount but to reconcile us to our finitude. It invites us to accept ourselves as limited beings who are loved and embraced by a wider sacred mystery precisely *with* our imperfections. One of religion's most obvious teachings, though often forgotten by humans, is that we ourselves are not God. We are subordinate, derived, finite beings. Hence, according to religion, we do not have to burden ourselves with the impossible task of overcoming our finitude. Religions teach that the mystery embracing our existence is deeper and stronger than the anxiety that threatens us in our finitude. Their almost unanimous message is that we may live confidently, without care about the big issues in life. Freedom from care about the big things that lie beyond our control can allow us, then, to struggle with those problems that we *are* capable of dealing with. By relieving us of impossible tasks religion frees us for those works that are proportionate to our limited capabilities. These would be the tasks of finding solutions to our scientific problems, our moral quandaries, and our emotional fears. The mark of religious wisdom is the ability to distinguish clearly between problems that we can deal with and anxieties that we are incapable of eliminating from the very structure of our being.

The attempt to transform unmanageable anxiety into manageable fear in the "emotional" arena is parallel to the reduction of mystery to problem in the intellectual one. It is the same impulse that leads the religious fundamentalist to expect religion to solve our intellectual puzzles. Paul Tillich writes that this shrinking of anxiety down to the manipulable status of fear is just the other side of an idolatry that attempts to reduce the infinite mystery of being to the finite objects that symbolize it. Reducing religion to the function of eliminating fear is a distraction from its proper objective of adventurously opening anxious human awareness to mystery. Only a courageous embracing of anxiety, and not attempts to remove it, will provide access to mystery in its fullness. Our typical way of avoiding anxiety by narrowing it down to a manageable fear is really a way of backing off from the risk of entering adventurously into mystery.

The Religious Origins of Secularism

Earlier we accentuated four distinct moments in the continuum of religious responses to mystery: sacramental, mystical, silent and active. And we noted a characteristic temptation in each way of relating to the world. If any one of them becomes untied from its natural bondedness to the other three it loses its religious character of openness to mystery. For example, if sacramental religion is not chastened by the mystical, apophatic and prophetic suspicion of images, it will become so obsessed with the symbols of mystery that it forgets about mystery as such. Thus it decays into idolatry. Mysticism, if it ignores the activist concern for transforming society, or if it abandons sacramental contact with nature, and the apophatic need for realism, can easily become a gnostic escapism. And the way of silence would become sheer nihilism if it were completely detached from sacramental, mystical and active approaches to mystery. Finally, the activist mode, if torn away from a sacramental devotion to nature, or from a mystical sense of the divine, or from the apophatic critique of language, would be reduced to a purely secular program to transform the world.

In a rough sort of way it is possible to insert into this typology several varieties of modern secularism. In general, secularism moves one step beyond the temptations we have seen in each religious mode. It fully ratifies the splintering of each religious type from its matrix of communion with the other three. Thus it is not inaccurate to say that secularism arises out of a context in which religion has already lost its integrity. More specifically:

1. When sacramentalism is isolated from the mystical, silent and active aspects of religion it has already become indistinguishable from *naturalism*, the view that nature is all there is. There are numerous secularists today whose interpretation of the world is purely naturalistic or "materialistic." Secularism and materialism ironically originate in a one-sided religious sacramentalism that has lost its mystical depths.

2. When mysticism becomes detached from the symbolic richness and ambiguity of sacramentalism, or from the this-worldly interests of active religion, or from the patience of the silent way, it turns into an escapist religiosity known as *gnosticism*. That is, it becomes an elitist and esoteric body of abstract teachings disconnected from the complexities of the real world. Gnosticism reduces human fulfillment to some form of "knowledge" or removal of "ignorance." There is a mystical temptation to reduce religion to "knowledge." But there are also secular forms of gnosticism, such as *rationalism* and *scientism*, both of which profess to provide definitive salvation from the shackles of ignorance. We shall examine these in the following chapter.

3. The way of silence can gradually become separated from the sacral, mystical and active dimensions of religion. And this apophatic distrust of words and images, if not held in check, will eventually become a kind of *nihilism*. This is the view that reality is completely empty of permanent truth, value and meaning. We shall look at this intriguing interpretation of secularism in Chapter 15.

4. Finally, the prophetic temptation to transform history, if divorced from its symbolic, mystical and apophatic religious context, is not fundamentally different from the phenomenon known today as *secular humanism*. Karl Marx's philosophy is a good illustration of this humanistic interpretation. We shall examine the doctrine of "humanism" more carefully in Chapter 16.

14

Skepticism

Even if it can be plausibly argued that religion is an indispensable response to existential anxiety, we might nevertheless wonder whether it is a truthful one. If it provides *ultimate* reassurance, we still have to ask whether there is *in fact* an ultimate basis of trust. Religion in all of its modes, but most explicitly in mysticism, posits an objective transcendent unity underlying the multiplicity of things, events and persons. Mystics are absolutely certain that they have perceived a divine oneness far deeper and more real than anything we experience in ordinary or "secular" life. But in spite of the assuredness with which they write or speak it is difficult for us to suppress the obvious critical question: if the divine is so real, then why is it not obvious to all of us? Why should the most real of all beings be so elusive? This is the question posed by "skepticism."

Three Levels of Skepticism

Skepticism is the intellectual component of the set of attitudes that we called "secularism" in the previous chapter. In the modern intellectual world a good deal of skepticism about religion has appeared. It has three distinct layers, though all three interpenetrate. We shall call them respectively rationalism, scientism and suspicion.

Rationalism. This first level of skepticism questions the *reasonableness* of religion. It wonders how people can still sincerely accept ideas about the sacred or divine mystery after the so-called Age of Reason.

During the eighteenth century and afterwards the rallying cry of intellectual integrity has been that of Immanuel Kant: *sapere aude*, "dare to know." Though Kant himself allowed a special place for faith, many others since the Enlightenment have taken his words to mean that we should follow reason *instead of* faith as the authentic path to truth. Such a view is called *rationalism*. It is a philosophy that makes "reason" the only reliable way to reach true knowledge. (By "reason" is meant here simply the faculty which experiences the world, understands it and makes judgments of fact about it.) And because the teachings of mystics and religious do not always seem reasonable, since they rely so much on authority and trust instead of "knowledge," advocates of rationalism consider religious faith an inferior and even erroneous mode of understanding.

The most intriguing aspect of rationalism, as far as any critical examination of religion is concerned, is its questioning the reality of a dimension of sacred mystery transcending the secular world. Rationalists admit, of course, that there is still much that we do not know about the immediate world, and they may even be willing to call this region of the yet unknown by the name "mystery." But they really mean "problem," and they typically insist that there is nothing about the universe that cannot be mastered by the human mind, at least in principle. Religious people hold that there is a distinct (though not necessarily separate) "mysterious" and "sacred" dimension that no amount of human ingenuity will ever fully master; and this dimension is considered to be inviolable, eternally evasive of all human efforts to understand it completely. Rationalism, on the other hand, thrives on the conviction that *all* reality is potentially capable of being comprehended by the human mind.

Rationalism raises the question whether intelligent people can plausibly believe in and practice religion today. It forces us to ask whether being religious, thinking religious thoughts and behaving in a religious way are consistent with the demands of reason that seem to be built into all of us. If religion were in any way irreconcilable with the full deployment of our rational faculties then it would be asking too much of reasonable people to accept it.

Precisely because of its apparent contradiction to our native rationality many sincere and thoughtful individuals spurn religion. Belief in "another dimension" or in universal purpose, eternal life or divine care seems uncongenial to rational confirmation. Reason firmly resists such "mystical" notions and is more at home in the realm of the profane. Furthermore, the claims of the various religions cannot possibly all be true if they are in such blatant contradiction to one another. For example, the apparently atheistic ideas of the Buddha seem irreconcilable with theism. And the Christian claim to the primacy of Christ or belief in the Trinity is in conflict with Islam's interpretation of monotheism. We could multiply such examples of religious disagreements almost indefinitely.

As rationalists behold this welter of confusion in the religious world, they cannot help but ask whether *any* of the various religious teachings may be accepted as reasonable. The fact that a particular religion holds its doctrines to be absolutely true is no evidence that they actually are so. Is it reasonable to accept any ideas simply on the authority of others? And would it not be better simply to let our own rational faculties figure out what the real world is all about, instead of looking at things through the filter of religious myth and tradition? To let the world come into our minds without the distortive mediation of any doctrines or a priori assumptions—this is the ideal of rationalism.

Further support for the rationalist position comes from the fact that religion relies so heavily on trust, an attitude that goes far beyond what reason can touch. Trust is the inner core of all religion. Religious trust thrives on the unknown and the unknowable, whereas reason is apparently oriented only to the known or the knowable. Reason finds it hard to follow religious trust into the obscure realm of "mystery." The testimony of the mystics that they have experienced the "really real," beyond all appearances accessible to reason, is unacceptable.

Scientism. Scientism is also a major component of modern skepticism. It is the view that science alone can lead us to the truth. This is a position similar to and often supported by rationalism, except that it makes the methods of experimental science the privileged road to reality. This stratum of modern skepticism questions whether the teachings of religion are compatible with or supportable by empirical (that is, experientially grounded) methods of knowing. At a time when scientific method has given us an exact, mathematical way of explaining so many things, the ideas of religion seem exceedingly vague. We can easily verify the existence of what science talks about, but can we do the same with the realm of mystery to which the mystics refer? Today the various modes of religious awareness stand under the close scrutiny of those who have taken science as the exclusive road to genuine knowledge. Scientism judges religion and mysticism to be scientifically indemonstrable, and that seems to be sufficient cause for our ignoring them.

Scientists and religious teachers have often collided with each other in the past. The two best known examples are the dispute between Galileo and the Roman Catholic Church in the early seventeenth century, and the opposition by Christians to Darwin and evolutionary theory during the past century. In both cases religious dogmaticians refused to look at the scientific evidence, and as a result of their stubbornness religion has now been widely discredited in the minds of many scientifically enlightened people.

The conflict of science with religion is also rooted in a disagreement about what constitutes true knowledge. Scientism maintains that scientific method is the only way our minds can reach the *real* world. Religion is full of assumptions and beliefs, whereas science, at least allegedly, takes nothing for granted, has no beliefs, and makes no gratuitous assumptions. Science accepts no propositions (other than mathematical kinds) that cannot be verified by scientific method. Religion, on the other hand, affirms in a variety of symbolic ways that "all shall be well" without any actual evidence that things will in fact turn out for the best. Or mysticism *assumes* that reality is completely intelligible, in spite of the fact that we have not investigated much of the world yet. "How," scientism asks, "can we accept a religious way of thinking that makes such sweeping judgments before all the evidence is in? Is not the mystic jumping to conclusions in affirming a transcendent unity when scientific experience notices only a multiplicity of entities only loosely connected by natural laws?"

Suspicion. There is also a third level of skepticism present in some of the most important modern critiques of religion. Paul Ricoeur calls it *suspicion* since it "suspects" there is much more going on in religion than meets the eye. (Ricoeur, 1978, 213–22) The attitude of suspicion views religion not only as unreasonable and unscientific, but also as *covering something up*. Suspicion looks at religion almost as though its symbols, myths, rites, practices and prayers were a *text* that needs to be carefully deciphered in order for us to arrive at some repressed content beneath its overt expressions. This type of critique is exemplified especially by Friedrich Nietzsche, Karl Marx and Sigmund Freud. They all viewed religion as a dubious set of symbols whose surface meaning (such as belief in God, *nirvana*, paradise, immortality, ultimate love or perfect happiness) cannot be trusted or taken at face value. Instead, such direct symbolic manifestations of religion need to be "read" as though they are hiding something.

What are they covering up? Nietzsche, Marx and Freud have different ways of describing the hidden meaning of our religious symbolism, but they all agree that it is unflattering. According to these skeptics there lies hidden beneath the expressions of religion nothing other than childish fear, weakness, resentment, and escapism. And the task of suspicion is to bring this latent and unsavory material to the surface in order that we might face it and move beyond it toward a more "genuine," that is, non-religious mode of understanding and existing.

This philosophy of suspicion has an interesting way of coming at the subject of religion. It persistently presses forward the fascinating question, *why* do we "do" religion? What motivational forces are "really" at work deep down inside of the mystical mind or the religious group? Like the psychoanalyst who looks for the "real" motives underlying the patient's erratic behavior, philosophers of suspicion look for the "real" but hidden causes of that strange human phenomenon known as religion. They might ask, for example, what are the "real" reasons the mystic renounces "this world" for the sake of a divine being that cannot be immediately seen? What is the hidden, unconscious origin of our sense of God? Are not the religious responses to suffering merely concealing moral immaturity or a refusal to face the harsh facts of our existence? Is not mysticism perhaps a way of evading the task of coming to grips with the "real" world?

The Projection Theory

Rationalism, scientism and suspicion all embrace what has been called the *projection theory* of religion. This theory proposes that the ideas of religion are no more than the "projection" or fantastic creation of our own infantile wishes. It holds that mystics and religious simply *wish* for God and other religious ideals (*Brahman, nirvana,* paradise, immortality, ultimate meaning, etc.) so intensely that they imagine them into existence. But there is no firm evidence in objective reality for our religious ideas of ultimate unity and meaning.

According to the projection theory our sense of the sacred has its origins in human wishing. The gods of religion are nothing more than the projection ("throwing forward") of our own personal attributes onto the world or into the void. Centuries ago the philosopher Xenophanes (6th century B.C.E.) said that ". . . if cattle and horses had hands, or were able to draw and do the work that men can do, horses would draw the forms of the gods like horses, and cattle like cattle, and they would make their bodies such as they each had themselves." And, though he was not himself an atheist, his suspicion of projection in religion has been shared by modern skeptics such as Ludwig Feuerbach, Karl Marx, Emile Durkheim and Sigmund Freud. They all surmised that human fantasy is the exclusive origin of our sense of the sacred. Hence they could not help but question religion's compatibility with reason.

We may exemplify the projection theory by looking briefly at the ideas of three of its most famous proponents.

Sigmund Freud (1856–1939). This Viennese scientist-psychologist is best known as the founder of *psychoanalysis*. Psychoanalysis is both a therapeutic technique designed to help people overcome the crippling illness called neurosis, and a general interpretation of the human condition constructed for the purpose of giving us a "realistic" understanding of our situation in the world of nature and civilization.

Freud was convinced that humans are driven by natural instincts that run contrary to reason and civilization. In a special way the *libido*, the natural urge for sexual gratification underlies our entire psychic life. This aspect of our psyche urges us to seek as much pleasure as possible and gives rise to the "pleasure principle." The pleasure principle is the component of our mental life that constantly stirs us to wish for and dream of satisfaction. The impulse for pleasure remains a permanent and undeniable aspect of our psychic makeup. And, according to Freud, it ultimately supplies the dynamism beneath our religious longings.

In short, people "do religion" because of their insatiable urge for gratification. They want pleasure so badly that when they cannot find it in their present lives they imagine its fulfillment in some other world. The context of harsh nature and oppressive civilization leaves us unhappy, and so we turn to religion for consolation. We wish for its comforts so strongly that we begin to believe its ideas are true. But because it has its origin in wishing religion must be regarded as an *illusion*. (By "illusion" Freud means the fantasized product of wishful thinking.) Religion is nothing more than an illusion born out of the need to have our wishes fulfilled. Religion, like dreams, which also originate in wishing, has no basis in reality.

Ludwig Feuerbach (1804–1872). Freud was by no means the first modern thinker to theorize that religion is nothing more than projection. Perhaps the most fully developed form of the projection theory was provided by the nineteenth century German philosopher, Ludwig Feuerbach. Feuerbach, who exercised considerable influence on Karl Marx, advanced the interesting hypothesis that all the ideas we associate with God, qualities such as love, justice, compassion, etc., are really *our own* human characteristics. But religion, like a vampire, sucks these divine attributes out of us and gives them to the fictitious projection known as "God." And as long as we believe in God as a separate being "out there," our true essence remains "alienated" from us.

In fact, according to Feuerbach, the real essence of humanity is what religion calls "God." But religion prevents us from recognizing our species for what it is, namely a divine, loving community. Projecting our divinity away from ourselves and onto "God" leaves us with a false and lowly concept of ourselves. Religion has estranged us from ourselves, and so we remain stuck in a lack of appropriate godly self-esteem. This lamentable estimation of ourselves obscures from us our own capacity for love. And lacking a true consciousness of our species' divine essence we turn to hatred and hostility toward one another. Only atheism, therefore, can return us to a rational awareness of our true being.

Karl Marx (1818–1883). Marx agreed with Feuerbach that we humans are estranged from our true being. And he also agreed that religious projection has something to do with our sorry, alienated human condition. But he disagreed with Feuerbach's view that religion is the prime cause of our self-alienation. Rather, unjust working conditions and social arrangements have robbed us of the substance of our being.

For Marx, to be truly human means to experience and enjoy the product and benefits of our own labor. To be at one with ourselves we have to experience our work and creativity as our own and not as belonging to someone else. But the capitalist owners of the means of industrial production have taken most of the product of the workers' labor and funneled it into their own pockets, leaving the working class destitute. The only way to correct this situation is through a class struggle in which the laborers will take control of the means of production.

How does religion fit into this oppressive situation? Religion supports the alienation of the workers by distracting them from the real task of correcting the unjust conditions. It promises them another world in which they will be compensated for putting up with this one. But it does nothing to correct the reigning injustices here and now. If this "inverted world" were set right side up by revolutionary political action, then there would be no need to escape into heaven. If justice prevailed here on earth, people would not seek religious consolations in the hereafter. And religion would then disappear.

Thus, according to Marx, it makes little sense to attack religion head-on in the manner of Feuerbach. Religion is not the source of the problem of alienation. In fact it is a feeble, but touching, protest against injustice. The cause of alienation is not religion, but the present social, economic and legal structures which uphold the inhumane organization of labor and profit. True atheism should not waste its time attacking religion. Rather it should attack the unjust economic and social structures that make people turn to religion in the first place. Nevertheless, religion is a projection that reasonable people will eventually have to abandon.

Faith and Reason

The question of whether religion is compatible with reason was raised first not by modern skeptics, but by deeply religious thinkers themselves. It was an issue that troubled the likes of Shankara, the Buddha and Lao Tzu in the East. And in the West, especially during the Middle Ages, Islamic, Jewish and Christian scholars wrote volumes discussing the reasonableness of a religious outlook. They taught that reason, properly understood, fully supports a religious trust in the transcendent. They saw no contradiction whatsoever between sincere religious "faith" and reason.

The most renowned example of a defense of the reasonableness of faith is found in the writings of Thomas Aquinas, a thirteenth century Christian philosopher. Aquinas was familiar with the works of such philosophers as Aristotle, Augustine and Boethius, as well as with several Jewish and Islamic thinkers, all of whom thought it unreasonable to deny the existence of God. In his voluminous *Summa Theologica* he advanced five logical "proofs" of God's existence, presenting the reasonableness of religious belief in transcendent reality. Here is one of Aquinas' five arguments:

> In the observable world causes are found to be ordered in series; we never observe, nor ever could, something causing itself, for this would mean it preceded itself, and this is not possible. Such a series of causes must however stop somewhere; for in it an earlier member causes an intermediate and the intermediate a last (whether the intermediate be one or many). Now if you eliminate a cause you also eliminate its effects, so that you cannot have a last cause, nor an intermediate one, unless you have a first. Given therefore no stop in the series of causes, and hence no first cause, there would be no intermediate causes either, and no last effect, and this would be an open mistake. One is therefore forced to suppose some first cause, to which everyone gives the name 'God'. (*Summa Theologiae*, 1A. 2,3; Blackfriars trans., 1969)

A paraphrase of Aquinas' arguments for God's existence (especially the third) might go something like this: Why does anything exist at all? Things do exist, but there is no necessity that they exist. You and I exist, but we might well not have. Why then is there anything at all rather than nothing? None of the objects of our experience is the source of its own existence. Everything in our world depends upon and has received its existence from something other than itself. Think, for example, of how your own existence depends upon your parents', and theirs on their parents', and so on. Or consider how the page you are reading received its existence from a paper mill, which in turn received its existence from industrialists whose own existence was derived from another complex series of causes, etc.—all the way back to the existence of the world itself. Everything in our experience seems to depend for its actual being on a whole series of other aspects of the world.

And what about the world itself? Since it is composed of a series of dependent beings it cannot be the source of its existence either. Like everything in it, the world as a whole must have received its being from some source beyond itself. As our reason moves further and further back in its attempt to answer why things exist at all, it concludes that somewhere beyond the reach of our immediate experience there has to be an *ultimate* source of all the other sources of existence. There must be a self-existing wellspring of the world's very being. And this ultimate source of the world's being is what faith means by "God."

Of course, most people do not come to faith in God simply by way of logic. They pick up their religious sensitivities initially through a kind of "contagion" by living within a community of fellow believers. Belief in God arises spontaneously in the course of their being nurtured by a set of religious stories and symbols that grasp hold of them before they have had time to think philosophically about their faith. But in the life of a reason-respecting religious person there may come a point where he or she asks whether the beliefs acquired during childhood and afterwards, or during a moment of religious ecstasy, are consistent with sober rationality. Aquinas, for one, thought this was a good question to ask. And he would certainly have agreed with modern skeptics that it would be dishonest for us to believe doctrines that were in utter contradiction to reason. He thought the idea of God to be not only compatible with, but actually required by, reason. For Aquinas and numerous other theists, then, faith and reason may coexist without any conflict.

In the eighteenth and early nineteenth centuries, during the so-called Age of Reason, some religious thinkers in Europe even went so far as to claim that reason, not faith, is our primary access to God. Under the influence of Newtonian physics and the developing sciences they were struck by how intricately nature seems to have been designed. From the structure of insect wings to the predictable behavior of gases they were astounded by the orderliness of it all. The major premise of their so-called "design argument" for God's existence was that wherever there is design or order there must be an intelligent designer responsible for it. Their minor premise, fortified by the emerging scientific world view, stated that the natural world is far more intricately ordered than any human artifact. Therefore, they concluded that there has to be an intelligent designer of the cosmos in its totality.

In his *Natural Theology,* a work read widely during the early nineteenth century, William Paley compared nature to a watch. If you found a
watch lying alone in the wild, and then picked it up and examined its
intricate structure, you would have to conclude that an intelligent designer
was responsible for its existence and order. It could not have been made
just by accident. But the natural world around us, especially in something
as carefully patterned as the eye, exhibits many times more astounding
order than a watch. Therefore, we may reasonably conclude that there is
an intelligent designer responsible for nature's design. Such a designer
would have to possess the omniscience, power and goodness that we associate with the idea of God. Reason all by itself can lead us to posit the
existence of God.

Arguments like those of Aquinas and Paley are sufficient to convince
many theists of the rationality of their faith. And if you find yourself
attracted to them be assured that you are in the company of many respected philosophers and religious thinkers throughout the centuries. But
we cannot close our eyes to the fact that other intelligent men and women
view the arguments with suspicion and even disdain. David Hume and
Immanuel Kant are the most famous of the many modern philosophers
unconvinced by the arguments (though Kant, like Martin Luther before
him, accepted God on the basis of faith alone). And Darwin's evolutionary
theory has convinced many scientifically educated thinkers today of the
inadequacy of Paley's argument from nature's design.

Opponents of arguments such as Aquinas' and Paley's include not
only atheists and agnostics, but also famous theologians. For example, the
Swiss Protestant theologian Karl Barth and his many disciples view any
alleged "proofs" of God's existence as idolatrous attempts by the human
mind to take control of the infinite. The God of revelation far surpasses
what our weak rational faculties can encompass. It is the height of arrogance to pretend that reason can lead us to God. Barth follows the *"sola
fides"* theology of the Protestant reformer Martin Luther. Not reason, but
"faith alone," can put us in touch with the reality of God. Hence we do not
need to worry much about the problem of faith and reason, since reason
has been so distorted by human sinfulness that it could never make contact
with divine reality anyway. Faith alone is the way to knowledge of God.
God grasps us in revelation, but we cannot grasp God through our faulty
reason.

Moreover, some theologians insist that faith requires a life of prayer,
and that God can be known only in the act of praying:

Unless we meet God in prayer we never meet Him, for
prayer is meeting God. Unless we meet Him, He can never be-

come real to us. A person can be fully real to us only as we get to
know him personally. No amount of mere talking or thinking
about him can take the place of knowing face to face. . . . To
learn to know God, then, we must learn to pray. If we have
prayed and still do not know Him, we need to learn to pray
aright. (Ferré, 51)

Reason's Reliance on Faith

Thus for a number of religious thinkers reason is inappropriate to
knowledge of God. To them faith and prayer are the only avenues to God.
Many others, however, question whether an approach to God based on
distrust of reason is a good way for believers to come into conversation
with rationalism, scientism and suspicion. Such a belittling of reason will
likely provoke an even more rationalistic distrust of religion. Mysticism is
not enhanced by our maligning of reason. *Fideism* (the view that faith alone
gives true knowledge) is perhaps an understandable reaction to rationalism, but it is hardly a solution that would take an exchange with skepticism very far.

An alternative approach to the problem of faith and reason has been
proposed in recent years, and it has begun to gain more and more acceptance. It avoids the extremes of both rationalism and fideism by showing
that there is always a kind of faith already inherent in reason and science.
There is a very "personal" component of trust or "faith" present in *all*
types of human knowledge. (Polanyi, 1964) Whether we are talking about
philosophy, science or theology, all the disciplines that require reasoning
rely upon a prior posture of personal trust and commitment for which
"faith" may be the most appropriate name. Human reason and science do
not start out at point zero, with a blank slate, in complete neutrality.
Reason and science are not devoid of beliefs and assumptions, as scientism
insists. The human mind is not a simple calculating machine operating
impersonally. Reason and science are activated by persons-in-community
already moved by commitments to various values that have taken hold of
them in the act of living. Before we can even begin to grasp the order of the
world, whether through reason or science, we have already, usually without realizing it, made an act of deep interior faith in the worthwhileness of
pursuing the truth. And we have already *believed* that there is an intelligible order to be discovered.

At the basis of our reasoning processes there is an attitude of trust that
arises from the deepest and most mysterious reaches of our existence. The

basic confidence that lies at the root of our psychic existence also manifests itself in our rational faculties. Prior to questioning and thinking about the world, we have already performed a silent act of faith in the capacity of our own mental faculties to grasp the truth about things. But, even more, we have already trusted that there is intelligibility and rationally comprehensible truth resident in reality. A deeply personal commitment consisting of trust in ourselves, in truth, and in the value of searching along with other inquirers for intelligibility, is present as a pre-condition of all forms of inquiry. And every academic discipline gets off the ground only if those involved in such studies are *personally* motivated by faith in the worth and integrity of rational pursuit. Reason and science, in other words, are far from being devoid of faith.

According to this proposal, the faith-like aspect of rational knowledge is not completely separable from the kind of trust working in religion. It is not identical with it either, but there is an overlapping of, and not a conflict between, reason's trust and religious faith. Those who think there is a conflict, whether skeptics like Freud or believers like Barth, seem unaware of how inseparable "faith" is from reason.

Seen in this light, religion may actually support the work of reason and science. For the latter are rooted in a basic trust that truth is worth pursuing. If this trust were absent, then reason and science would not have the needed incentive to seek their goal. But human trust, as we have seen earlier, can sometimes sag. It needs reassurance if it is to be sustained. And religion is at least one such means of reassuring our basic trust. In the mystical reference to an *ultimate* truth at the heart of reality, religion points to a ground for our trusting that truth is worth pursuing. Understood in this foundational way, religion does not conflict with, but instead promotes, the work of reason and science.

Religion and Suspicion

One of the main objections by skeptics to religious belief is that the latter is so highly imaginative as to be untrustworthy. Religion, according to the projection theory, is the product of a wishful thinking that gives rise to powerful illusions. Religion requires the use of our imaginations, but the faculty of imagination can easily be held captive by the pleasure principle and the perverse motivations that "suspicion" has unmasked. Religion seems to be nothing more than a projection.

The projection theory and the "philosophy of suspicion" force us to ask about the origin of the human sense of sacred reality, or the sense of

"God." Does our sense of God, if we happen to have one, come from a transcendent reality or from our imaginations? Superficially it would appear that there are only two conceivable answers to this important question: (1) either our sense of God comes from God, presumably by way of some kind of "revelation," or (2) it comes from human imagining alone. Religious people would usually insist on the first, while rationalism, scientism, and suspicion would opt for the second.

At first these seem to be the only two possibilities, but there may be a third. Both of the above alternatives can be held together in a more comprehensive "hypothesis." John Bowker (1973) argues that the origin of our sense of God may be explained in part as the product of our imaginations while at the same time being the result of an encounter with the divine. Suppose God is real. In that case, as apophatic religion insists, our sacramental representations of God would only be approximations. But that would not necessarily make them completely unrealistic. The fact that we do wish for God does not logically invalidate God's existence. It may be that projective imagining is the only way we human beings, with our limited mental and spiritual capacities, could initially come into encounter with an ultimate mystery. But perhaps it is the presence of this mystery at the margins and depths of awareness that evokes in us our primitive religious imaginings in the first place. This interpretation may also help explain the diversity of religious symbolic systems as well as the apparent conflicts that exist among the various religious traditions. If none of our religious representations are adequate to mystery, it would not be surprising that they are not easily reconcilable with one another either.

According to this position we "do religion" both because we "wish" for ultimate reality *and* because an ultimate mystery has somehow grasped hold of us and invited us to seek it out. According to Bowker, it is not unreasonable to suppose that a divine mystery has aroused our religious sensitivity in the first place. And in response to this vague invitation we move imaginatively toward mystery, employing the wide variety of symbolic ways observable in sacramental religion. This theory allows for the possibility that there is much illusion in concrete religious life, as the skeptics have emphasized, without denying that religion can also be on the way to truth and realism. There may even be layers of childish motivation behind our religious projections, as Nietzsche, Marx and Freud suspect. Since we are incapable of comprehending mystery, we need not expect that our representations of it will ever be more than provisional and inadequate. But the fact of projection and illusion in our religious lives does not logically preclude the possibility that God is still somehow the source of our sense of God.

Religion itself expressed suspicion of projection and crudity in its sacramental imagery long before modern skepticism did so. The "way of silence" in all the religious traditions regards religious images as little more than inadequate approximations that we must eventually learn to abandon for the sake of openness to mystery itself. In that sense the skeptical suspicion of religious projection is not the enemy of religion but its ally. Yet, as we shall see in the next chapter, a complete abandonment of images leads to nihilism.

Conclusion

The quest for religious knowledge cannot be undertaken without an involvement of the whole person, and not just reason, in an ongoing struggle for truth. No religious tradition expects that the participant can achieve religious insight simply by way of automatic logical operations. Only a sincere personal commitment to the truth makes one adequate to receive it. Religious knowledge is gained only if the whole person's life, not just the rational component, undergoes the sea-change called *conversion*. Often a mature concern for religious truth is not aroused intensely until limit-experiences arise in the course of one's life and present a new challenge to one's entire way of living. It has been observed that "life is a pathway on which there is no knowing without going." The same is true of religion. Here, according to its sages, new truth does not come easily but has to be struggled for. "Even within science, truth comes to those who with zeal hunt for it, those who frame theories to catch the right data. Within religion, truth comes to those who in passion sacrifice for it, who compose lives to hear the Spirit-wind of God." (Rolston, 336)

Religious traditions generally teach that transcendent truth comes only to those who are "adequate" to receive it. And such adequacy often requires undergoing a struggle for the truth in which one's whole being undergoes a transformation that tunes one in to the specific "frequency" of mystery. The learning of commonplace truths, such as those of logic, mathematics and science, does not require as much personal investment and struggle as religion. We do not risk much of ourselves when we accept that $2+2 = 4$ or that the law of gravity is correct. But it is difficult seriously to accept the religious view that a gracious mystery encompasses one's life without feeling a deep challenge in such an intuition. Only in taking the risk of radically trusting mystery, and steering one's life and relationships accordingly, does one religiously acknowledge its presence and challenge. According to theology, this is why ultimate mystery is so elusive to common sense, reason and science. Unless we risk our whole being, and not just our rational faculties, we will not be able to taste mystery in its depths. Whether acknowledgement of mystery is reasonable or not—perhaps we cannot decide this in a logically dispassionate way and without a prior commitment of ourselves. Perhaps we will not know for sure that faith is reasonable until the leap has already been taken.

15.

Nihilism

Religions hold out the prospect of fulfillment. If they did not, people would hardly be drawn to them with such enthusiasm. Religions promise an *ultimate* deliverance from suffering and disappointment, and this assurance appeals to something deeply embedded in our nature. They speak more directly to our instinct for "perfection" than do any other ingredients of our culture or environment. They express holy dissatisfaction with present reality and with all mundane solutions to human problems. They seek a *final* liberation or salvation, often in some realm apart or in some extraordinary experience of "enlightenment."

But how do we know that disappointment and frustration do not ultimately define our existence? How many of us have actually experienced the perfection we long for? Might not "unsatisfactoriness" adequately define the outer limits of our lives? Might we not be circumscribed by sheer "nothingness" rather than by a gracious mystery? Perhaps the religious quest for ultimate fulfillment and a "peace that surpasses all understanding" is finally fruitless? Maybe we should simply learn to live, as Albert Camus suggested, within the limits of a world defined by tragedy and death? Possibly reality is not ultimately intelligible, but instead "absurd."

A number of influential writers and thinkers, especially in the present century, accept the latter sentiments as the only "realistic" philosophy of human existence. They suspect that beneath all appearances there is no transcendent ground of trust, no mystical "oneness," no state of final perfection, no ultimate "goodness." Instead there is an endless void of "nothingness." This way of thinking is often called by the name *nihilism*. Nihilism literally means "belief in nothing," from the Latin word for "nothing," *nihil*. According to nihilism, under all appearances of reality, beneath our sense of values, truth and meaning, there is simply—*nothing*.

There is no transcendent ground of truth, goodness or meaning. These are all inventions of ours, mere masks imposed over the abyss of nothingness that gapes open beneath the world and human existence.

Nihilism, therefore, seems to be the most extreme refusal of any religious vision of reality. Religion, after all, arises out of a sense of wonder at the being, unity, beauty and goodness of the world. Unlike nihilism, religion (except perhaps for some kinds of Buddhism) holds that behind these so-called "transcendental" qualities there exists an *ultimate ground*. The amazement by religious people that things and persons have "being" gives rise to the response of gratitude and trust that we saw exemplified in sacramental religion. The feeling of gratitude at the sheer being of things often leads religions to posit the reality of a divine creator at the foundation of the world's being. The coherence or "unity" of being is so impressive to certain individuals that they become mystics. To a degree of intensity that few of us ever reach the mystics are overwhelmed by an impression of the ultimate oneness of all things in the universe. When religious mystics perceive their inability to image adequately the "perfection" of mystery they fall back into the contemplative silence of apophatic religion. And the "goodness" they intuit in the world, especially when they experience the love of others, tempts religious people to the "hypothesis" that the universe is itself the product of a transcendent goodness and love that exists beyond the world itself.

Thus religion is not content just to observe the reality, unity, beauty and goodness of the world. What is special about it—and this makes it different from anything else humans do or think—is that it generally seeks a transcendent foundation of the "transcendentals," that is, of being, unity, beauty and goodness. (These are called "transcendentals" because they "transcend" individual items in the world and are aspects of *all* things that exist.) Religion looks for a *ground* of the transcendentals. The idea of God and other religious notions of an ultimate order are indicative of the attempt to express symbolically the mysterious origin of the transcendentals. Religion attempts to establish the absolute "truth" of the transcendentals by pointing to a sacred origin eternally independent of our own valuations. It insists upon the inherent reality of being, unity, beauty and goodness apart from our own projective imaginings.

Nihilism, on the other hand, rejects any divine foundation for the transcendentals. Being is really only an illusion. Unity is only appearance. Beauty is our own creation. Goodness is arbitrary human convention. Thus nihilism implies that any meanings we live by, including those of religions, are precarious sketches. They are built on the shifting sands of our own whims and are in no way to be taken as representations of any ultimate reality. Symbols and myths are inherently empty of any content other than what we breathe into them. Any consistently skeptical interpretation of the world would have to draw these conclusions.

Our attempt to understand what religion is all about, and why most humans have been religious, must also ponder what the alternative to religion might be. And nihilism presents itself as the most consistent alternative. Attention to the modern phenomenon of nihilism, therefore, is enormously significant in our critical assessment of religion.

The Incoherence of Secular Humanism

Less radical forms of skepticism also acknowledge the fragility of our world of meanings and values, but only nihilism brings this suspicion to its logical conclusion. Nihilism is a radical interpretation of the implications of all secularism and skepticism. It attempts to state fully and without blinkers just what is implied in any godless interpretation of reality. Usually secularists do not think out fully and clearly the implications of their denial that there is an ultimate ground of the world's being, unity, beauty and goodness. If they did, there would be no reason for them to cling so tenaciously to the meanings and values they still idealize. According to nihilism, there is no eternally established reason to espouse any humane cause or to get involved in any value-centered activity. In the absence of God or transcendent mystery there would be no unquestionable basis for such commitments.

Secularists typically reject the idea of God while still embracing many of the same moral values and myths about the meaning of life that religious people do. For example, Soviet president Mikhail Gorbachev, in a recent speech at the United Nations, insisted that we must build a new international order on the basis of "universal human values." Although his ideas arise out of an avowedly atheistic ideology, the values he publicly promotes are not fundamentally different from the traditional biblical ideals of justice, freedom and individual human rights. These values were originally nurtured by prophetic religion. They are, almost by momentum, still present in the cultural systems of the West, and even atheists are not immune to their influence. But when they are taken over into a religionless context they give rise to what has been called "secular humanism." Secular humanism denies the existence of God but still cultivates values such as love, justice and peace originally associated with religion. Most serious atheists today would accept the tenets of secular humanism. These are articulated in the "Humanist Manifesto," first published in 1933 but recently updated. And there is now a journal called *The Humanist* which carries articles interpreting and applying the philosophy of secular humanism to social, political and environmental problems that beset us all today. Many scholars in the universities of the world today embrace the philosophy of secular humanism.

The humanist philosophy is a very positive endorsement of life and the values of love, justice, compassion, freedom, truth, beauty, etc. Humanists are very ethically committed people. They are often the first to endorse activist issues, and many make considerable sacrifices for the sake of improving the natural environment and the quality of human life on this planet. Their moral courage and integrity often puts to shame that of religious believers. The significant difference between the humanist and the believer, though, is that the former explicitly rejects or doubts the reality of God whereas the latter thinks it necessary to base values and meanings in an ultimate reality. The humanist argues that belief in the sacred is not essential or even helpful in the pursuit of goodness.

Nihilists, however, assert that secular humanism is inconsistent and illogical. They insist that if "God is dead," and there is no divine mystery, then there can be no eternal source of the meanings and moral values espoused by secular humanism. Secular humanism ironically accepts the traditional biblical ideals of love, justice, peace, and freedom as inviolable. But nihilism explicitly denies that there is any permanent basis for such "absolute" values. If there is no God, it argues, then there is no transcendent and universal source of ethical ideals and values either. There simply cannot be any "universal human values" such as Gorbachev wants us to follow. Without God, values lack any fixed or eternal foundation. They are the transient projections of perishable people and cultures.

Religion holds that if values are to have an unconditional claim upon us they require a transcendent *source* radically independent of fragile human existence. But, like all atheists, nihilists insist there is no transcendent source, no "God" to ground our values and endorse our meanings. And if there is no eternal ground it follows that there are no absolute criteria of right and wrong, and no reason to believe there is a final purpose to our lives. If God is not real, then there is no eternally valid reason to continue espousing the ideals originally gestated by religious traditions. If, as all skeptics suspect, the sacred is only a projected fiction, then there can be no source of good and evil outside of ourselves. And if each of us is an autonomous source of values, who is to say any longer what is right and what is wrong, what is true and what is false? Relativism, the view that there are no absolutes and that "all is relative," would then be the only acceptable interpretation of skepticism.

Nihilistic atheism, in other words, considers secular humanism to be half-hearted in its atheism. On the one hand humanists reject the idea of God, but on the other they continue to think and act "as if" God actually exists. They uphold the filmy web of traditional values and meanings as though they were handed down from heaven. When humanists promote the values of love, freedom, justice, compassion, truth, beauty and peace as though they were inscribed eternally in the scheme of things, they are deceiving themselves. How can there be universal values unless there is an absolute, transcendent source of values that makes them universal? Nihilists try to be more consistent than the humanists. They claim that if there is no divine source of ideals, then all our values are relative. There can be no truly universal values in the absence of God. Any alleged universality, such as that suggested by Gorbachev, is itself a fiction.

Secular humanism, therefore, has not radically left behind the world of religion. It is still tied to the apron strings of a theistic culture. Like Hindus, Buddhists, Jews, Christians and Muslims, secular humanists act "as though" there were still some transcendent order of "rightness" that measures and judges their conduct, even though in their philosophical theories they explicitly deny it. They still feel guilty when they have violated the goodness they idealize, even though they have rejected the reality of anything that would render a value inviolable. To the nihilist, this kind of thinking is simply dishonest.

The most famous exposition of nihilism can be found in some of the writings of the nineteenth century philosopher, Friedrich Nietzsche (1844–1900). He is best known for his declaration that "God is dead." Nietzsche discovered that for all intents and purposes the idea of God had little meaning for most of his contemporaries. God had already died in their culture and their hearts. And yet they had failed to realize the dramatic implications of the death of God. Nietzsche tried to think out fully the consequences of atheism, beyond the half-hearted impiety of his contemporaries. If God is dead, he prophesied, should we not feel the emptiness and nothingness of a universe devoid of any eternal meanings, truths and values? In the absence of God, should we not be terrified at the abyss of meaninglessness gaping beneath our existence. The truly sensitive skeptic will take note of this abyss and shrink back from it in horror.

But the true skeptic might also realize what a tremendous opportunity exists for humanity now that the sun of religion has set and the darkness of atheism has come over us. If God is dead there is now no longer any above or below, no absolute standard by which to measure our conduct. This is initially disorienting. We would prefer to hide ourselves in the security of the "herd" that simply conforms to reigning ethical standards. But the truly strong and courageous atheist will take the death of God as the occasion for a new beginning. Now it is possible to construct for ourselves a "higher history than any history hitherto." This higher history will be fashioned by individuals who accept the death of God and the absence of

any transcendent values. Such individuals will accept their responsibility
for creating new meanings. They will have the courage to "transvalue all
values," to go "beyond good and evil." They will no longer look to some
eternal heaven for guidance, but will undertake to build a new humanity
over the graveyard of dead gods. This new type of humanity, the
"overman," will leave behind not only religion but also the tepid skepticism of those humanists who still cling nostalgically to the old epoch of
religious morality. (Kaufmann)

According to Jean-Paul Sartre, whose own nihilist leanings have been
influenced by Nietzsche, secular humanists have concocted a logically
incoherent position that goes something like this:

> God is a useless and costly hypothesis; we are discarding it;
> but, meanwhile, in order for there to be an ethics, a society, a
> civilization, it is essential that certain values be taken seriously
> and that they be considered as having an *a priori* existence. It
> must be obligatory, *a priori*, to be honest, not to lie, not to beat
> your wife, to have children, etc., etc. So we're going to try a little
> device which will make it possible to show that values exist all the
> same, inscribed in a heaven of ideas, though otherwise God does
> not exist. In other words . . . nothing will be changed if God
> does not exist. We shall find ourselves with the same norms of
> honesty, progress, and humanism, and we shall make of God an
> outdated hypothesis which will peacefully die off by itself.

This is a dishonest way of thinking, according to Sartre. Most atheists, he insinuates, really fail to take their atheism seriously. If you're going
to be an atheist, he seems to be saying, go all the way. Carry your atheism
out to its logical conclusion. As Sartre would put it, taking a line from one
of Dostoevsky's characters, "If God does not exist, then everything is
permitted." If God does not exist

> . . . all possibility of finding values in a heaven of ideas
> disappears along with Him; there can no longer be an *a priori*
> Good, since there is no infinite and perfect consciousness to
> think it. Nowhere is it written that the Good exists, that we must
> be honest, that we must not lie; because the fact is we are on a
> plane where there are only men.
> . . . if God does not exist, we find no values or commands
> to . . . legitimize our conduct. So in the bright realm of values,
> we have no excuse behind us, nor justification before us. We are
> alone, with no excuses. (Sartre, 1957, 22)

But few atheists go this far. Like Gorbachev in his United Nations speech, they continue to cling to the same system of values we saw in prophetic religion. Only they drop the need to ground this system in a transcendent realm. Thus, according to nihilists, the secular humanists are as spineless as the religious. And in the substance of their approach to life they are really not different from believers in God. They drop God like Santa Claus but then go on with their lives as before, living according to the same values for which religion requires an ultimate foundation. They are in fact even less consistent than the religious. If God does not exist, it should make a dramatic *difference*. It should drastically alter the way in which people interpret their lives and their morality. But most skeptics do not have the stamina to "transvalue all values," that is, to create a whole new world of meanings consistent with thoroughgoing atheism.

Thus the only honest form of atheism would be one that rejects the absolute values derived from religious traditions. Nihilism, it would appear, does not compromise with theism as does secular humanism. It takes the "death of God" with utmost seriousness. If God is not a reality, then there is no absolutely secure reason for our holding on to religiously endorsed meanings as do the humanists. Once we discard the deity who is said to be the origin of the transcendentals, we should recognize that our "values" no longer have any universal foundation either.

Nihilism Examined

Nihilism insists that our basic trust and religious reassurance are misguided. Our mystical faculties are faulty attempts to cover up the radical plurality of beings. The way of silent waiting for perfection is sheer futility. Morality is groundless. In rejecting a transcendent unity beneath appearances nihilism repudiates the project of seeking an ultimate meaning to our existence. In affirming the finality of frustration it renounces the possibility of an ultimate peace and perfection. And in denying that there are any universal values it shakes loose the foundations of any consistent morality. It would be difficult to imagine a more radical refutation of religion.

A critical examination of religion needs to take seriously the protestations of nihilism. For no other type of skepticism strikes more forcefully at the very heart of the religious outlook. In denying that there is a transcendent basis for truth, unity, beauty and goodness, nihilism brings out into the open what a world devoid of religion should look like. And nihilism is also important because of the questions it raises about the logical plausibility of secular humanism.

But is nihilism itself a rigorously self-consistent position? Are the nihilists themselves fully coherent in their thinking? Is it really possible to be a *serious* nihilist? Or would not such seriousness already remove one from the ranks of nihilism? If nihilists are so offended by the dishonesty of the theists and the humanists, that they even bother to take the time and spend the energy to write passionately about it, is this not because they *cherish* honesty as a universal value by which we must all be judged? And if honesty is a value to which we should unconditionally bow, how does such obedience differ from the posture of the secular humanists who still (according to nihilists) remain theists at heart?

It is puzzling, for example, that Nietzsche considers it *absolutely* important that we start existing all over again in a more courageous and creative way. Even though Nietzsche rejects the reality of any transcendent ground of absolute values, he develops a rigorous secularist ethic according to which it is never permissible to "sin against the earth." There is a deadly seriousness about his philosophy. He clearly exhibits what Tillich calls "ultimate concern" about certain values that have taken hold of him. And it is also intriguing that Jean-Paul Sartre continues to affirm the value of freedom consistently and unconditionally, even after rejecting the existence of any unconditional values. Even though Sartre asserts that if God does not exist "everything is permitted," he certainly does not think it permissible for us to deny our freedom. (Ogden, 120–43) And even though Albert Camus develops an "absurdist" philosophy in which the abyss of meaninglessness lurks beneath our lives, he ends up endorsing the unconditional values of honesty (in *The Stranger*) and of compassion (in *The Plague*).

In the final analysis many of the most notorious "nihilists," in their lives and in their writings, often seem to drift back toward the humanism that they have already rejected for its logical inconsistency. Thus we may question whether nihilism is itself possible as a serious theory of reality. Of course, *practical* nihilism, understood as a disregard of the claim of any values on us, remains a possibility in our actual lives. We all become practical nihilists whenever we refuse to allow our lives to be molded by any standards or values. But nihilism as a formal, theoretical interpretation of reality is very unstable. Almost before it establishes itself as a serious alternative to religion or humanism, it begins to slide back into the humanist camp. It finds these quarters uncomfortable, however. For according to its own assessment, humanism is still at heart religious.

Nihilism and Religion

Initially nihilism seems to be absolutely opposed to religion. But it is really a caricature of one of our four religious ways, the "way of silence." We have observed that atheism is best understood as an outgrowth or radicalizing of certain temptations that reside in religion itself. Nihilism is the understandable result of carrying to an extreme the tendency toward *iconoclasm* (the destruction of images) which is a central feature of apophatic religion. If the way of silence, with its renunciation of the world and of images, loses touch with the sacramental, mystical and active modes of religion it becomes indistinguishable from nihilism.

To repeat, religion in any of its four modes of expression contains an inclination which can lead to an eventual loss of its integrity if the ways are not held in balance with one another. We have noted, for example, that sacramentalism may degenerate into idolatry or ritualism as a way of avoiding the depth and breadth of mystery. Mysticism can also lose touch with the needs of the social world and degenerate into escapism. Activism can easily break its ties with the sense of the transcendent, as in the case of secular humanism. And the way of silence can lead to nihilism if it is not carefully qualified. We have suggested that these temptations can be offset only when each of our four religious modes allows itself to be qualified by the other three.

The possibility of such deviations requires a constant struggle by people to sustain their religious authenticity. We may usefully understand the temptations of religion in terms of the notion of adventure discussed in Chapter 11. In each mode there is a tendency to swerve away from the adventurousness that we have located at the heart of the religious quest. The theme of adventure implies a wholesomeness and vitality that appeals to our passion for beauty and breadth of vision. It is hard to dispute the merits of such a standard in our assessment of the value of any set of ideas or expressions. But how does religion measure up to this standard?

Each type of religion potentially contributes something to the broadening of our vision of reality, but accompanying each religious approach to mystery and to the world there is also a peculiar kind of temptation to veer away from the goal of adventure. Each of the four ways can sustain the spirit of adventure only if it stays in touch with the other three and participates to some degree in their own dynamics as well. The authenticity of each of our four religious ways demands that it live in communion with the central insights and inclinations of the others. If not, religion loses its adventurousness and slides back toward either monotony or chaos. The decline of religion, with its corresponding loss of adventure, is the direct result of one religious way's disconnecting itself from the dynamism that comes from interacting with the other types.

Sacramental religion's attitude toward the material world is one of enjoyment, but the temptation that goes with such enjoyment of particular realities is *idolatry*. Enjoyment can gradually slip into an enslaving obsession. The classic name for this obsession is idolatry. Idolatry opposes the spirit of adventure by narrowing our interest to a specific aspect of reality and closing us off from the larger world. This is why it has been condemned so forcefully in post-axial religion. The religious protest against idolatry is an attempt to liberate human life and consciousness from the monotony of single-vision. Sacramental religion may avoid this temptation by generating a wide variety of images of God, so that none of them will be taken with absolute seriousness. And it may also maintain its integrity by assuming into itself aspects of the other three religious types.

Mystical religion, in its concern for union with the One beyond the many, relativizes the world of particular things and selves. This viewing things within the perspective of ultimate mystery provides an obstacle to the sacramentalist inclination to idolatry. But in its relativizing of particular goods mysticism may itself surrender to a narrowing and monotonous fall from its intrinsic adventurousness. It may little by little devolve into a severe disregard for the value and uniqueness of individual things and persons. The specific temptation of mysticism is that it may neglect the contrast and plurality required by adventure. It may so accentuate the unity of reality that it suppresses the sense of multiplicity, novelty and diversity associated with the spirit of adventure. Or it may seek refuge in some transcendent sphere untouched by history and the messiness of everyday existence. People attached to mystically oriented religious traditions have sometimes withdrawn from involvement in the complexities of social and political life. They have followed the religious tendency known broadly as *gnosticism*. Gnosticism is a kind of religiousness that gives up on this world and its complicated affairs, often portraying the whole realm of physical and historical reality as inferior to the world of spirit "up above." At times gnosticism is a disguised infatuation with social privilege, teaching that only a few special people are worthy of being saved. Those attracted to mysticism have more than once ended up in some kind of gnosticism. Their religion then becomes a deliberate form of escapism, confined to a closed circle of enlightened elite. Set apart from the ignorant masses, gnostics become ensconced in a sacral world disconnected from this one. Such a temptation can be conquered only if the mystical instinct is constantly chastened by the colorfulness of sacramentalism, the patience of apophatic religion, and the social involvement of the activist way.

Activist religion contributes to adventure by seeking to alter and renew the world, by bringing fresh forms of order and justice into it. Such a concern for justice is filled with unsettling risk and adventure. It thrives on the conviction that there is a mysterious and more inclusive region of future possibilities seeking to interrupt the monotony and social narrowness of the present. But religious activism also contains a certain bias that can lead it to slip away from its intrinsic openness to the novelty of surprise. It may be tempted at times to what we may call, for lack of a better term, *impatience*. Activists seek to reshape human history, but they are tempted to tyranny when there is resistance to their designs. They abandon the prophetic idea of a divine plan beyond our narrowly conceived social projects. Religious activism torn away from its sacramental, mystical and apophatic matrix becomes a purely secular humanism.

Finally, silent or apophatic religion is uneasy about any of our words or images of ultimate reality. It is suspicious of all symbolic language about God. And so it advocates extreme reserve as the most appropriate response to mystery. But such advice, if taken to an extreme, might lead us to a nihilist position. If our religious awareness is totally divested of sacramentalism it will become completely empty. Nihilism would be the consequence of a too relentless suspicion of symbols. And it would deviate from adventure, not in the usual manner of absolutizing a narrow form of order, but in the opposite way of absolutizing chaos. Perfection can only be found somewhere between these extremes.

Nietzsche himself observed that nihilism has its origins in the devaluation of the world prevalent in religions. In Brahmanism, Buddhism and Christianity there is a negation of the world that, if unchecked, leads to the view that reality is empty. Nietzsche merely brought out the nihilist implications of a one-sided world-negation already latent in mystical and apophatic religion. Atheism is the understandable consequence of a fragmentation that starts inside the world of religion. When religion fails to preserve some sort of balance among its four ways, the resulting caricatures of individual ways leads directly to an abandonment either of mystery or the world. Nihilism, like other kinds of atheism, begins with the disintegration of religion.

16.

Humanism

Nihilists, in spite of their explicit intentions, generally "regress" to a form of humanism. They still have a hidden value system and an implicit code of morality. Nietzsche tells us to "remain faithful to the earth." And Sartre insists that we accept our freedom. They hold these imperatives out to the rest of us as universal values. They imply that we should surrender ourselves to their unconditional claim upon us. But if we affirm the universal and unconditional character of any values, we must raise again the question of how these values acquire their universal and unconditional character.

Religion and theology hold that the acceptance of universally binding moral imperatives leads us inevitably to the idea of an ultimate ground of goodness. But we are compelled to ask today whether commitment to moral values actually requires a religious justification. Is religion essential for morality? This is the critical question raised by many skeptics today. Earlier we noted that religion and morality both share a common human attraction to "the good." And it is hard to find a religion that does not promote morality. The prophetic religions, for example, insist that worship of God includes caring for the needy. Hinduism, Buddhism and other traditions all see "good works" and compassion as part of religion. But is religion absolutely essential for morality? And if so, in what sense?

Today skeptics, especially the so-called secular "humanists," question whether we need religion to justify morality. Humans seem to be quite capable of vigorous moral ambition in the absence of any specifically religious commitments. So, what might religion add to morality, if anything? If religion adds nothing to morality, then why should morally inclined people bother about it at all? If we can be "good" without God, as many people obviously are, then talk about God or sacred mystery becomes

238

morally superfluous. If religion has no other function than shaping our conduct, it can easily be replaced by non-religious ethics.

In this chapter we shall look at three distinct ways of answering the question whether religion is necessary for, or adds anything to, morality. The first way is that of post-Enlightenment "modernity." This "humanist" interpretation has no need for religious legitimation of morality. The second, which we shall call the "classical" answer, seeks to root moral imperatives *directly* in some religious vision. According to this interpretation we cannot remain consistently moral without an explicit religious ethic to guide us. And the third position, the "post-modern," argues that religion may not be necessary as a source of specific moral imperatives, but that it remains "existentially" vital as a source of reasons why we should strive to be moral at all.

I. "Modernity's" Dismissal of Religiously Based Ethics

In the latter part of the eighteenth century, the "Age of Reason," the German philosopher Immanuel Kant (1724–1804) questioned the commonly accepted belief that religion is essential for morality. He argued that the moral law is already written within each person. At the most, a specific religion like Christianity might *exemplify* morality, but it cannot be its primary source. The source of morality abides within each one of us, written on our own hearts. For Kant, a Christian himself, Jesus is significant as an exemplar of virtue, but he is not essential as a source of moral directives. Each one of us already possesses the very same moral impulse that Christ felt. We can look to him as an "example" of how we should respond to the moral law, but the proximate source of obligation exists within each person, apart from any religious affiliation. We all experience a "categorical imperative," an internal demand to do our duty and to act in a manner that we would expect everyone else to follow also. So we misunderstand religion if we look to it primarily as a source of the ethical intentionality that is already inscribed in our souls.

Kant himself thought that the existence of the moral law within us implies that God exists (as the one who wrote it into our souls), and that the religious outlook is valid. Furthermore, he specified that religion still remains necessary as a seal on the human quest for happiness. But many post-Kantian thinkers have forsaken religion altogether. They have focused only on Kant's project of making morality autonomous, that is, independent of religion. And so today, partly as a result of the impact of Kantian philosophy, secularist thought fully endorses the notion of an ethics without religion. The idea of God and other religious notions of ultimate reality are considered morally superfluous. If morality can flourish without any reference to the divine, then what possible purpose does religion serve? Religion even interferes with the cultivation of values, diverting people's attention to heaven when they could be improving things on earth. Why mystify the consciousness of the masses by giving them religious motivation for conduct that could be justified more securely on purely rational and secular grounds?

In the present century the philosopher Max Otto expressed this secularist position on religion and morality:

> Whenever men and women have been able to act as if there were no divinity to shape human ends, and have themselves assumed responsibility, they have discovered how to turn their abilities to good account. . . . Not believing in God has worked well. It has worked better than believing did. (M. Otto, 1940, 382–83)

Nevertheless, Otto observed, people still cling to God. They do so partly to find an answer to the facts of suffering and death, but most of all they do so to have some reason for committing themselves to moral ideals. The reason for the retention of theism, he wrote,

> . . . is man's low opinion of himself as a moral being. Thousands who leave God out when engaged in practical pursuits, or in following the promptings of desire, are careful to keep him on hand for the sake of ideals. They feel that God is needed to validate and enforce the moral life. This they believe is especially true of "the masses." Without God, man is a purely natural creature and must act, so they think, like any other animal . . . Generosity, ethical idealism, civic-mindedness, interest in moral growth can be expected from none but those who are inspired by God. (384)

Otto, on the contrary, argued that moral aspiration does not require belief in the supernatural. Instead, religion and the idea of God are themselves outgrowths of our natural moral idealism. Moral aspiration is much older than the gods, and it is still around after the gods are gone. In the absence of God and religion there is still

> . . . devotion, heroism, self-sacrifice, loyalty to causes. What is it but this original virtue in human beings that faith in God draws upon to give itself vitality? No; the conclusion cannot be with

stood that greatness, from every point of view, has been achieved by individuals and by whole peoples in the absence of faith in God. (385)

Kai Nielsen, a contemporary philosopher, also questions any need to invoke religion to justify our morality. He takes issue with those theologians who emphasize that morality is baseless unless it has its origin in the decree of God's eternal will. God is not necessary to give authority to moral decrees. Rather it is our moral nobility itself that gives rise to the idea of God.

> Morality cannot be based on religion. If anything, the opposite is partly true, for nothing can be God unless he or it is an object worthy of worship, and it is our own moral insight that must tell us if anything at all could be worthy of worship. (1976, 254)

> A religious belief depends for its viability on our sense of good and bad—our own sense of worth—and not vice versa. . . . A moral understanding must be logically prior to any religious assent. (256)

Thus Otto and Nielsen think the human moral impulse is primary, and religion secondary and superfluous. Some skeptics go even further than Otto and Nielsen. They find religion not only morally unnecessary but even intolerable. Friedrich Nietzsche, for example, thought Christian morality was a cover-up for a defeatist attitude toward life. The moral imperatives associated with Christian religion are representations of a refusal to live life to the fullest. Nietzsche declared the "death of God" in order to signal his sense of the collapse of a culture based upon a "conventional" morality adhered to without real conviction. His atheism was an expression of his desire for a "higher" morality surpassing the mediocrity sanctioned by religion. He wrote that people could get along morally quite well without being watched over by the all-seeing eye of a God whose essential function seemed to be that of moderating human behavior. Noble people would have to "transvalue all values," that is, place morality on an entirely new, this-worldly, foundation. But they would not necessarily be less moral for all of that. For they would discover a new and better reason for being moral than simply trying to please a supernatural being whose arbitrary decrees robbed them of their own life. They would root their morality directly in an aspiration to *live*. The desire to live fully, the simple desire to *become*, would spontaneously give rise to a more vigorous ethic than we have ever had under the watchful eye of religion.

Many other critics have also found religion morally defective. Karl Marx thought that religion was an understandable response to human misery, but in his opinion it lacked moral substance. Because of its promise of happiness in the next world religion had promoted an escapist attitude toward oppressive conditions in this world. Thus religious ideology had undermined rather than strengthened the natural impulse toward compassion, justice and liberation of the oppressed. Religion for Marx was not moral enough.

Likewise, Sigmund Freud doubted that religion promotes morality any more vigorously than rationalism and scientism can. And Albert Camus, through one of his characters (Dr. Rieux) in his novel *The Plague*, wondered whether belief in a deity who permits human suffering might not even legitimate our own indifference to the plight of others:

> ". . . since the order of the world is shaped by death, mightn't it be better for God if we refuse to believe in Him and struggle with all our might against death, without raising our eyes toward the heaven where He sits in silence." (1948, 116f.)

Other skeptics have pointed out that a good deal of the butchering of humans has been carried out in the name of religion. Religion is often mixed up with the most savage and barbaric deeds. On this basis more than any other, we have reason to question whether religion actually adds anything of substance to our moral aspirations. To many honest thinkers religion is not needed as a support for moral behavior, and in some cases it is even an obstacle to ethical uprightness. And Jean-Paul Sartre, more forcefully than any other modern philosopher, taught that morality is our own, not God's, creation. For all of these reasons religion seems, to skeptics at least, to have little importance for the moral life of humans.

II. The "Classical" Religious Reaction

Not surprisingly, this "modern" impeachment of the moral value of religion has drawn vigorous rebuttals. A classic illustration is provided by the tormented Dmitri in Dostoevsky's *The Brothers Karamazov*.

> It's God that's worrying me. That's the only thing that's worrying me. What if He doesn't exist? What if Rakitin is right—that it's an idea made up by men? Then, if He doesn't exist, man is the chief of the earth, of the universe. Magnificent! Only how is he going to be good without God? That's the ques-

tion. I always come back to that. For whom is man going to love then? To whom will he sing a hymn . . . Rakitin says that one can love humanity without God . . . only an . . . idiot can maintain that. (721)

Dostoevsky (1821–1881), along with other religious writers, is asking here: if there are no eternally established standards of right and wrong, then what is to keep us from a moral relativism where each person is left alone to decide what is good and evil? And if relativism becomes widespread, what is to prevent the upsurge of barbarism and nihilism? In an earlier novel, *Crime and Punishment*, Dostoevsky's character Roskolnikov finds no reason, in the absence of an eternally prescribed ethic, not to chop open the head of an innocent woman for the sake of a little pocket change. And Ivan, Dmitri's atheist brother, concludes on the basis of simple logic that if there is no God then literally anything is permitted.

Dostoevsky's apprehensions have been amplified by numerous contemporary religious thinkers. They claim that the most horrific crimes of our century, perhaps of all human history, have been prompted by godless ideologies. And they cannot help drawing a connection between the modern religious vacuum and the complete disregard of personal rights that has allowed the slaughter of literally millions of people in the twentieth century. They contend that if the ethical track record of religions is hardly clean, that of modern atheism is much worse.

All the great religious and philosophical traditions point to some transcendent and timeless order of "rightness" as the basis for a potentially universal moral consensus. Generally speaking, the morality of a people is related to and measured by some intuited eternal cosmic order. Egyptian religion called this universal transcendent order *Ma'at*. Judaism speaks of the "Wisdom" or the "Word" of God. Taoism referred to the eternal *Tao* or "Way" as the standard for our moral life. Muslims and Christians also see the basis for morality in the "Word" and "Will" of God. Plato postulated an eternal realm of "Ideas" which contains "the Good" toward which we naturally aspire in our moral life. Buddhists submit to *dharma*, which means both duty and universal rightness. And so forth. The modern experiment with the supposition that we humans are the sole origin of our own morality is not even conceivable in these traditional frameworks. Today classical religious ethicians from the various traditions argue that we must hold onto or recover this venerable view of morality wherein goodness is written into the book of the universe independently of our human existence. Moral values are indeed *a priori*, that is, derived from a prior, eternally established set of standards. They are not our own creations, and if we start thinking they are we will end up in a moral relativism in which literally anything goes. Authentic existence requires *obedience* to an eternal moral order. The solution to modern social and political ills is to recapture a feeling for the eternal moral order set forth by religions. One of the main values of religions is that they can put us in touch with the eternal moral will of the divine. This is the "classical" point of view.

III. A "Post-modern" Alternative

However, our question still persists: what exactly is the connection of religion to morality? Should we dispense with religion in our efforts to live truly ethical lives, or do we need religion in order to be moral? So far we have looked at two extreme responses to these tough questions. The "modern" stance maintains that morality will spontaneously radiate out of a life lived purposefully. The instinct to live, if allowed to express itself, will all by itself give rise to wholesome moral aspiration. Religion is neither necessary nor desirable as a motivator to moral idealism. The reason people have not always had moral aspirations is that their instinct for life and creativity has been so often thwarted by fear and repression, the latter sometimes sanctioned by religion itself. Where people are fully alive, we do not need to worry about whether they will be moral. Working together they can formulate their own purely human moral codes and also discover a purely rational motivation for adhering to them. This is the secular humanist conviction.

The opposing "classical" position holds that we need direct moral imperatives dictated from "on high" in order to prevent the slide of modern civilization toward an ethical void. We require an authoritative and unambiguous divine source of moral precepts, something like the Law-giver God of the Bible, who sets out in stone tablets what is right and wrong, and who commands unwavering adherence to these decrees. Modernity's dismissal of religion as a source of morality has obliterated any clear authoritative criteria of right and wrong. The collapse of religion has prepared the way for the bloody purges of this century and for the moral decadence that now threatens life on our planet. According to this second position we cannot be good without religion.

There is yet a third kind of response, though. We shall call it "post-modern" because it accepts some, while rejecting other, aspects of modernity's understanding of morality. Like modernity it seeks an "autonomous" morality that avoids the triviality of "conventional" religion and morality. At the same time it embraces the classical position's positive assessment of the ethical value of religion. But it avoids a too direct and uncritical association of religion with specific moral imperatives. The "classical" stance leaves itself open to being taken over by what we earlier called "pre-conventional" morality. What is needed today is a more critically refined formulation of the precise relationship of religion to our moral aspirations.

The post-modern proposal follows the Kantian idea that in a certain qualified sense religion is indeed morally superfluous. It is a simple fact that most non-religious people are also moral, many of them admirably so. They do not need religion in order to be upright in their conduct. They have moral aspirations even where they are not religious. How then does religion relate to morality? Our third position answers that religion is not needed in order to formulate moral codes, but it is eventually required as part of an adequate answer to the question: why should we bother about morality in the first place? Religion shows its distinctive colors not when it gets into the morality business (which of course it cannot help doing to some extent), but when it arms people with *reasons to trust in life* in spite of all the temptations to despair. In other words, the location of religion in relation to morality may be formulated in terms of the distinction we made in Chapter 9 between problem and mystery: religion is not so much the provider of answers to our specific moral problems as it is a response to the "limit-question": *why should we be moral at all?* (Tracy, 100–04)

Post-modern theology agrees with some aspects of both the modern and the classical ethical theories, but it disagrees with others. On the one hand, it accepts the observation by Kant and his humanist disciples that a genuine morality must be autonomous. It should emanate in an unforced manner from a life of trust rather than as a fearful response to a set of authoritarian decrees, even if the latter are presented under the heading of "God's eternal will." For "the will of God" may easily be interpreted in preconventional or conventional ways. When that happens, as it often does, divine authority may be given to precepts that can suffocate rather than promote human life and happiness. Often in the past the notion of "God's will" has been accompanied by threats of punishment and hopes of reward that have perpetuated moral immaturity. Or it has sanctioned stuffy and repressive social arrangements. But in the post-modern view any adherence to a code of conduct out of fear or desire for consolation is immature morality. Behaving ourselves in order to receive a reward or to avoid punishment, or purely in order to be accepted by the group, is childish and unworthy of authentic ethical and religious existence. So the idea of a moralistic God who arbitrarily issues commandments that seem to have nothing to do with the intrinsic energy of human life and the quest for happiness is morally intolerable. To repeat, the "classical" approach sometimes leaves itself open to the pre-conventional and conventional ethical dispositions.

On the other hand, our third approach cannot dispense with religion and its notion of an ultimate, transcendent mystery. Together with the "classical" position it acknowledges the need to provide a transcendent ground for ethical conduct. But the question is where to locate this transcendent reality. How can we understand the idea of God and morality in a manner that prevents a return to pre-conventional or conventional religious morality?

The post-modern answer is as follows. Morality flourishes only whenever people have a firm conviction that life is worth living. The fact is, however, that people do not always have such trust. As we have observed several times before, our original trust is subject to erosion by negative experiences that inevitably occur in the course of our lives. Religion then comes into the picture not to make us moral but to provide the reassurance that life is worth living at all. Religion points to a *ground* of trust, an ultimate graciousness of mystery, a final perfection behind our feeling of dissatisfaction. In doing so it makes reality appear meaningful, and it is this impression that activates our moral instincts. If we were fully convinced that life is not worthwhile it is doubtful that we would have the incentive to act ethically in a consistent way. By pointing to an ultimate reason why reality is trustworthy, religion makes its central contribution to morality.

Post-modern theology shares the "modern" position that genuine moral aspiration follows only from a prior conviction that life is worth living at all. Without such an animating premise, perhaps felt only implicitly for the most part, there can be no genuine moral aspiration. Whenever the will to live weakens, so also does the desire to do good. The place of religion is not to interfere with our moral autonomy by providing an alternative and competing set of moral norms. This would be "pre-conventional." Instead religion's role is to articulate visions of ultimate mystery and perfection that would motivate people to trust in the final meaningfulness of life. A mature (post-conventional) morality will follow from this trust more easily than it would from the idea of a deity issuing the arbitrary moral decrees of pre-conventional morality.

Does this third interpretation make religion morally superfluous? In one sense "yes," but in a deeper sense "no." The post-modernist puts religion in a much more important and foundational place than is allotted to it by the classical view. It does not situate religion in competition with autonomous ethics. Religion is not an alternative source of commandments. Rather, religion is a source of symbolic reassurance concerning *why* we should be ethical at all. For example, when the myths of sacramental religion narrate the possibility that suffering and evil will end and that redemption is possible, this serves to reassure people that there is a way through the most intransigent limits, and that therefore they can go on in confidence with their lives. Braced by an *ultimate* reassurance that life is worth living in spite of suffering and death, people will be more naturally inclined to give ethical substance to their lives than if they were convinced that existing is finally futile.

To reiterate, religion does have an indispensable role with respect to ethics. But it is not one of competing with our natural impulse to morality. We noted earlier that religion does not need to compete with science either. Instead it can function to ground the trust in the value of truth-seeking that underlies the entire scientific enterprise. And religion may play an analogously foundational role with respect to our moral life. If religion is understood as providing a foundation for the moral life, it is in no danger of being replaced by ethics.

Philosopher John E. Smith, who is one of the most articulate defenders of this third alternative, emphasizes the foundational (rather than competitive) role that religion plays in relation to morality:

> Ultimately, no view of the good life, no serious doctrine of what man ought to do, is ever possible apart from some view of his final destiny; and such a view introduces the religious element. This is the most important consideration in showing that morality is necessarily related to religion. (200f.)

The main issue here is not so much whether we will be moral, although that is always a legitimate question. Rather, especially today, a more basic question is whether we have something worthwhile to live for, some goal or destiny to fulfill, something that will guarantee the significance of our lives and endeavors. This trust in life can no longer be taken for granted. There are too many aspects of our experience that can lead us to doubt the validity of trust. Despair about the very meaning of life is the main concern of many. Questions about what we should do morally speaking with our lives are secondary to the question whether life is worth living at all. If religion has a contribution to make to morality it will lie primarily in the area of responding to this more fundamental question.

A fully moral life can blossom only out of the soil of a vision of reality that seeks to maximize the meaning of life. In other words, a vigorous moral life can follow only from a meaningful vision of reality as a whole. The *primary* function of religion, therefore, is not to issue moral decrees (since these can be given even in the absence of any religion), but to present a vision of reality that will make for a coherent and meaningful life. If religion does that part well, it will also have provided the basis for moral existence. It will have shown that, after all, religion is needed for morality, but in a much deeper sense than the classical position imagines. Understood in this light, Smith says,

> . . . religion is a genuine foundation for morality without at the same time being an authoritarian force behind it compelling the good life through fear. Since it is the threat of authority that the opponents of religious morality usually deplore (and rightly so), a religious foundation that eliminates this threat and that at the same time provides the basis without which all morality must be destroyed is able to overcome the objection. Morality is both unsure and incomplete without a living connection with religious faith. (202)

Religion, Morality and the Stages of Moral Development

Wholesome moral aspiration arises only out of a basic confidence that life is meaningful and that the world is trustworthy. If we had no such confidence we would have no inclination to be genuinely moral either. The people who are most interested in doing good are those who *already* trust in life. Be it observed, too, that they are often skeptics as far as religion is concerned. For such individuals morality flows out of an implicit prior conviction (a "faith," if you will) that there is value in living and in making life enjoyable for others as well. Their moral activism does not stem from a desire to please authorities or to avoid the consequences of violating taboos. Instead it is guided by the belief that pursuit of values is worthwhile in its own right. An authentic morality accepts the burden of ethical action not out of fear, or because of a desire to be accepted by one's social group, but from a conviction of the universal and unconditional character of the values one is pursuing. A truly moral person is one who loves his or her neighbors because they are intrinsically valuable, not because one will be rewarded for doing so or punished for not doing so. Virtue is its own reward.

But, as we noted in Chapter 12, there are different *stages* of moral development, and it is necessary to distinguish among several levels of ethical maturity as we assess the relationship of religion to morality. For, viewed developmentally, a certain kind of religiosity does seem necessary to those arrested at moral levels one and two. Ideas of God and the sacred add an awesomeness to taboos and conventions that makes them all the more staunch in their imperialism. Purely human standards, when soaked in the sacred, become intractable, inviolable. But when their sacral legitimation is questioned, the moral force of taboos and conventions is weak-

ened also. Therefore, people committed to such norms, no matter how
oppressive the latter might be, defend "religion" fanatically at times. They
need the sacred primarily to uphold what they consider to be "moral."

So if we are asked whether religion is needed in order for us to
behave, we may first have to make a rather complicated self-examination
about our own particular level of moral development. If we are fixed at
levels one or two (and probably no one has fully outgrown these stages) it
would not be surprising if we answered that we would become rather
mischievous if we had no sense of divine control. The first two levels of
moral development do seem to "need" religion. Each of them clings desperately to the sacred in order to shore up the moral force that it intrinsically
lacks. Taboos and conventions are themselves often devoid of inherent
moral authority, so we have to appeal to the idea of God's authority to
compensate for their own emptiness. When we are fixated at levels one or
two, we are more inclined to identify morality with religion than when our
moral life is operating at the third level. But when we act for the sake of
goodness itself, we no longer do so because a divine authority tells us to. So
religion does indeed seem to become morally superfluous at the "post-
conventional" level. Ironically, we might say that this mature type of
morality is *least* in need of religion as a source of moral imperatives. It is
the most autonomous or independent of the three types. But precisely
because it does not need religion as a source of ethical directives, it can
establish the healthiest relationship to religion as reassurance. It can appreciate the role of religion in giving shape and support to our original confidence in life's meaning, without which morality will wither and die.

The real wonder is not so much that people are moral, but that they
have so much trust in life in spite of all its negativities. Religion attempts
to justify this trust. A religious vision seems, at least to its advocates, to be
the most coherent way of interpreting and justifying our spontaneous
trust.

The Religious Origins of Humanism

Skepticism, as we have seen, is the outgrowth of a dismantling of the
four-fold character of religion. Whenever one of religion's four ways is
isolated from the others it swerves into a form either of secularism or a
religious escapism that inevitably evokes a secularistic reaction. What we
are calling secular humanism is the inevitable consequence of a severance
of the "active way" from its former connection to the sacramental, mystical
and apophatic aspects of religion. Whenever the human impulse for moral
action is divorced from symbols of the sacred, or from a sense of an

ultimate meaning and inexhaustible mystery, the context for action is then shrunk down to the sphere of "this world." It then becomes necessary to find perfection within this sphere alone, since there is no other. If there is no infinite expanse of mystery the secular domain then takes on an almost infinite importance. And it becomes absolutely imperative for the activist to make "this world" fulfill our deepest longings.

It goes without saying that religions would find the humanist approach to be inadequate and, ironically, dehumanizing. In the short run, it is true, the activist energy of secular humanism can provide needed improvement of our immediate environment. The humanist approach appeals to our instinct for reform. But religion in its whole, four-fold fullness would offer a caution to the humanist. In the long run, religion insinuates, our own reforms are not enough to bring about the coherence and perfection that the human spirit requires. And to pretend that human action alone can do so will sooner or later lead to even more frustration.

Conclusion: Prayer

Probably nothing is more central to religion than praying. And since religion comes to concrete expression especially in prayer, we may conclude by noting that each of our four religious ways gives rise to a correspondingly characteristic way of praying.

"Prayer," says Friedrich Heiler in his classic work on the subject, "is the great bond of union of Christendom; and not only of Christendom, but of all mankind. Prayer is the most tangible proof of the fact that the whole of mankind is seeking after God; or—to put it more correctly—that it is sought by God. For it is precisely in prayer that we have revealed to us the essential element of all religion . . ." (1932, iv) According to the Protestant reformer Martin Luther, faith is "prayer and nothing but prayer." The great nineteenth century German theologian, Friedrich Schleiermacher, also said: "To be religious and to pray—that is really one and the same thing." His contemporary, the poet Novalis, thought that "praying is religion in the making." And Richard Rothe, a famous evangelist, strongly insists: ". . . the religious impulse is essentially the impulse to pray. . . . the non-praying man is rightly considered to be religiously dead." (Heiler, 1932, v)

Thus in coming to the phenomenon of prayer we arrive at the very core of religion. Members of our species have probably prayed, in one way or another, ever since their earliest appearance in evolution. Praying is the act, perhaps the only act, in which religion becomes concretely real. Aside from prayer, religion is really an abstract notion for the most part. Its ritual formulas, creeds, temples and churches are mere shells unless they are animated by acts of prayer addressed to mystery. Religion lives only in a rather willowy sense in symbols and stories until these are concretely recited in a worshipful spirit by actual people. There are ageless and venerable religious traditions, but these too are abstractions until they come alive in present moments of prayer. Religion becomes concrete or actual only at those points where an individual life intersects prayerfully with a tradition. It is especially in the person's or community's sincere act of praying that the language and meanings embodied in a religious tradi-

251

tion become actualized. To study religion, then, means in a special way to study prayer. (W.C. Smith)

This implies, however, that all the critical questions that have been raised about the reasonableness and respectability of religion converge with a special urgency on the matter of prayer. Religion in the eyes of both its defenders and critics stands or falls with the plausibility of prayer. Today the same questions are asked about prayer as about religion as such. What is going on when we pray? Is not prayer perhaps merely a conversation with ourselves? Is it reasonable for people to pray as though there were powers able to respond to them? If praying is effective, then why does it appear sometimes that so few of our prayers are answered? Is prayer any different from magic? Does it do us any good psychologically? Is it a childish attempt to manipulate God or the gods? In short, is it really possible to pray any more?

Skepticism has questioned the genuineness and viability of prayer. But it is fascinating to read the results of sociological questionnaires on the religious habits of people today. Often they indicate that people who consider themselves non-religious and even atheistic nevertheless pray. (Greeley) Non-believers sometimes spontaneously call upon the heavens or some hidden and anonymous powers for help, especially in tough circumstances. They even occasionally invoke the name of God. Though in calmer circumstances they are embarrassed at having broken down or "regressed" to prayer, their spontaneous orations still provide interesting data to interpreters of religion. It seems that praying is often an unpremeditated outburst of ineradicable human trust.

However, prayer in the context of the major religions often has a formal, stylized quality that allows us to understand and categorize its several main types in terms of our typology of religion. Prayer, as the heart of religion, may be broadly defined as the conscious surrender to mystery. But, following our four-fold breakdown of religious ways, we may take notice of four correspondingly distinct ways of praying in response to the sense of mystery.

A. Sacramental Prayer. In sacramental religion prayer is often ritualized, especially in the form of rites of passage and of sacrifice. Ritual is a communal celebration of life, ideals and identity; and in sacrificial offerings it is an expression of petition and gratitude. It usually goes hand in hand with myths, the most significant sacred stories in the lives of people. Thus its mode of worshipping mystery is *dramatic*. It *acts out* in the form of a drama the conviction of being related to an ultimate mystery. Its dramatic character sets sacramental prayer apart from the contemplative, quietistic and activist modes of worship associated with the other three types.

If ritual is the typical form of sacramental prayer its content is *thanksgiving and petition*. The enjoyment that accompanies sacramental religion's appreciation of nature fills its participants with an almost spontaneous feeling of gratitude for the gifts of the earth. And, in response, "eucharistic" rituals of shared thanksgiving and petition arise in the life of a community. The Christian eucharistic celebration is a modern remnant of a kind of ritual worship that goes back into the darkness of prehistoric religion. The rites of Vedic Hinduism, of native Americans, Australian aborigines, African tribal societies and other peoples that live close to nature also exemplify this sacramental mode of prayer.

The specific temptation of sacramental prayer, corresponding to the temptation to idolatry in sacramental religion, is *ritualism*. Sacramental religion can slip from wholesome enjoyment of nature toward an acquisitive obsession with the goods of the earth. Likewise the rituals that celebrate the gifts of life and nature can gradually become ways of possessing and manipulating the beneficent sacred sources from which they seem to emanate. Ritual can degenerate into magic. When this happens the criticisms of skeptics become religiously significant as a needed corrective.

B. Mystical Prayer. The defining feature of mysticism is its quest for and experience of union with mystery. To the extent that all of religion manifests such a tendency, it might be accurate to say that mysticism is a dimension of all religion. However, at times the quest for intimacy or union with God becomes so explicit and self-conscious that we may speak of mysticism as a distinct type of religion. Likewise, its specific style of prayer is that of longing for union with the divine. The prayer of union, or unitive prayer, is less dependent on symbols, rituals and sacrifice than sacramental prayer. At times it seems as though it dispenses with them altogether. Its prevailing passion is that the distance between the participant and God will be conquered in the experience of a oneness of the soul with its sacred destiny, the Godhead itself. This type of prayer may be called *contemplation*. Whereas sacramental prayer of petition humbly begs for further gifts from the gods or God, contemplative prayer seeks God alone. It is content with nothing less than the infinite.

However, in its haste for encounter with transcendent unity it risks the temptation of *monism*. That is, it may overlook and deprecate the richness of religious life that accompanies a multitude of symbolic expressions. Contemplation at times may give too short shrift to the many nuanced ways in which mystery is mediated to religious consciousness by way

of particular goods. An overreaction to the dangers of idolatry and ritualism may lead the contemplative to a state of mono-tony.

   C. Apophatic Prayer. This is the prayer of silence. Usually it does not
take place until one has already had a taste of sacramental, mystical and
activist modes of religious existence. It is a kind of prayer in which God
seems so radically "other" than anything human imagery can represent
that it is best not to imagine ultimate reality at all. Hence it is a prayer
without images. Whereas most religious devotion requires the use of images or "icons" (the Greek term for images) to represent the Godhead,
apophatic prayer puts these aside as inadequate. The purpose of silent
prayer is to prevent the worshipper from acquiescing in too narrow an idea
of mystery.
   The apophatic approach emphasizes that images of God are not to be
taken too literally. It teaches a renunciation of obsessive clinging to particular "icons," mental or artistic, when we pray. Such detachment in prayer
will expand one's religious horizons. However, there is a temptation in this
kind of prayer, parallel to the excesses of asceticism. It is the temptation to
iconoclasm ("destruction of images"). Eventually a rigorous iconoclasm will
impoverish the human sense of mystery. Without our dwelling in images
and stories our religious life will lose its content altogether. Iconoclasm
may be essential as a moment within the religious process of purifying the
sense of mystery, but it cannot without considerable peril be made the sum
and substance of religion.
   In the history of spirituality there is much controversy, and even
occasional armed strife, between the iconoclasts on the one hand and the
sacramentalists (those who rely on sacred images and symbols) on the
other. For example, in 726 Byzantine Emperor Leo III issued a decree
against the use of icons of Christ, his mother and the saints. His actions
provoked a riot as well as the condemnation of popes. The controversy
lingered and has made a lasting imprint on the character of Christianity,
some factions of which have always been suspicious of images while other
factions have been positively disposed toward their use in worship. Islam
has generally abandoned the use of icons as a temptation to idolatry, while
popular Hinduism is inseparable from their use. And while the Buddha
would have been suspicious of sacramental religious representations, his
followers' devotional life is filled with vivid and abundant images of the
Buddha himself. We have argued that it is essential for the integrity of
religion that there be a balance of sacraments with silence. The same must
also be true of prayer.

D. Activist Prayer. For activist religion, action itself is prayer. Action, especially the doing of justice, is a way into mystery, no less than sacramentalism, contemplation and renunciation. Therefore, the prophets identified it with prayer and worship. Good works carried out on behalf of others is the supreme form of sacrifice. As far as the prophets are concerned, the most sincere worship of God lies not in rituals or contemplation or silence, but in the love of one's neighbor and one's enemies. In the history of religion there have also been bitter disputes as to whether charitable action is sufficient to be called prayer, but to the activist such discussions are fruitless. If religion, prayer and theological discussions do not bear fruit in the world of actual human existence, then the activist questions their authenticity.

The characteristic temptation of activist prayer, as it is evaluated by representatives of the other types, might be called *profanity*. Literally "profane" means "outside the temple," that is, outside the sphere of the sacred. Religion itself is a rebellion against sheer profanity. "Profanity," in this connection, simply means the failure to acknowledge explicitly a distinct realm of the sacred. When religious life is too oriented toward the affairs of the world, it runs the risk of losing touch with the *mysterium tremendum et fascinans*.

Prayer, as the most concrete expression of religion, involves a constant struggle to balance its symbolic, mystical, silent and active elements.

Appendix A:
Religion and Cults

There is much discussion among social scientists as to just what makes a "cult" distinct from a religion, or whether all religions are perhaps varieties of cult. Usually, however, a cult is understood as a small religious group cut off from the main religious bodies, and attached to a living charismatic "cult figure" (like Jim Jones of Jonestown, or Sun Myung Moon of the Unification Church). This cult leader exercises a tight management of the lives and minds of the participants. In addition, he or she may insist on financial control of the members' lives. Many cults demand that people surrender all their worldly possessions as a condition of membership.

It is still difficult to know exactly where to draw the line between a cult and the larger religious movements called "sects," and even the major religious traditions themselves. The lines are blurry, especially once we notice that major traditions themselves developed out of sects and perhaps to some extent out of groups almost indistinguishable from cults. Furthermore, in the major traditions individual leaders are also often endowed with an unusually intense sacral meaning, and their special personal attractiveness allows some of their followers to treat them almost like cult figures. Some Roman Catholics, for example, are often attached to the person of the Pope in a way that may seem to share at least several of the features of a cult. But the Pope does not, at least in principle, seek to be the center of Christian faith. According to Catholic theology he is simply a "sacramental" representative of Christ, and his formal mission is to turn the attention of Catholics to the Savior, and not to himself.

The major historical religious figures, such as Moses, the Buddha, Jesus or Muhammad, tried, sometimes unsuccessfully, to divert attention away from themselves by pointing toward an ultimate mystery or an exceptional religious destiny. A cult leader, on the other hand, usually wants the members' attention to be focused on himself or herself.

Although an adequate discussion of the cult phenomenon today would require more than a few books, we might usefully distinguish religion from cult in terms of the criterion of adventure. Accordingly, a "cult" would be a sect that has *unnecessarily* closed itself off from the expansiveness and openness to novelty and mystery that we have associated with the spirit of adventure. The key term here is "unnecessary," for at times in the social development of any distinct group it seems necessary to draw clear boundaries between its specific teachings and the larger social consensus. Perhaps it is even essential momentarily to suspend dialogue with the wider world of ideas, and not allow too much novelty in for a while. Some time might be required to put structure and definiteness into a new sect's thinking. Without some definition sects and religions, like anything else, would fade off into a vagueness that would make them unidentifiable. Thus there may be need for a momentary tightening of the boundaries that enclose the religious system. During such a phase too much novelty might be taken as a threat to the life-ways of the religious group. (Bowker, 1988)

A partial exclusion of novelty is required in any organized entity. No finite structure can entertain all possibilities. At certain times in the evolution of religion and society, as well as that of the cosmos itself, the introduction of novelty is inappropriate. For example, when the evolution of life was still at the phase of unicellular organisms, it was not yet time for dinosaurs. When society was still at the tribal phase, it was not yet time for the invention of the computer. Likewise in the evolution of a religion there is perhaps a time to circle the wagons and get the teachings in order before becoming too open to the outside world.

But there also comes a time to open up to the infusion of novelty without which any body, whether a cell, a social group or a religious sect, will decay and die. A "cult" results from the untimely, irrelevant obsession with religious harmony and order when it would be more enlivening to allow individuals in the religious system more autonomy and room for creativity. A cult is the product of a group's clinging to a strong leader's fixed religious ideas about order when the time is ripe for change, diversity and growth. It is the mark of religious wisdom to be able to discern *where* and *when* to draw the limits that define how religion fits into the totality of life. The cult leader often lacks such wisdom, and so he or she tends to place limits around the membership in a way that is restrictive of their growth. In a cult there is usually a firm "clinging" to a particular person. The great traditions of Islam, Judaism, Christianity, Hinduism and Buddhism would find this infatuation with a finite human being to be an undue narrowing of the base of religious life. Some early Christians were tempted to form cults of such powerful personalities as Paul and other Christian leaders, but Paul vigorously repudiated such attempts.

A cult can be extremely attractive, however. Today the major religious traditions often seem irrelevant, especially to young people. If there is

considerable sadness in an adolescent's life, the warmth and family atmo-
sphere of a cult can be extremely inviting. The failure of the churches to
speak to the needs of these sensitive people has driven them in search of
social units that can provide immediate solutions. And the cults are there
to take them in. If there is little structure in one's life the natural human
instinct for order will drive one to a place where he or she can find a
harmony that keeps chaos away. A cult, precisely because it has already
excluded much novelty and diversity, often seems to provide the safest
haven from the threat of disorder.

A cult, then, is understandable as the solution to the natural need for
order and meaning in one's life. But the risk of such self-enclosure is that
the relevant novelty essential for vitality might also be ruled out. In a cult
too much of a burden of authority is often placed on the shoulders of a
single individual to guide the group to the "truth." And if the leader is a
particularly attractive or charismatic figure, he or she might serve as the
focus of the members' need to surrender themselves religiously. The leader
can become the principal cult object. In such fusion of themselves with the
personality of the cult leader, people might find a sort of security, but in
the process they will lose themselves and their freedom. By thus imprison-
ing themselves in the cult they forfeit the possibility of growth and expan-
sion that can only come through the assimilation of novel and creative
ideas. A cult is so attached to the will and whim of its leader that it soon
begins to stagnate. It sacrifices all novelty for the sake of a trivial order. In
terms of the theme of adventure, it has opted for monotony rather than
risking the disorientation that arises from any invigorating encounter with
the larger world. For that reason the life expectancy of a cult is relatively
short in comparison with a sect or a religion.

Often when a religion is in its infancy it is composed of a social
minority which, in order to maintain its distinct identity, almost has to seal
itself off momentarily from the larger cultural context against which it
struggles. This was true in some sense, for example, of early Buddhists,
Hebrews, Christians and Muslims. These started out as "sects," but they
all continued to grow like living organisms, embracing much variety and
including new elements down through the centuries. They opened themselves, though sometimes reluctantly, to the conflicts that inevitably occur
when new elements are entertained. The Scriptures of all the major faiths
contain evidence of tension and sometimes bitter internal strife. A sect is to
some degree willing to accommodate this complexity and confusion, and
such tolerance allows it to grow into an adventurous religion. A cult, on
the other hand, is not willing to expand its sense of limits or of life's
meaning beyond those tolerated by the leader.

At many points in their histories, of course, sects and religions have been tempted to close the circle of "truth" around themselves and ward off the invasion of novelty. By giving in to such a temptation they sometimes revert to the kind of obsession with order that is operative inside a cult. But the breadth of complexity within the major religions helps to inhibit such narrowness, allowing for the intersection of many different ways of being religious. The major traditions are impressive for their tolerance and nurturing of all four ways of being religious. The richness and tension that follows from the effort to keep all four ways alive contributes much to the vitality of these traditions. A cult, on the other hand, is at a disadvantage because it is too narrow in scope and traditional memory to accommodate the self-correcting elements present when a variety of religious ways is tolerated and promoted.

Appendix B:
Is Marxism a Religion?

It is tempting to include Marxism among the religions of the world. In its "myth" of dialectical materialism it provides the basis for trust. It gives people a goal to strive for. It has its own sense of origins and order. It has a symbolic language for the "compound of limitations" that confront people in their lives, especially concerning the oppressive conditions of "capitalism." And it holds out the prospect of final "freedom" from this oppression. Moreover, its central teachings invite people into an adventurous struggle to bring about a kind of redemption from evil as it is understood in Marxist terms. How then is it different from "religion" as we have been using the term?

The main difference is that Marxism fails to accentuate the dimensions of *sacrament, mystery* and *silence* that are indispensable to religion. Religion rejoices especially in the intuition of a domain of mystery that will forever remain beyond the bounds of human mastery. Marxist doctrine, however, follows the methods of scientism and secular humanism according to which all reality is in principle capable of being brought under the domination of human knowledge and work. And so it explicitly rejects, as sheer illusion or "mystification," the sacramental character of nature and the symbolic reference to a distinct realm of mystery.

Buddhism also refuses to say anything about "another dimension." But it never denies such a reality in the doctrinaire manner of Marxism, and it even cultivates the religious sense of mystery precisely because of its silence. Marxism, however, refuses to be silent, and in its materialism it reduces all reality to matter. Its materialism is a repudiation of sacramentalism, and there is little room for a *mysterium tremendum et fascinans*. Thus it does not fully fit our understanding of religion as sacramental adventure into *mystery*. Like other kinds of secular humanism it isolates the active strand of religion from its primordial linkage to sacrament, mystery and silence. In doing so it loses three of the characteristics essential to religion.

Bibliography

Aquinas, Thomas. *Summa Theologiae*. Blackfriars trans. New York: Image
Books, 1969.
Barnes, Michael. *In the Presence of Mystery*. Mystic, Connecticut: Twenty-
third Publications, 1986.
Berger, Peter. *A Rumor of Angels*. Garden City, New York: Doubleday
Anchor Books, 1970.
Berger, Peter. *The Sacred Canopy*. Garden City, New York: Doubleday
Anchor Books, 1969.
Berry, Thomas. "The Dream of The Earth." *Cross Currents* XXXVII
(1988), pp. 200–215.
Bhagavad-Gita. In *Indian Philosophy*. Ed. by S. Radhakrishnan and C.
Moore. Princeton: Princeton University Press, 1957. Pp. 101–63.
Bowker, John. *Problems of Suffering in Religions of the World*. Cambridge:
Cambridge University Press, 1970.
Bowker, John. *The Sense of God*. Oxford: Clarendon Press, 1973.
Bowker, John. *The Religious Imagination and the Sense of God*. Oxford:
Oxford University Press, 1978.
Bowker, John. *Is Anybody Out There?* Westminster, Maryland: Christian
Classics, 1988.
Camus, Albert. *The Plague*. Trans. by S. Gilbert. New York: Modern
Library, 1948.
Carmody, Denise L. and John T. *Shamans, Prophets and Sages*. Belmont,
California: Wadsworth Publishing Co., 1985.
Chesterton, G. K. *Orthodoxy*. Westport, Connecticut: Greenwood Press,
1974.
Chung-yuan, Chang. *Tao: A New Way of Thinking*. New York: Harper &
Row, 1975.
Copleston, Frederick. *Religion and the One*. New York: Crossroad, 1982.
Cox, Harvey. *The Secular City*. New York: The Macmillan Company, 1965.
Dawkins, Richard. *The Blind Watchmaker*. New York: W. W. Norton &
Co., 1986.

de Bary, William Theodore, ed. *The Buddhist Tradition*. New York: Vintage Books, 1972.

Donahue, John R., S.J. "Biblical Perspectives on Justice." John C. Haughey, ed. *The Faith That Does Justice*. New York: Paulist Press, 1977. Pp. 68–112.

Dostoevsky, Fyodor. *The Brothers Karamazov*. New York: Modern Library, 1950. Citation by Anthony Padavano, *The Estranged God* (New York: Sheed and Ward, 1966), p. 65.

Dunne, John. *The Way of All the Earth*. New York: Macmillan. 1972.

Einstein, Albert. *Ideas and Opinions*. New York: Bonanza Books, 1954.

Eliade, Mircea. *Patterns in Comparative Religion*. Trans. by Rosemary Sheed. New York: Sheed & Ward, 1958.

Eliade, Mircea. *Myth and Reality*. New York: Harper Torchbooks, 1968.

Eliade, Mircea. *Shamanism*. Princeton: Bollingen/Princeton University Press, 1972.

Ferré, Nels. *Making Religion Real*. New York: Harper & Row, 1955.

Fowler, James. *Stages of Faith*. San Francisco: Harper & Row, 1981.

Frankfort, Henri, *et al. Before Philosophy*. Baltimore: Penguin Books, 1951.

Frazer, James. *The Golden Bough*. Abridged edition. New York: Macmillan, 1922.

Freud, Sigmund. *The Future of an Illusion*. Trans. by James Strachey. New York: W. W. Norton & Co., 1961.

Greeley, Andrew. *Unsecular Man*. New York: Delta Books, 1974.

Gustafson, James. "Religion and Morality from the Perspective of Theology." Gene Outka and John P. Reeder, Jr., eds. *Religion and Morality*. Garden City, New York: Doubleday Anchor Books, 1973. Pp. 125–54.

Haught, John F. *The Cosmic Adventure*. New York: Paulist Press, 1984.

Haught, John F. *What Is God?* New York: Paulist Press, 1986.

Heiler, Friedrich. *Prayer*. Trans. and ed. by Samuel McComb. New York: Oxford University Press, 1932.

Heiler, Friedrich. "The History of Religions as a Preparation for the Cooperation of Religions." Mircea Eliade and Joseph M. Kitagawa, Ed. *The History of Religions*. Chicago: The University of Chicago Press, 1959. Pp. 132–60.

Huxley, Aldous. *The Doors of Perception*. London: Chatto & Windus, 1954.

Huxley, Aldous. *The Perennial Philosophy*. New York: Harper Colophon Books, 1970.

Jacob, Louis. "The Relationship between Religion and Ethics in Jewish Thought." Gene Outka and John P. Reeder, Jr., Ed. *Religion and*

Morality. Garden City, New York: Doubleday Anchor Books, 1973. Pp. 155–72.

James, William. *The Varieties of Religious Experience*. New York: Collier Books, 1961.

Jaspers, Karl. *The Origin and Goal of History*. New Haven: Yale University Press, 1953.

Johnston, William, ed. *The Cloud of Unknowing and the Book of Privy Counseling*. Garden City, New York: Doubleday Image Books.

Jonas, Hans. *The Phenomenon of Life*. New York: Harper & Row, 1966.

Jung, C. G. *The Undiscovered Self*. Trans. by R. F. C. Hull. New York: Mentor Books, 1958.

Kaufmann, Walter, ed. *The Portable Nietzsche*. New York: Penguin Books, 1976.

Kohlberg, Lawrence, *The Psychology of Moral Development*. San Francisco: Harper & Row, 1984.

Küng, Hans. *Does God Exist?* Trans. Edward Quinn. Garden City, New York: Doubleday, 1980.

Küng, Hans. *Eternal Life*. Trans. Edward Quinn. Garden City, New York: Doubleday, 1984.

Küng, Hans. *Christianity and the World Religions*. Trans. Peter Heinegg. Garden City, New York: Doubleday, 1986.

Leech, Kenneth. *Experiencing God*. San Francisco: Harper & Row, 1985.

Lienhardt, Godfrey. *Divinity and Experience*. Oxford: Clarendon Press, 1961.

Lonergan, Anne, and Richards, Caroline, ed. *Thomas Berry and the New Cosmology*. Mystic, Connecticut: Twenty-third Publications, 1987.

Lonergan, Bernard. *Insight: A Study of Human Understanding*. New York: Philosophical Library, 1958.

Marcel, Gabriel. *Being and Having*. Westminster: Dacre Press, 1949.

Maringer, J. *The Gods of Prehistoric Man*. New York: Knopf, 1960.

Moltmann, Jürgen. *God in Creation*. Trans. by Margaret Kohl. San Francisco: Harper & Row, 1985.

Moltmann, Jürgen. *Theology of Hope*. Trans. by James W. Leitch. New York: Harper & Row, 1967.

Monod, Jacques. *Chance and Necessity*. Trans. by A. Wainhouse. New York: Vintage Books, 1972.

Müller, Max, ed. *The Sacred Books of the East*. Oxford: Clarendon Press, 1897.

Neihardt, John C. *Black Elk Speaks*. New York: Washington Square Press, 1972.

The New English Bible. Oxford and Cambridge: Oxford and Cambridge University Presses, 1970.

Nielsen, Kai. "Morality and the Will of God." Peter Angeles, Ed. *Critiques of God*. Buffalo: Prometheus Books, 1976. Pp. 241–57.

Ogden, Schubert. *The Reality of God*. New York: Harper & Row, 1977.

Otto, Max. "The Non-Existence of God." *Issues in Religion*. Allie M. Frazier, ed. New York: D. Van Nostrand Co., 1975. Pp. 382–87

Otto, Rudolf. *The Idea of the Holy*. Second Edition. Trans. by John W. Harvey. New York: Oxford University Press, 1950.

Pagels, Heinz. *Perfect Symmetry*. New York: Bantam Books, 1986.

Polanyi, Michael. *Personal Knowledge*. New York: Harper Torchbooks, 1964.

Polanyi, Michael. *The Tacit Dimension*. Garden City, New York: Doubleday Anchor Books, 1967.

Prabhavananda, Swami, and Manchester, Frederick, trans. *The Upanishads*. New York: New American Library, 1957.

Rahner, Karl. *Foundations of Christian Faith*. Trans. by William V. Dych. New York: Crossroad, 1978.

Reynolds, A. ed. *A Shewing of God's Love*, by Julian of Norwich. London: Longmans, Green and Co., 1958.

Ricoeur, Paul. *The Conflict of Interpretations*. Ed. by Don Ihde. Evanston: Northwestern University Press, 1974.

Ricoeur, Paul. *The Philosophy of Paul Ricoeur*. Ed. by Charles Reagan and David Stewart. Boston: Beacon Press, 1978.

Roberts, Bernadette. *The Experience of No-Self*. Boulder & London: Shambala, 1984.

Robinson, J. A. T. "Can a Truly Contemporary Person Not Be an Atheist?" *The New Christianity*. Ed. by W. R. Miller. New York: Delta Books, 1967.

Rolston, Holmes, III. *Science and Religion*. New York: Random House, 1987.

Sartre, Jean-Paul. *Existentialism and the Human Emotions*. Trans. by Bernard Frechtman. New York: Philosophical Library, 1957.

Skinner, B. F. *Beyond Freedom and Dignity*. New York: Bantam Books, 1972.

Smith, John E. *Reason and God*. New Haven: Yale University Press, 1961.

Smith, Wilfred Cantwell. *The Meaning and End of Religion*. New York: Macmillan, 1963.

Teilhard de Chardin, Pierre. *The Future of Man*. Trans. by Norman Denny. New York: Harper Colophon Books, 1969.

Thomas, E. J., trans., *Pali Sermons, Samyatta, V, 420*. London: Kegan Paul, Trench, Trubner & Co., Ltd., 1935.

Thompson, William M. *Christ and Consciousness*. New York: Paulist Press, 1977.

Tillich, Paul. *The Courage to Be*. New Haven: Yale University Press, 1952.

Tillich, Paul. *Dynamics of Faith*. New York: Harper & Row, 1957.

Toulmin, Stephen. *An Examination of the Place of Reason in Ethics*. Cambridge: Cambridge University Press, 1970.

Tracy, David. *Blessed Rage for Order*. New York: The Seabury Press, 1975.

Ward, Keith. *Images of Eternity*. London: Darton, Longman and Todd, 1987.

Weinberg, Stephen. *The First Three Minutes*. New York: Basic Books, 1977.

Whitehead, Alfred North. *Science and the Modern World*. New York: The Free Press, 1967a.

Whitehead, Alfred North. *Adventures of Ideas*. New York: The Free Press, 1967b.

Wilber, Ken. *Eye to Eye*. Garden City, New York: Doubleday Anchor, 1983.

Zaehner, R. C. *Mysticism, Sacred and Profane*. New York: Oxford University Press, 1961.

Index

illusion, 217
immediate environment, 21
immortality, 7, 63, 138, 215, 216
impermanence, 50
initiation rites, 22ff., 87
injustice, 70
Isaac, 66
Isaiah, 134, 137, 160
Islam, 62, 74ff., 81, 89, 101, 117, 137, 139, 254
Israel, 67, 70

Jacob, Louis, 187, 262
Jainism, 35, 43, 56
James, William, 78, 99–103, 263
Jaspers, Karl, 35, 263
Jägerstätter, Franz, 192
Jeremiah, 134
Jesus, 71, 78, 90, 121, 128, 135, 136, 137, 179, 191, 208, 239, 256
Jewish scriptures, 74
Joan of Arc, 191
Job, 114ff.
John of the Cross, St., 106, 123
Johnson, Samuel, 19
Johnston, William, 122, 263
Jonas, Hans, 18, 263
Jones, Jim, 256
Judah, 67, 70
Judaism, 62, 67ff., 81, 101, 117, 139
Julian of Norwich, 99, 157, 264
Jung, C. G., 193, 263
justice, 70, 71, 77, 131, 134

Kabir, 111
Kali, 45
Kant, Immanuel, 213, 221, 239, 245
karma, 32, 43, 50, 53, 129, 132
karma yoga, 129

Katha Upanishad, 36
King, Martin Luther, Jr., 191
Kingdom of God, 73
Kohlberg, Lawrence, 188, 263
Krishna, 40, 41, 45, 129, 208
Kshatriyas, 43
Küng, Hans, 78, 139, 263

Lao Tzu, 110, 113, 219
Leary, Timothy, 105
Leech, Kenneth, 123, 136, 263
legitimation, religious, 177ff.
liberation, 62, 227
liberation theology, 136f.
Lienhardt, Godfrey, 180, 263
life beyond death, 138
limit-experience, 166
limit-questions, 168ff., 245
limits, 5, 21, 158, 260
Lonergan, Anne, 263
Lonergan, Bernard, 263
love, 128–143, 183, 185, 215
lust, 53
Luther, Martin, 90, 179, 221, 251

ma'at, 176, 243
magic, 57, 82, 91, 158
Mahavira, 56
Mahayana Buddhism, 53–57, 183
Manchester, Frederick, 36, 264
Marcel, Gabriel, 263
Marduk, 151
Maringer, J., 263
marriage, sacrament of, 91
Marx, 139, 211, 215, 216, 217, 218, 224, 242
Marxism, 83, 260
materialism, 211
maya, 33, 34, 38, 202
Mecca, 75–77
Medina, 75
Meister Eckhart, 110, 129